MEL BAY'S COMPLETE BOOK OF BLUES GUITAR LICKS & PHRASES

By Austin Sicard, Jr.

A cassette tape of the music in this book is now available. The publisher strongly recommends the use of this cassette tape along with the text to insure accuracy of interpretation and ease in learning.

Contents

Introduction

Often I tell my students that an endless barrage of notes is not what guitar playing is all about — that sometimes "less is more." Knowing when to play and when not to play is essential to the feel and emotion of a song. Nowhere is that concept of feel more apparent than in blues music.

The guitar and the blues live side by side in music history — each contributing to the popularity of the other. Many of the techniques that dominate guitar music today have their origins in blues guitar. The blues remains a fascinating style to which all rock players attribute their roots, but very few know why. With this book, I have compiled an extensive anthology of great blues licks that I consider "necessary" in a blues guitarist's repertoire.

This anthology is intended for anyone who is interested in blues guitar, whether a beginner or an established guitarist. Over 400 licks are presented here in tablature and feature easy fingering. Speed is not of utmost importance, but accuracy certainly is.

I transpose each basic lick into each of the ascending keys of the guitar fretboard. I do this to introduce the concept of voicing — that by changing the key, the sound and feel of each lick will be different from the previous one. You might find that what sounded like gritty Delta blues in E becomes a country solo in G or perhaps a soaring rock lead in C# minor.

Blues is also steeped in rhythm techniques, and the various licks presented here will lend themselves to whatever rhythm or style you choose. I feel that after studying and practicing from my book, you will be more versed in whatever style you play due to the universality of blues.

The most important factor of all is one of "feel." Feel is an intangible quality that every great guitarist has. It's knowing you're in the groove of the rhythm, and the guitar becomes an extension and expression of yourself. You feel the song and, much like an artist with a paintbrush, you paint your style across an acoustic canvas.

These blues licks convey the feel and spirit of the blues masters — the tortured bends of Jimi Hendrix and Stevie Ray Vaughan, the driving blues of Eric Clapton, and the smooth baritone of Albert King. I hope you enjoy them as much as I do.

Special thanks to Steve Fontenot (for his Korg A-3 effects unit), Rodger Filiberto, Marshall Williams, Sean and Tevis Vandergriff, and my family for their support. Also thanks to Todd Schulz for letting me use his custom-made Foster guitar and Reels on Wheels Studio. Above all, this book is dedicated to Jimi Hendrix and Stevie Ray Vaughan for sharing their music with us.

Austin Sicard

The Fingerboard Dictionary

To better acquaint you with the fingerboard, here is a notation chart for all six strings from open string to 12th fret in correlation to the fingerboard drawing.

Guitar Fingerboard

How to Read Tablature

Tablature is a drawing of six horizontal lines representing the six string on the guitar.

The numbers written on the lines represent the frets on which to place your fingers. "O" indicates an open string.

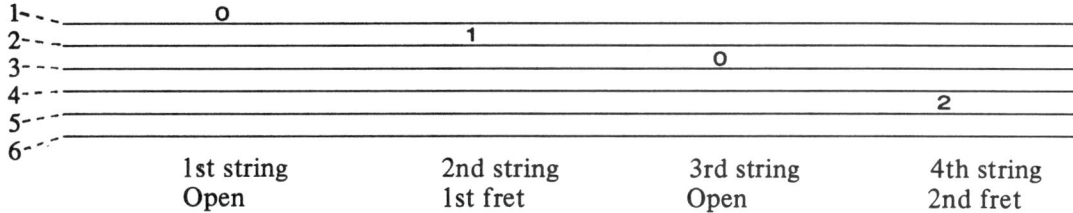

| 1st string | 2nd string | 3rd string | 4th string |
| Open | 1st fret | Open | 2nd fret |

In this book, the tablature numbers will appear directly under each note of music, showing which string and fret to play.

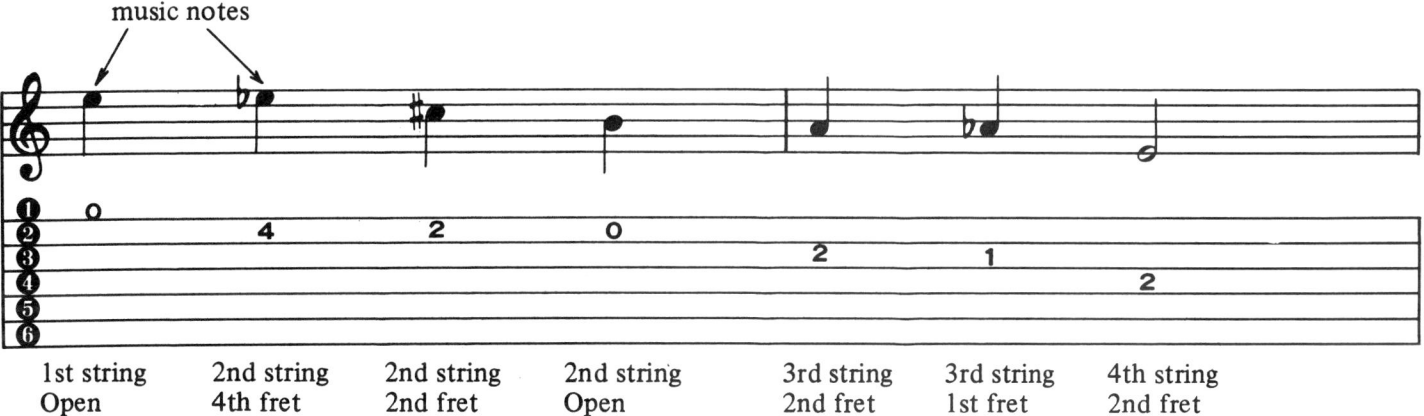

| 1st string | 2nd string | 2nd string | 2nd string | 3rd string | 3rd string | 4th string |
| Open | 4th fret | 2nd fret | Open | 2nd fret | 1st fret | 2nd fret |

When two or more notes are played at the same time, the numbers are above one another as shown below. Suggested left-hand fingers will be numbered next to music notes.

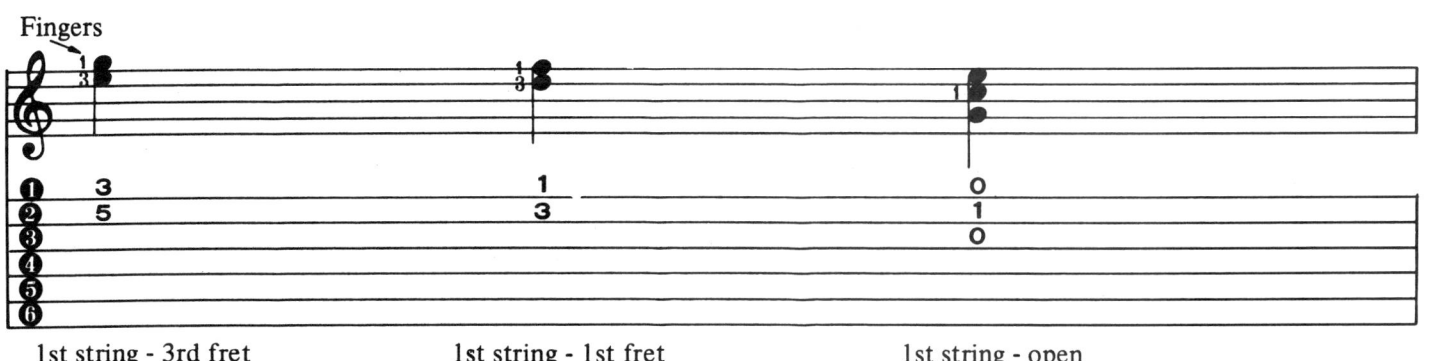

1st string - 3rd fret
2nd string - 5th fret

1st string - 1st fret
2nd string - 3rd fret

1st string - open
2nd string - 1st fret
3rd string - open

Things to Know About Notes

𝐨 = the whole note; receives 4 beats.

𝅝 = the half note; receives 2 beats.

♩ = the quarter note; receives 1 beat.

♪ = the eighth note; receives half of 1 beat. When two are written together, they look like this:

They are counted as: 1 and   2 and   3 and   4 and.

When written together, they are referred to as eighth-note couplets.

𝅘𝅥𝅯 = the sixteenth note; receives half the count of the eighth note. In rock guitar solos, sixteenth notes are written mostly in quadruplets and look like this:

Counted as: 1 e and a   2 e and a   3 e and a   4 e and a

To make quadruplets easier to understand, use a four-syllable word like "Mississippi."

Example 1
The Slide
(Which way is up?)

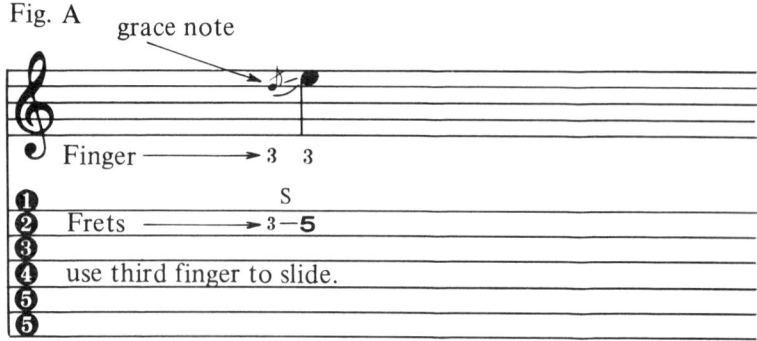

Fig. A   grace note

Finger ⟶ 3 3
                 S
Frets ⟶ 3—5
use third finger to slide.

Above is a quick slide using a grace note one whole step away from the desired note we wish to acheive.

Fig. B Below is a long slide up and a long slide down.   C

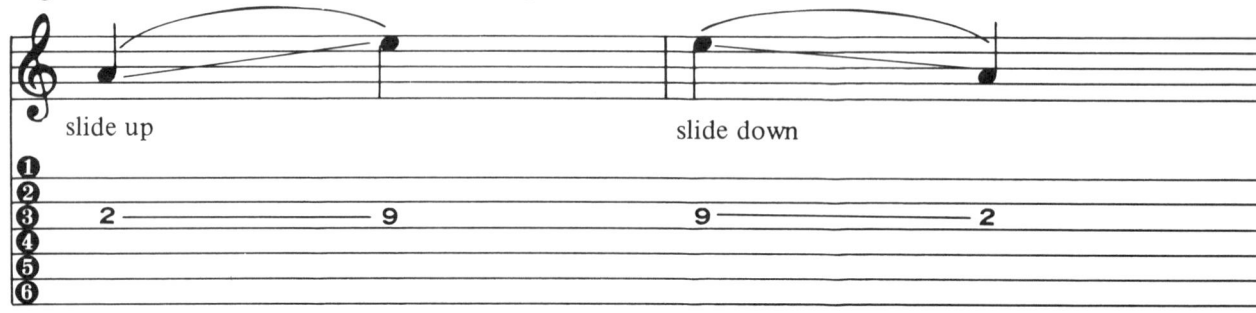

slide up   slide down

2 ——————— 9   9 ——————— 2

On the guitar, the direction "up" starts from the fret closest to the tuning keys up to the fret closest to the body of the guitar.

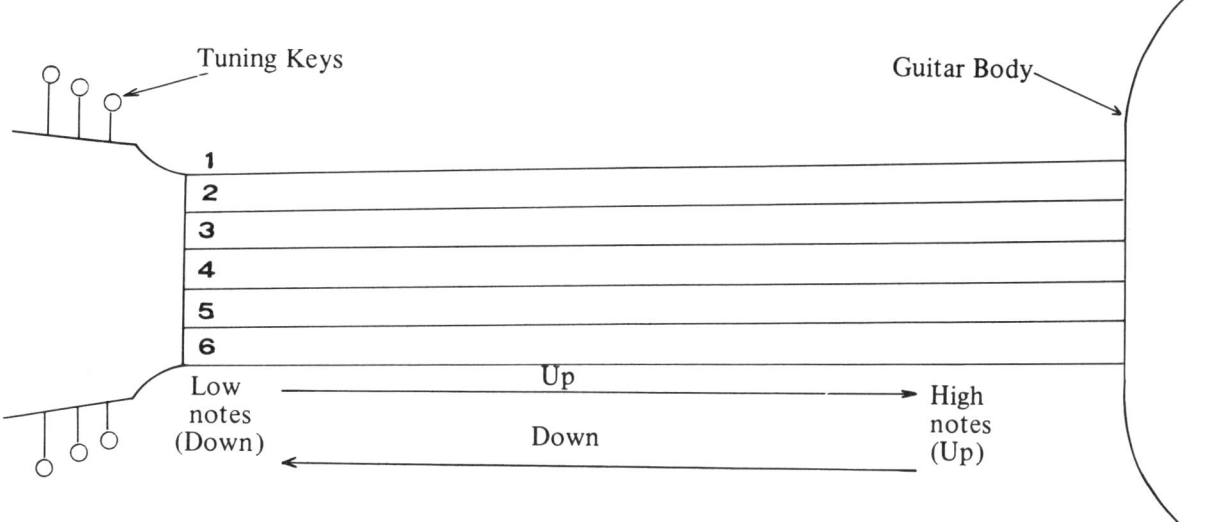

Example 2
The Slide Versus the Bend

Here's how the bend looks in notation and tablature:

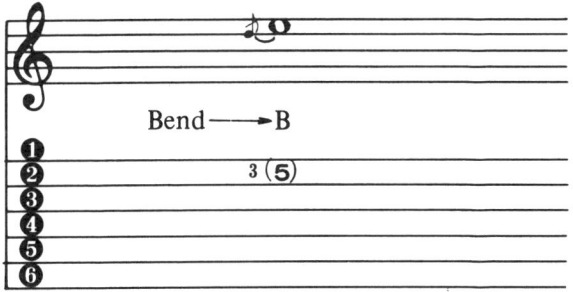

The tablature shows the 3rd fret on the 2nd string is to be bent to the 5th fret (number in parentheses). Practice until the bend is smooth sounding with sustain.

Here's how the bend looks in "box" diagram form:

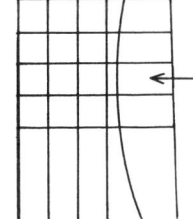

On the second string, place the 3rd finger on the 3rd fret and bend the string up towards the ceiling to the sound of the 5th-fret note.

The Bend

Pick this note and bend the string to the sound of the number in parentheses.

Bend & Reverse Bend

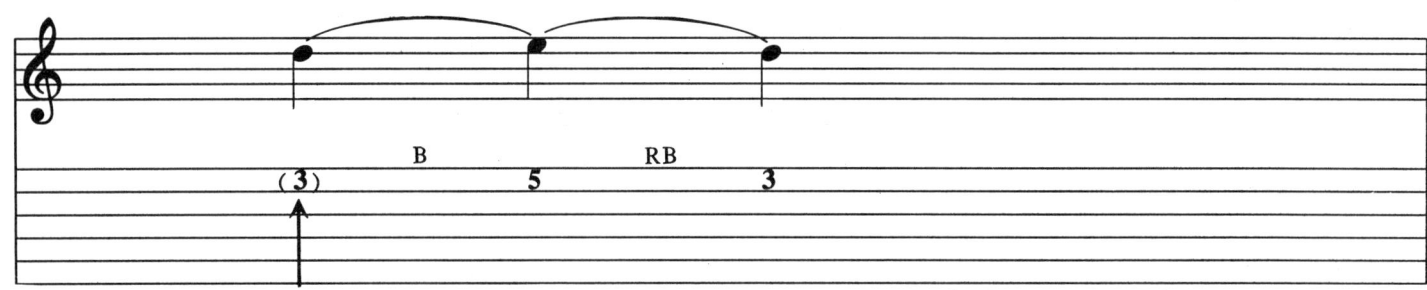

Pick this note (3) and bend to No. 5. Release the bent string back to a straight-string position, which is No. 3.

Reverse Bend

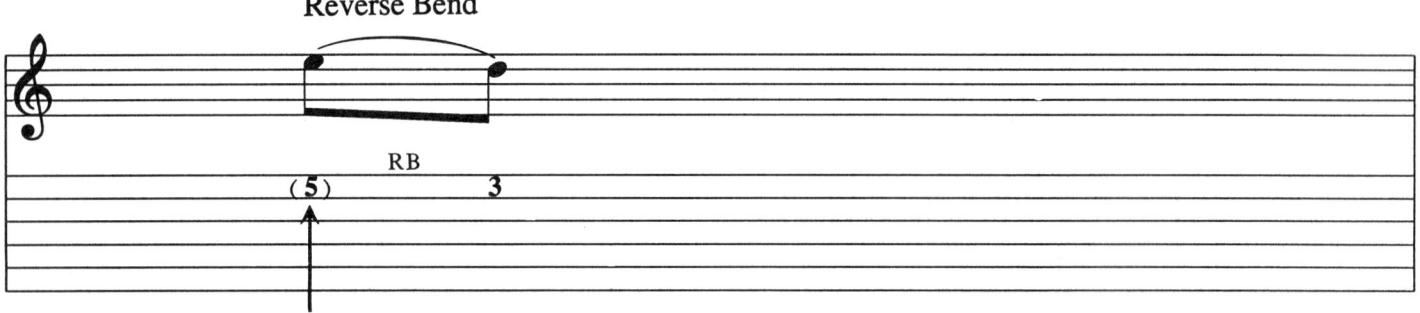

Ghost bend (pre-bend) to this number (5), starting from the number you're going to reverse string to, which is No. 3 (after the parentheses). When you feel you've reached the number in the parentheses (5), pick the string and reverse back to the straight-string position. Don't take your finger off of the string when reversing. Let the string maintain sound from high note to low note when reversing the bend from (5) to 3.

In other words, pick an already bent string, then allow it to return (reverse) to a straight-string position.

> **B = Bend**
> **B, RB = Bend and Reverse Bend**
> **RB = Reverse Bend**

Note: Bending strings can be a task on some guitars. If so, simply slide (instead of bending) to or from the number in parentheses when playing the above procedures.

Example 3
Hammers, Pull-Offs, and Grace Notes

Hammers (H) and *pull-offs (P)* are also some of the most important techniques needed to play lead guitar.

Practice the two examples below:

Fingers →

Fig 1: The hammer is a low to a high note. Start by picking the 5th fret, 3rd string, then tap the left-hand third finger on the 7th fret down hard enough to produce a "hammered note."

Fingers →

Fig. 2: The pull-off is a high note to a low note. Start by placing the left-hand third finger on the 7th fret, 3rd string. Pull off the third finger in a snapping motion to sound off the 5th-fret note.

Grace Notes

Grace notes are one or more notes preceding a principal note, but the count is **emphasized on the principal note.** In other words, the little notes move "gracefully" to the count of the note they precede.

Observe below:

As you can see, grace notes move in many ways; the slide, bend, hammer, and pull-off are the examples shown below.

Fig. 3.

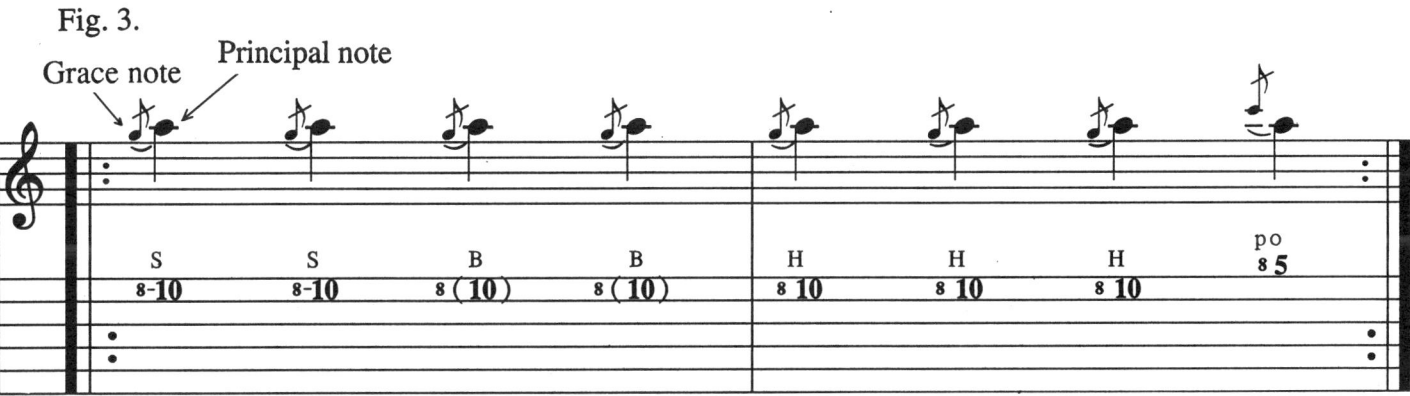

Grace note   Principal note

Different Shuffle Triplet Notations

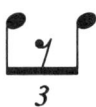

This means to play a triplet without the middle triplet note. The eighth-count rest (ɤ) replaces the middle note, causing a moment of hesitation (or silence) betweent the other two. (This notation sounds like a heartbeat.)

This is another way of writing the above triplet, except that this one holds its first note a little longer before playing the next note. Even though it looks like a quarter note and eighth note notation, it's played like a triplet with the first two notes tied:

Ex. ← tie

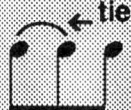

The bracket (L⎯⎯⎯J) with the number 3 also defines the triplet feeling for the two notes. To sum things up, this notation sounds like a lazy heartbeat.

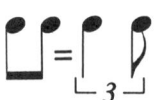

This means to play this 🎵🎵 like this 🎵🎵

When you see this written at the top corner of a musical piece, it indicates that all eighth-note couplets are to be played like a shuffle triplet.

Section 1
Licks and Phrases in the Key of E

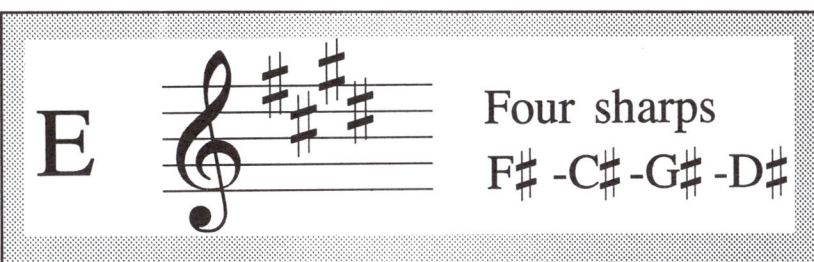

E   Four sharps
F♯ -C♯ -G♯ -D♯

Solos used in this section are based on the two blues (pentatonic) minor scales below.

Low Octave

Open Pattern

High Octave

12th Fret

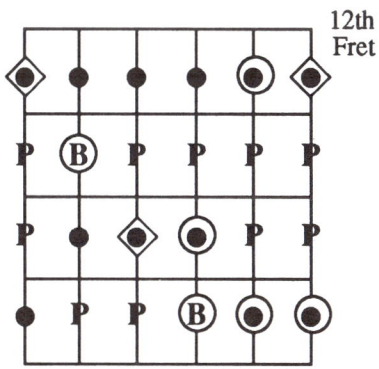

◈ = **Root (key) note E**

◉ = **Popular notes to bend**

Ⓑ = **Blue notes (flat 5th tones)**

P = **Passing tones (notes that connect neighborly as well as chromatically to the root and principle tones of the scale)**

Standard Single String Triplets in E

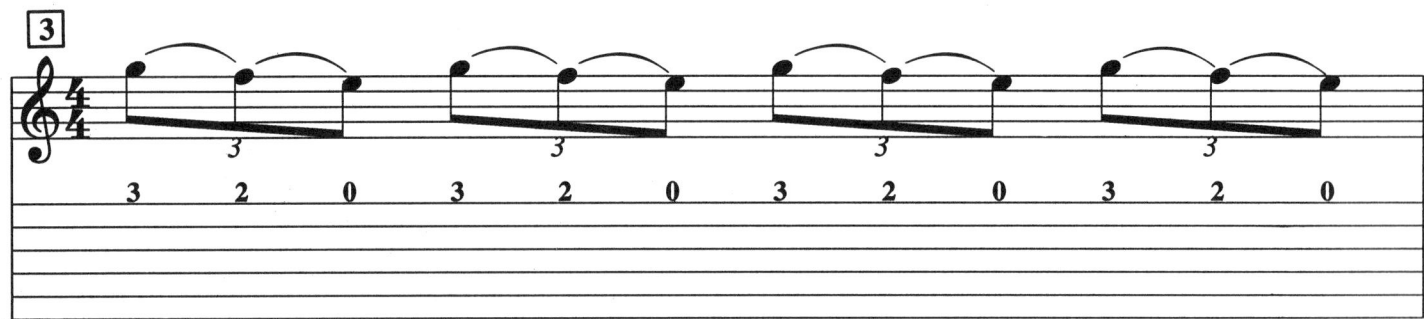

Note: For smoother picking, keep edge of pick at an angle instead of parallel to string.

Licks 1 through 19 can be played to the E shuffle rhythm track, which is recorded on the tape that accompanies this book.

Two String Triplet Combinations
(Using Hammer-Ons and Pull-Offs)

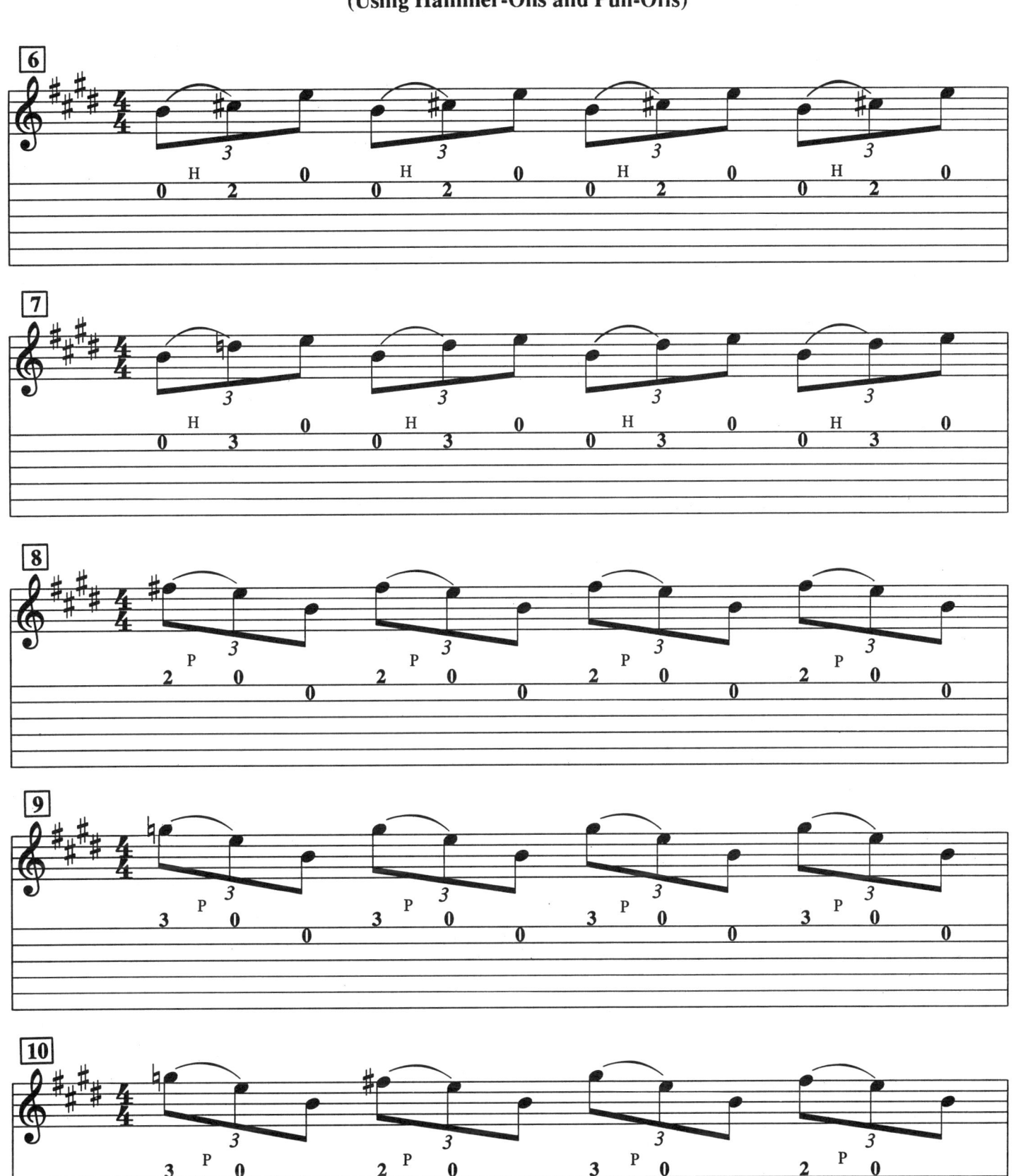

Two String Triplets Continued

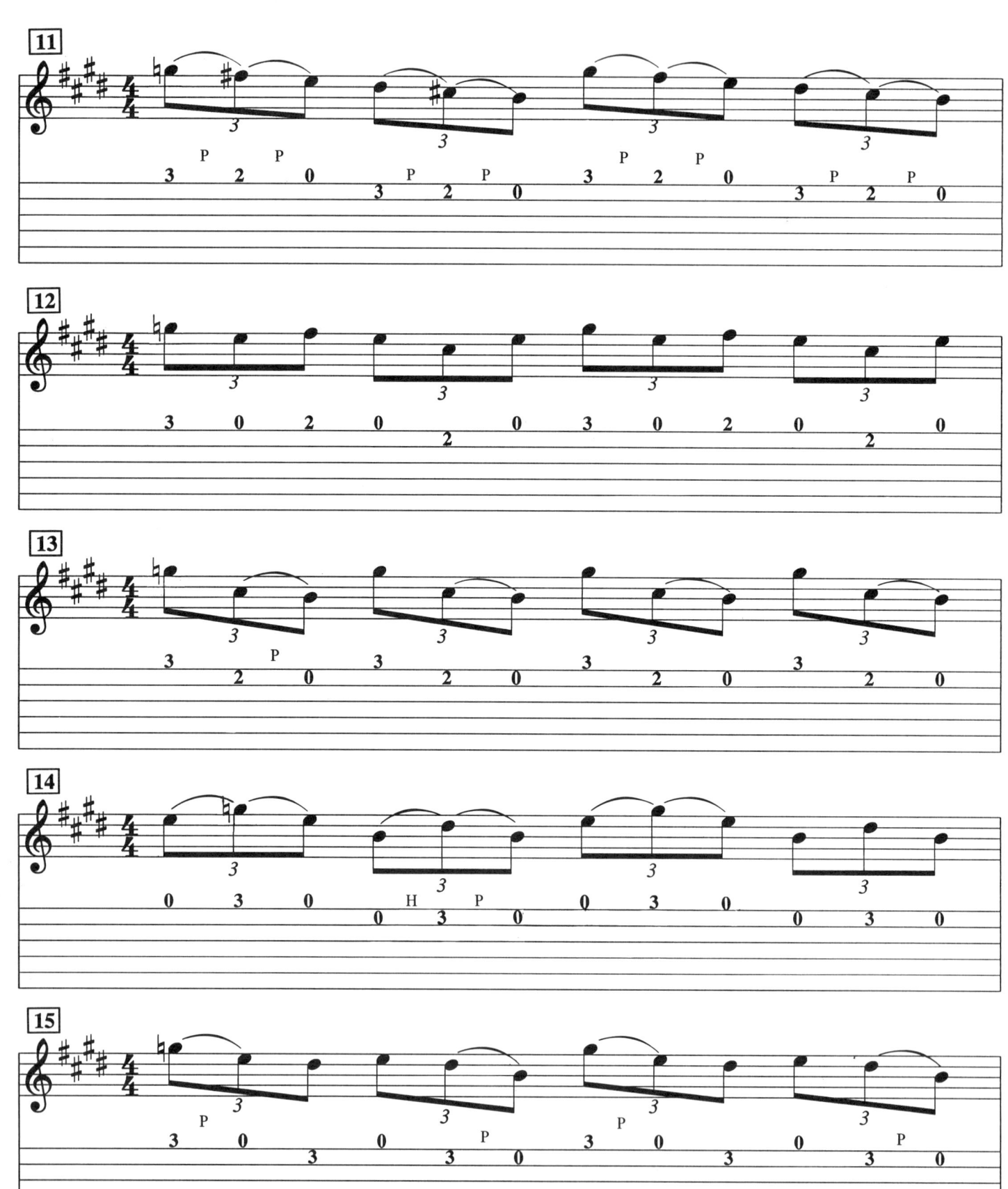

Triplet Licks Using the Finger Slide ($\underline{\textbf{S}}$)

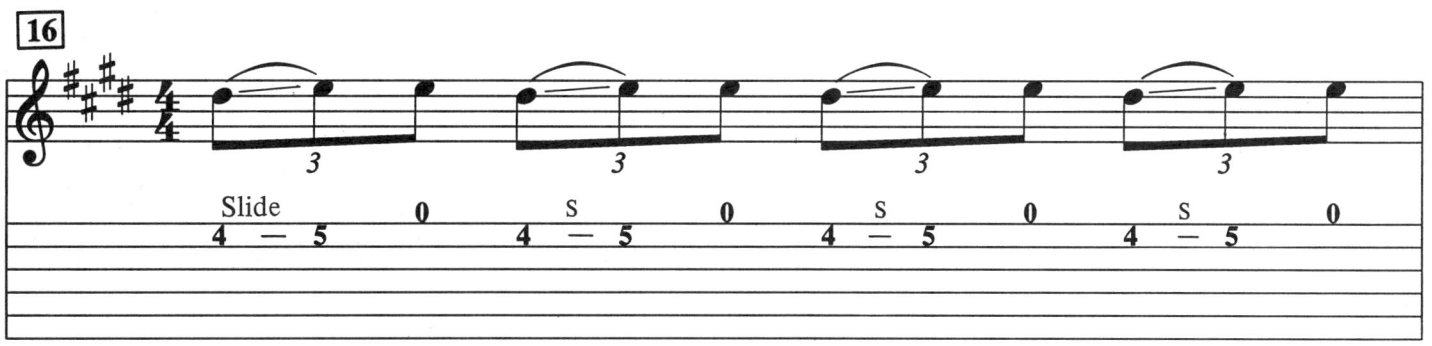

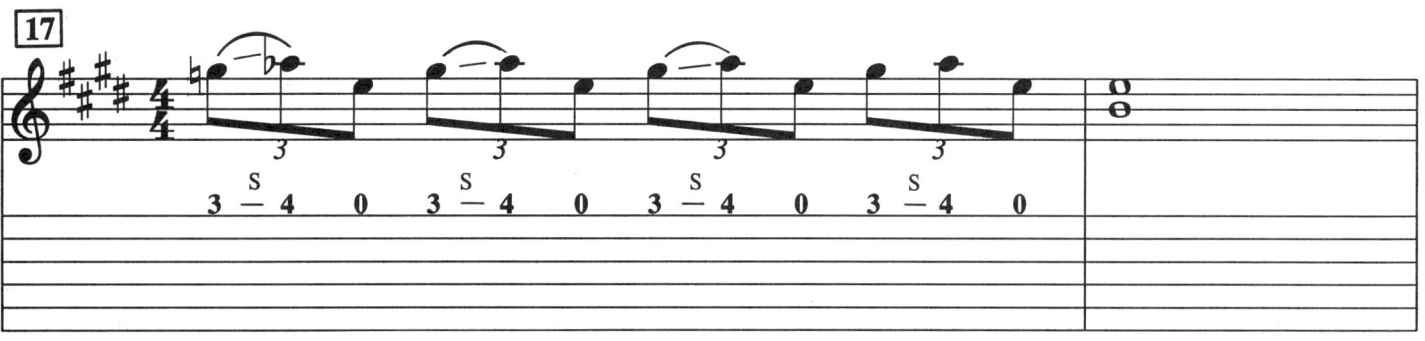

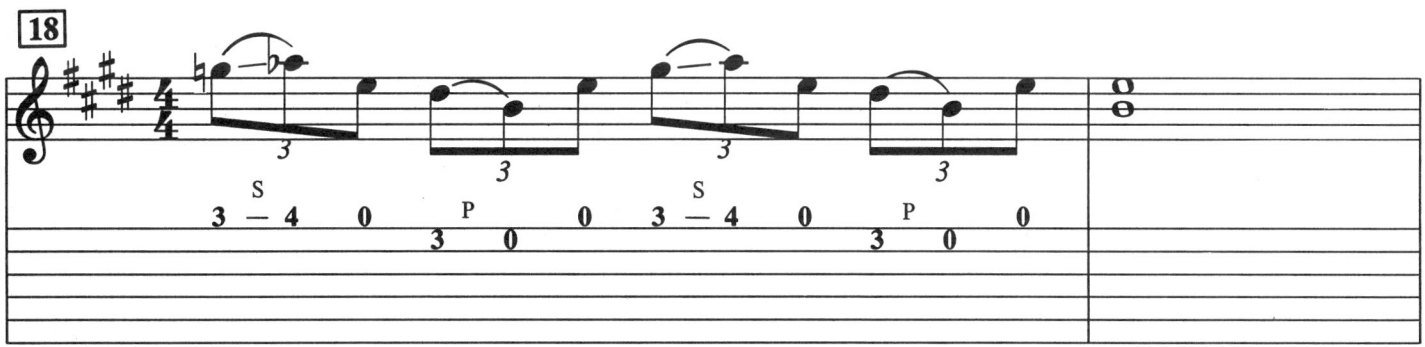

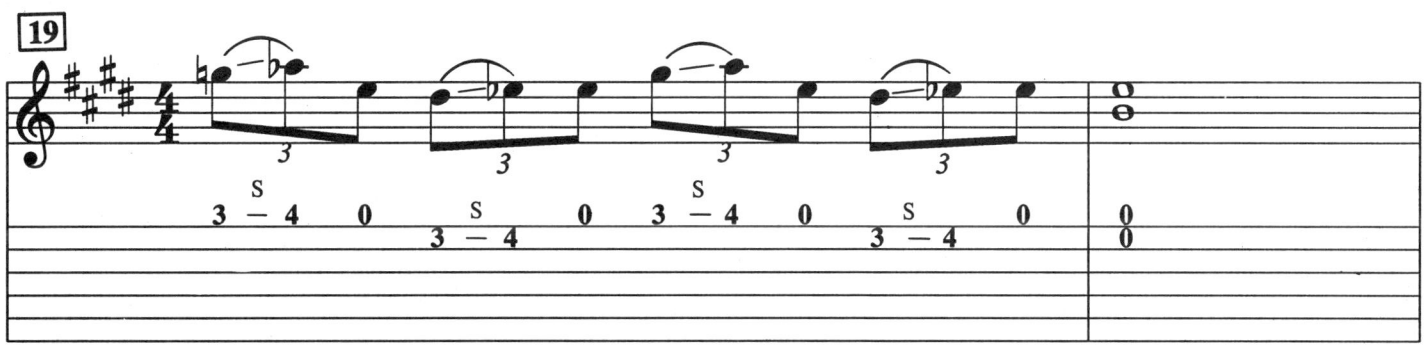

Finger Slide and String Licks in E

Solo From East to West

Slide Rule Boogie in E

Straight or Shuffle

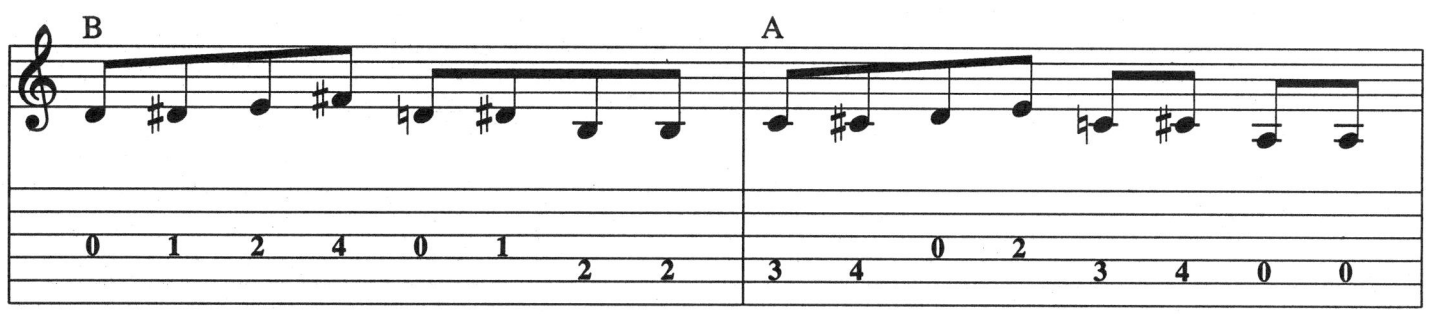

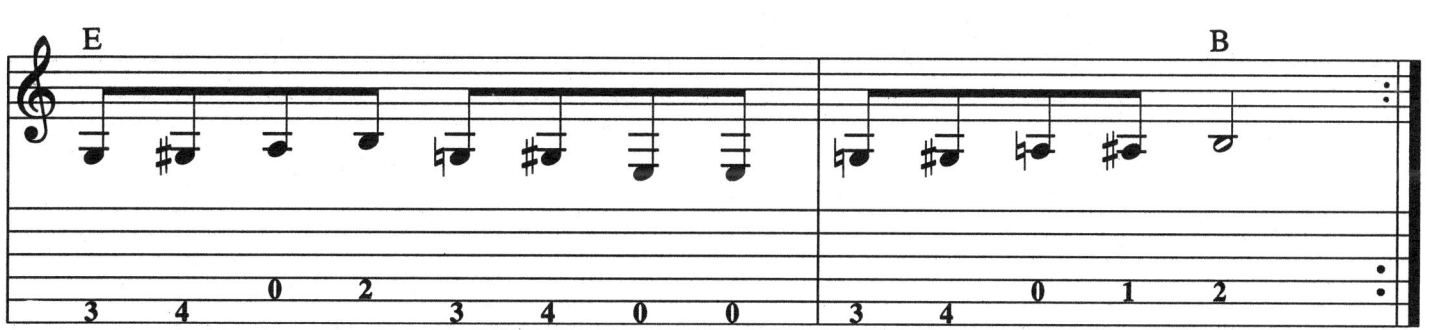

Running on "E"

Cool Blue

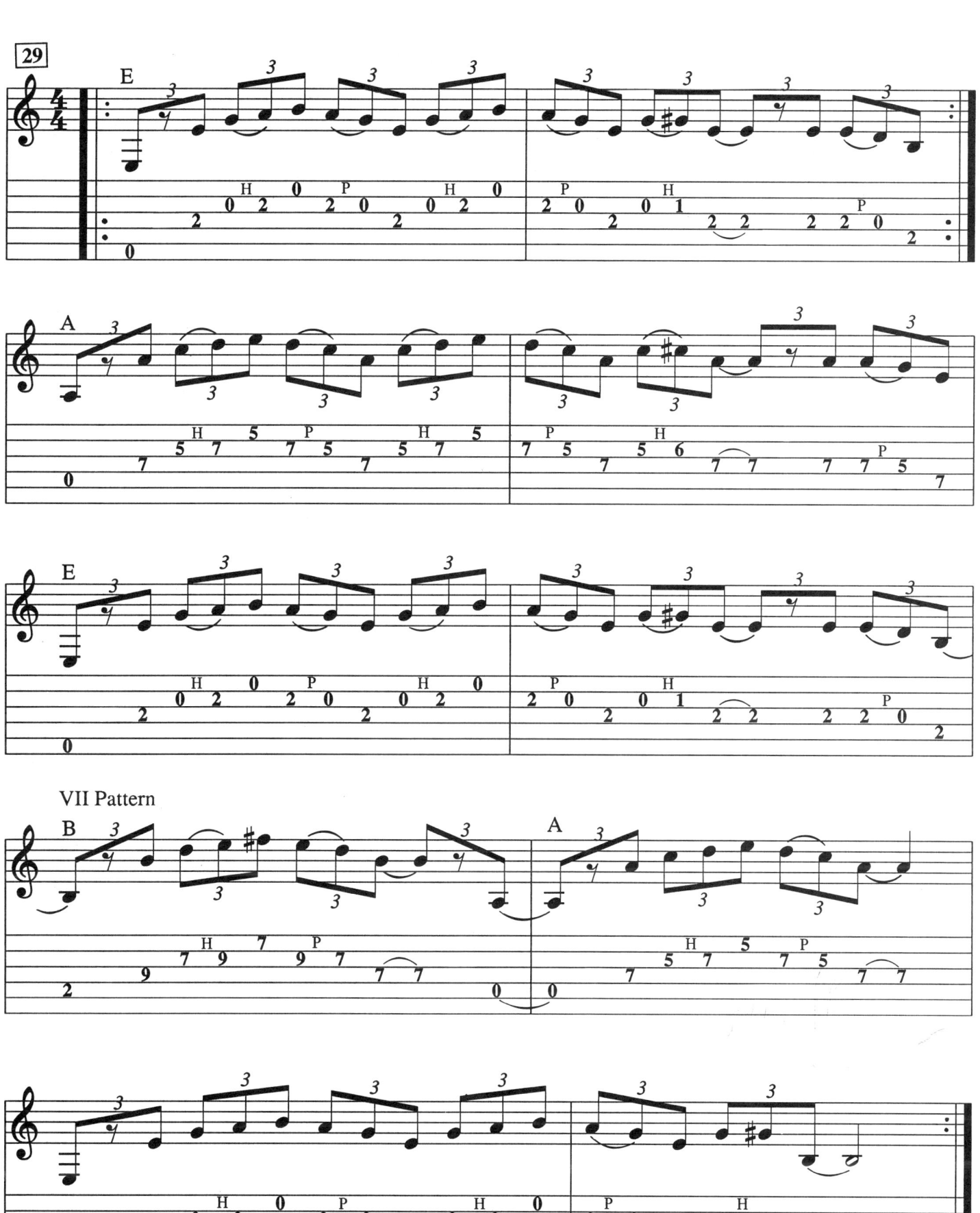

Personality Licks in E

More Personality Licks in E

Personality Licks (Cont.)

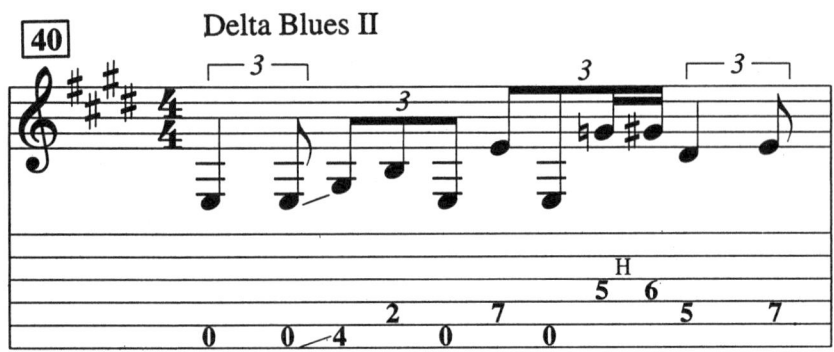

40 Delta Blues II

41 Double Stop Blues Rock Cliché

42 Double Stop Blues Cliché

43 In the style of Robert Johnson

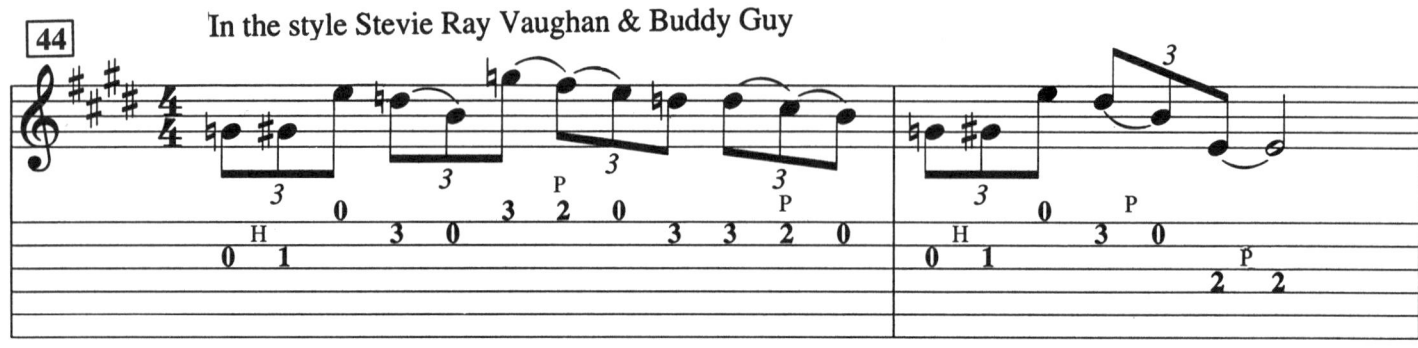

44 In the style Stevie Ray Vaughan & Buddy Guy

Traditional-Style Blues in E

25

Funky Licks and Phrases

In the style of Stevie Ray Vaughan

In the style Z Z Top

In the style of Jimi Hendrix and Johnny Winter

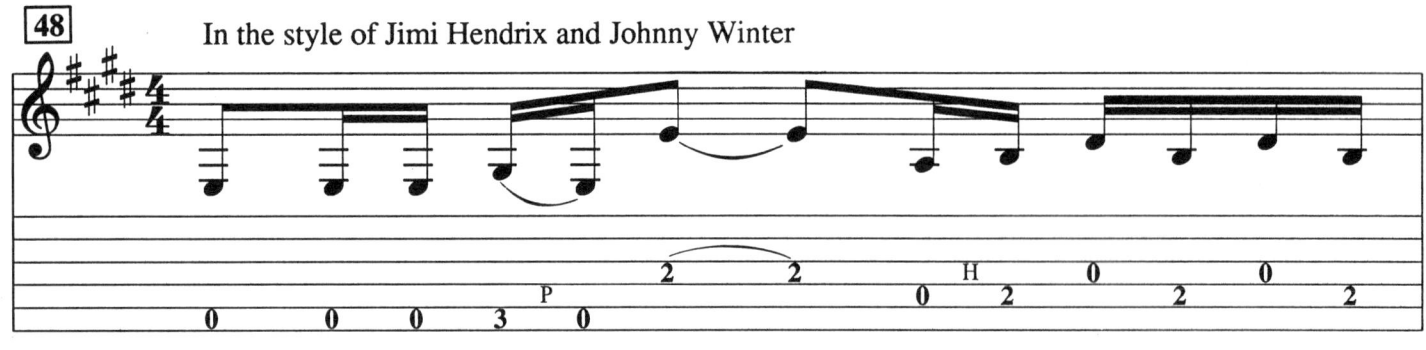

In the style of SRV and HRZ

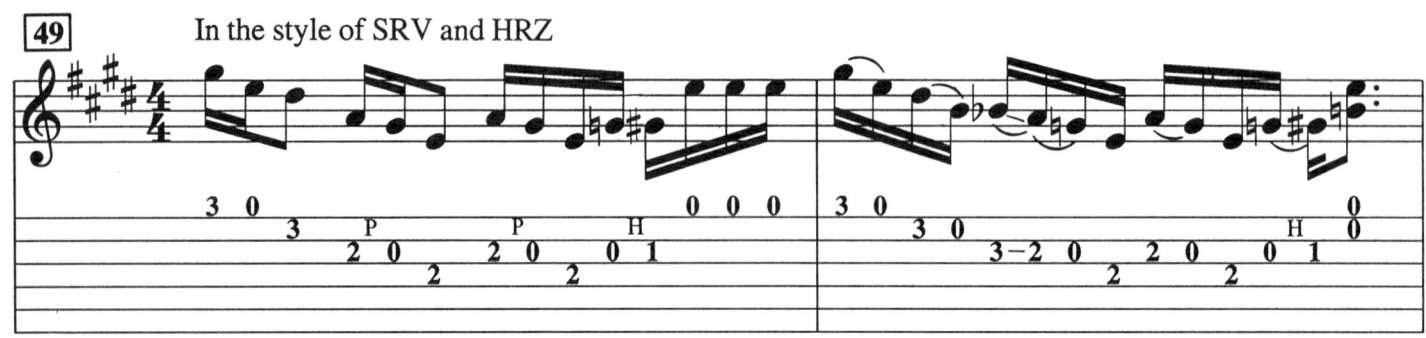

Triplet Solos

Solos Playing on the 4th (Extension)
Scale Pattern in E

Also see page 126.

Key of E

More Licks in the 7th Fret Position
(Using the 4th Extension of the E Blues Scale)

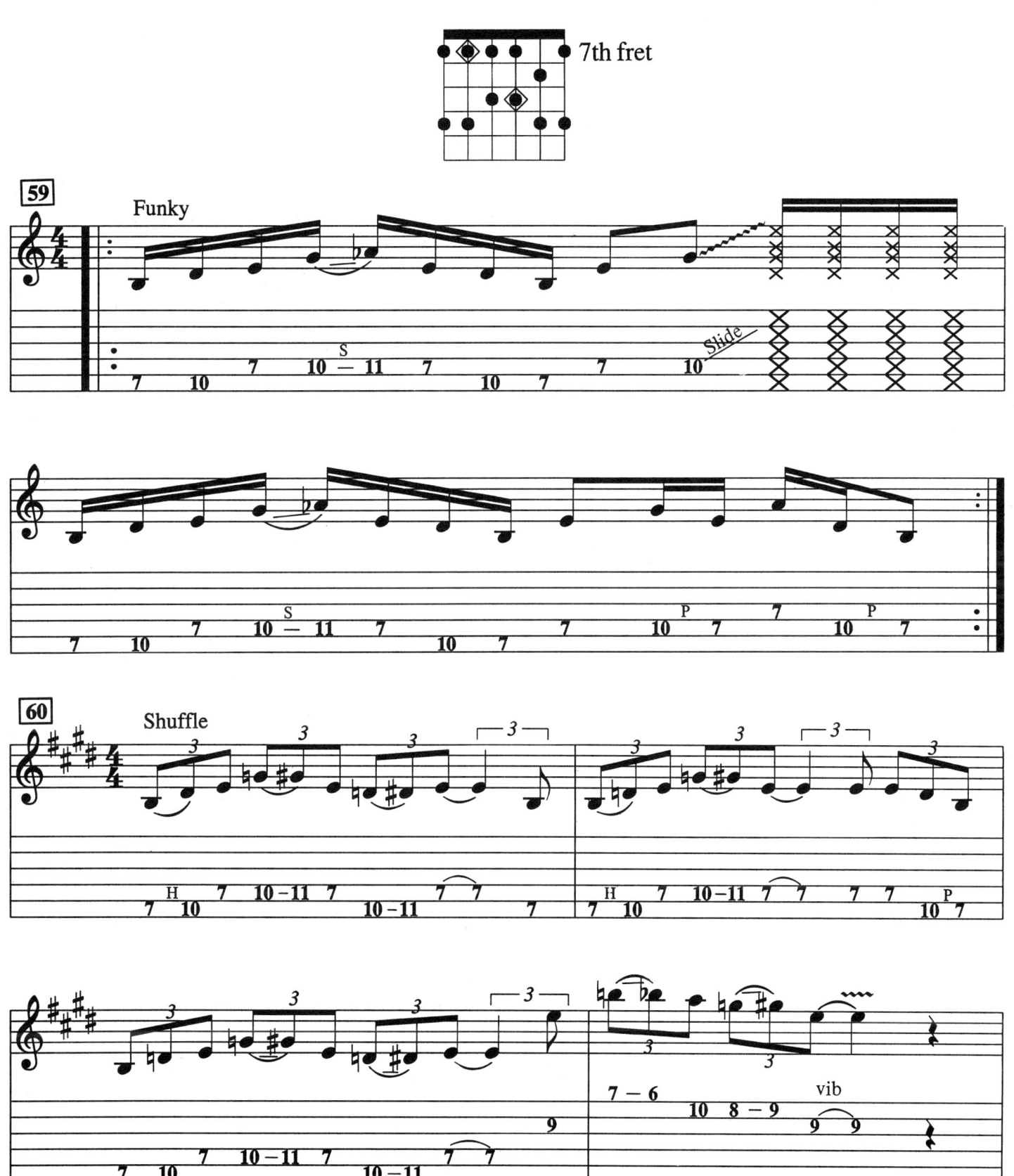

Double Stops in E

Licks in the Style of Stevie Ray Vaughan
and Jimi Hendrix

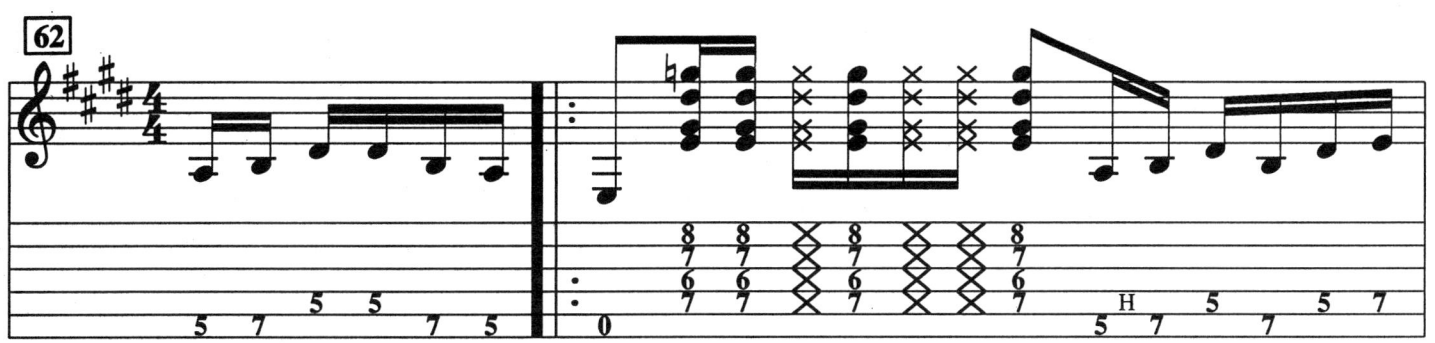

In the style of Jimi Hendrix

Shuffle Solo in E

In the style of Buddy Guy and Freddie King

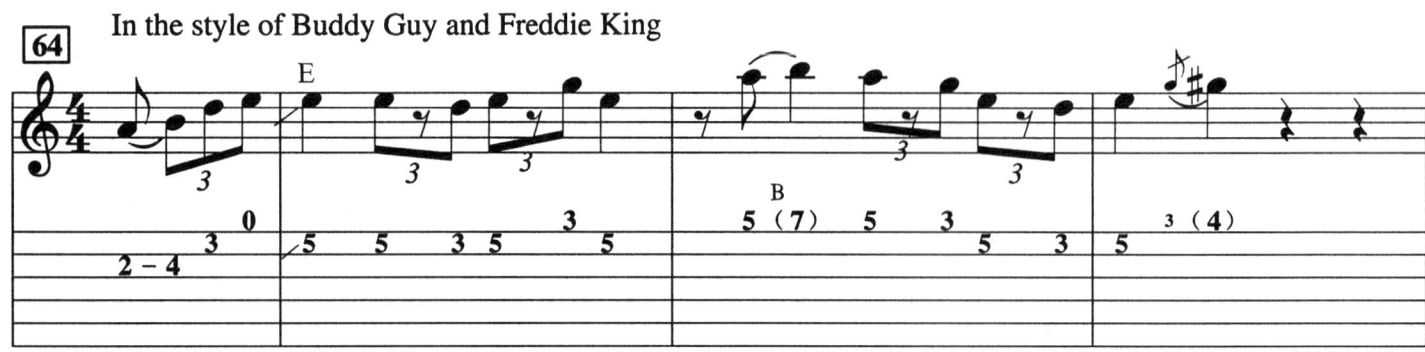

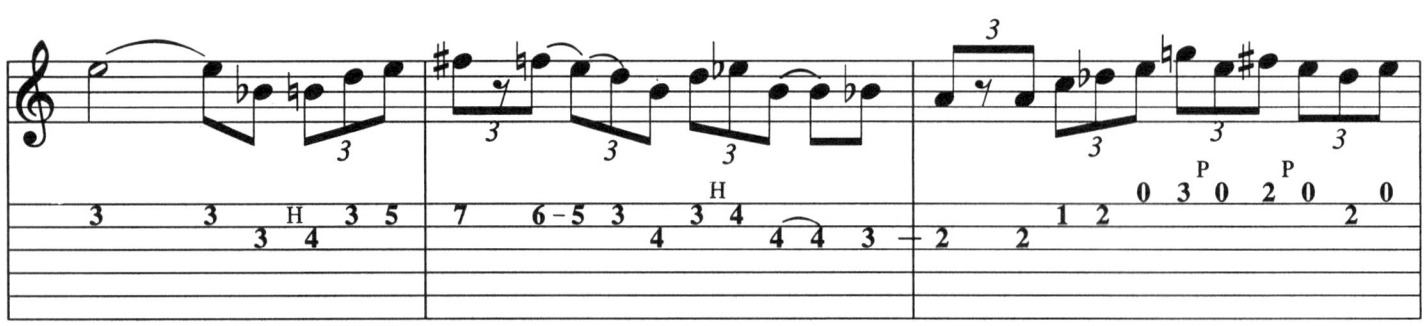

Bottom-End Boogie in E

More Bending String Licks in E

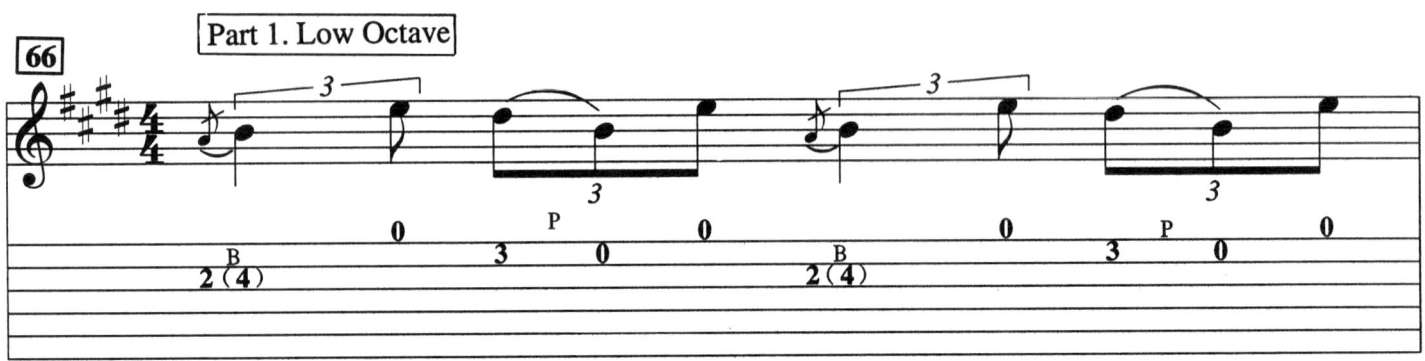

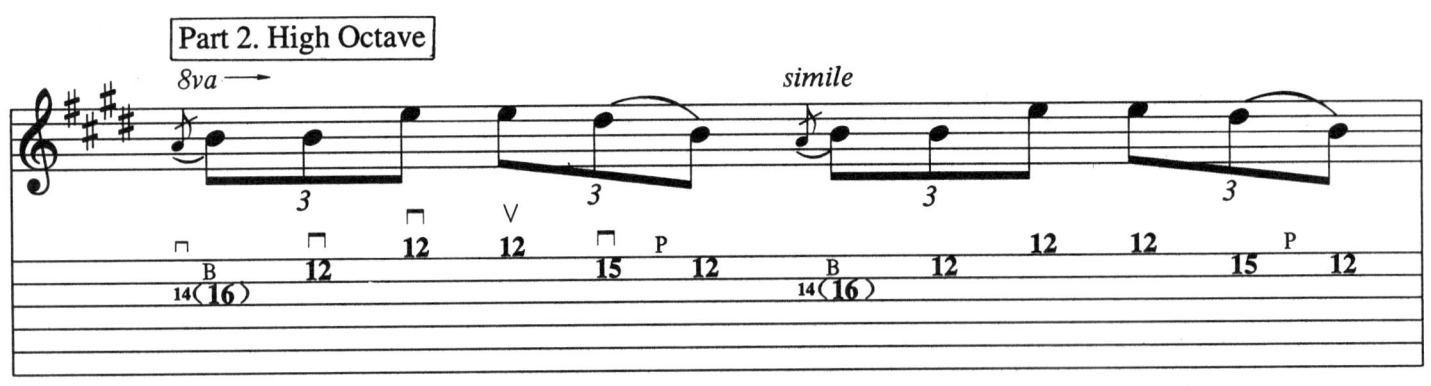

Slide Guitar Licks

(Open E Chord Tuning)

Section 2
Licks and Phrases in the Key of F

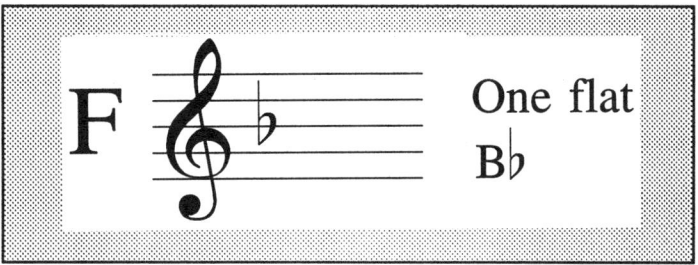

F   One flat
B♭

Solos used in this section are based on the blues minor scale below.

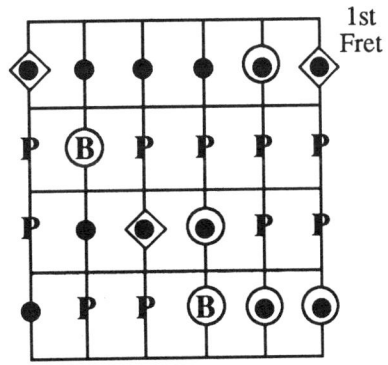

1st Fret

◆ = Root (key) notes
F

◉ = Popular notes to bend

Ⓑ = Blue notes
(flat 5th tones)

P = Passing tones
(see explanation in Section 1)

Standard Triplets in F

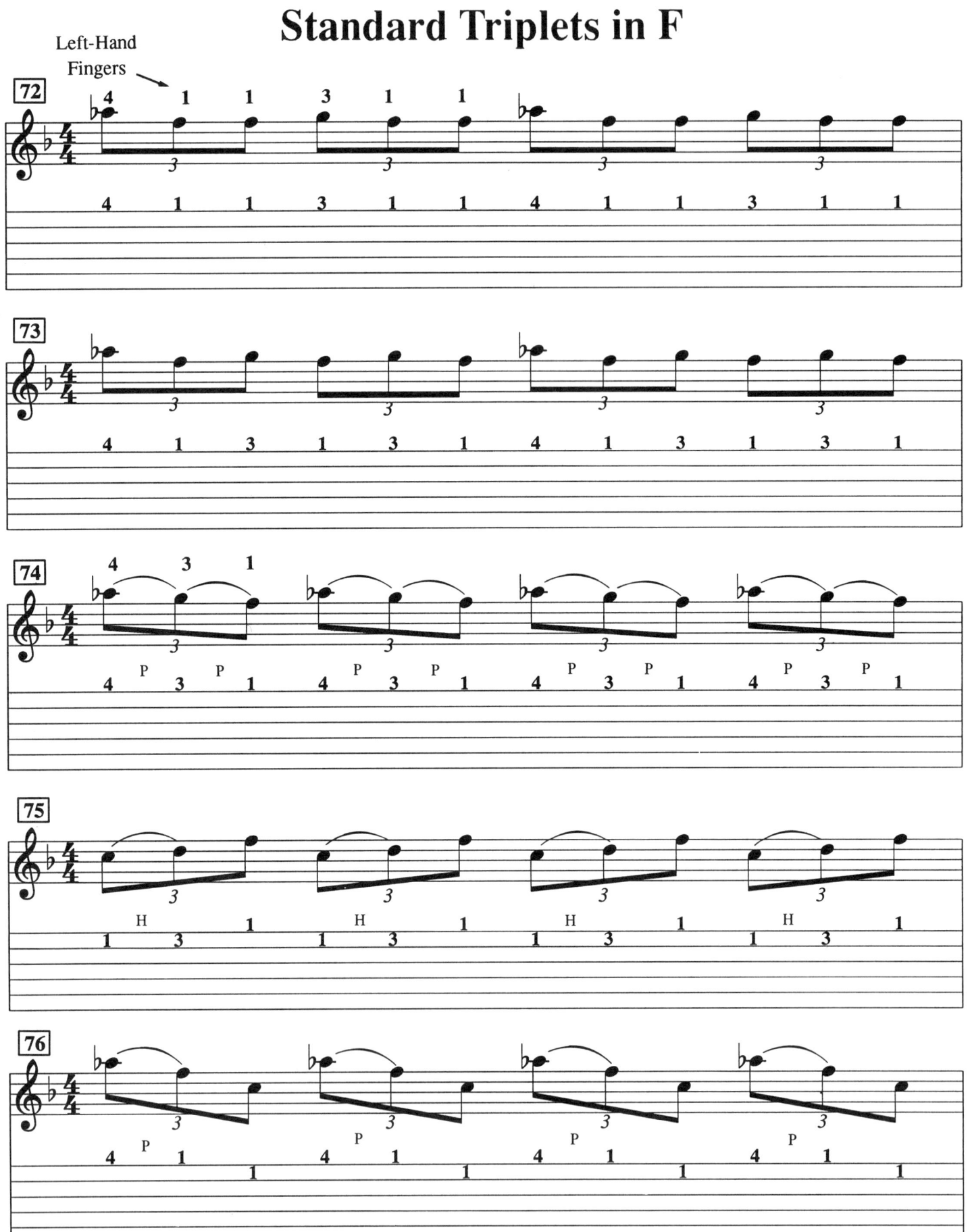

Note: Bar first finger over first and second strings for Solos 75, 76, 77, 78, 80, 81, and 82.

Standard Triplet Licks in F

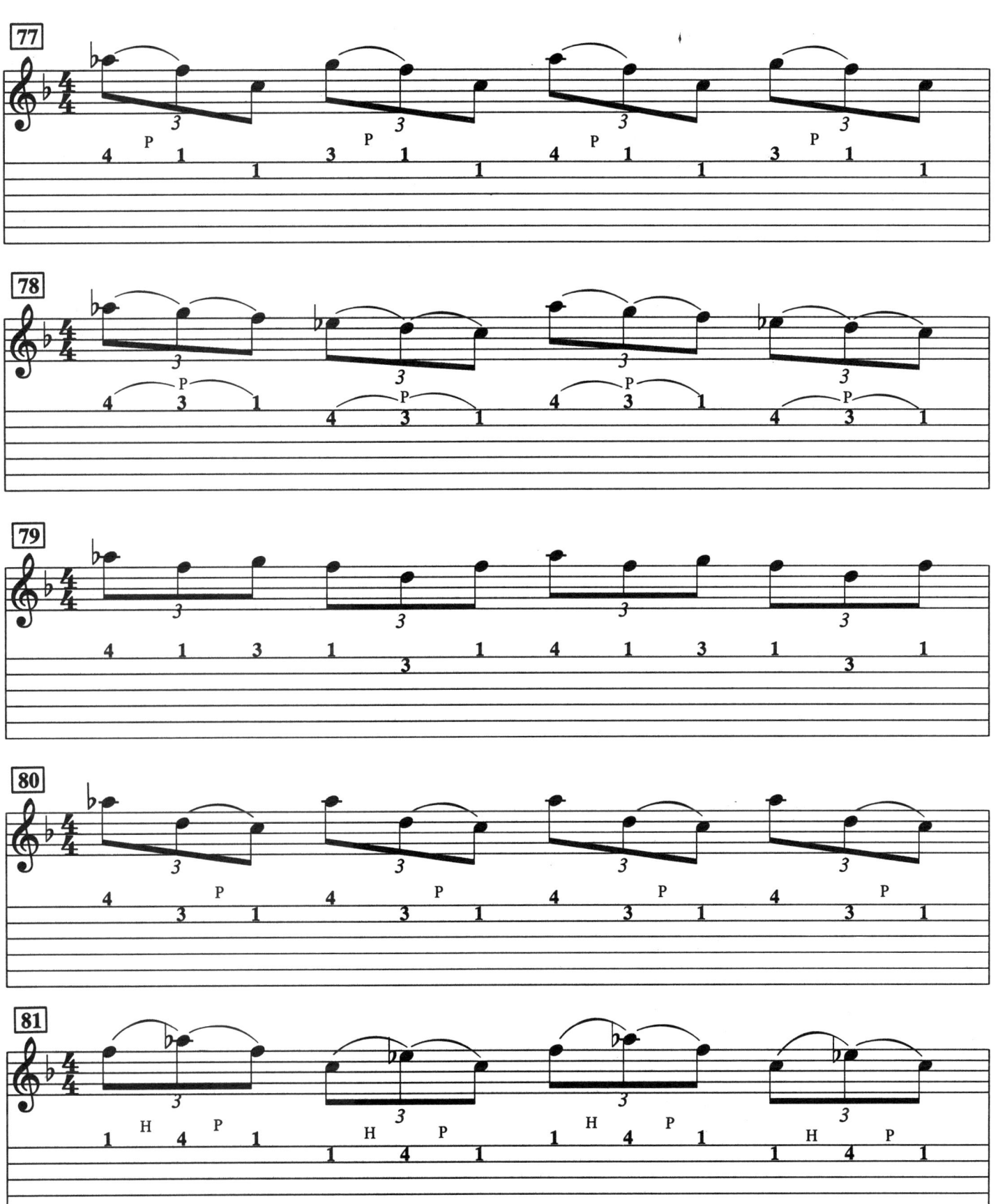

F

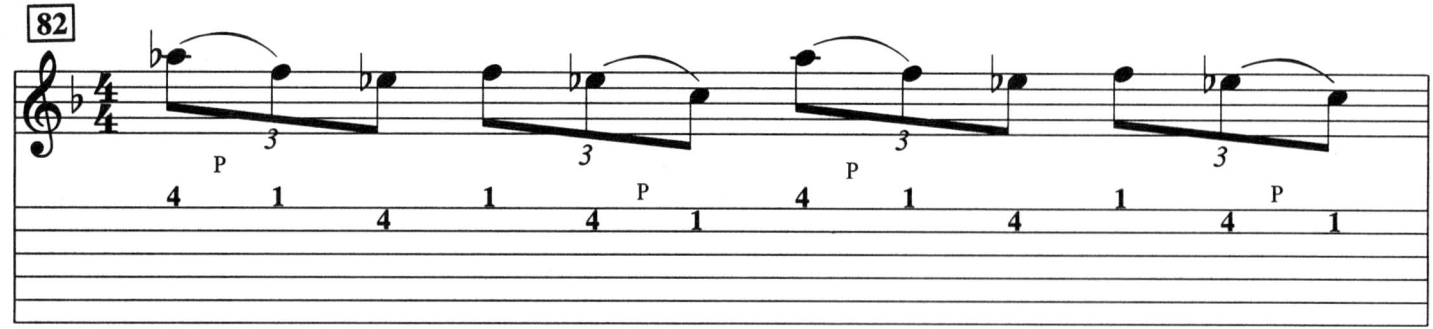

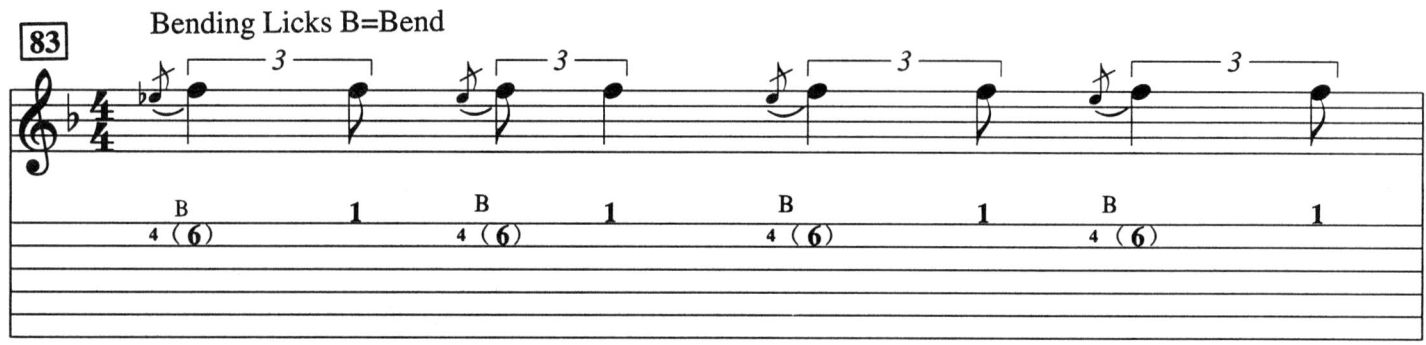

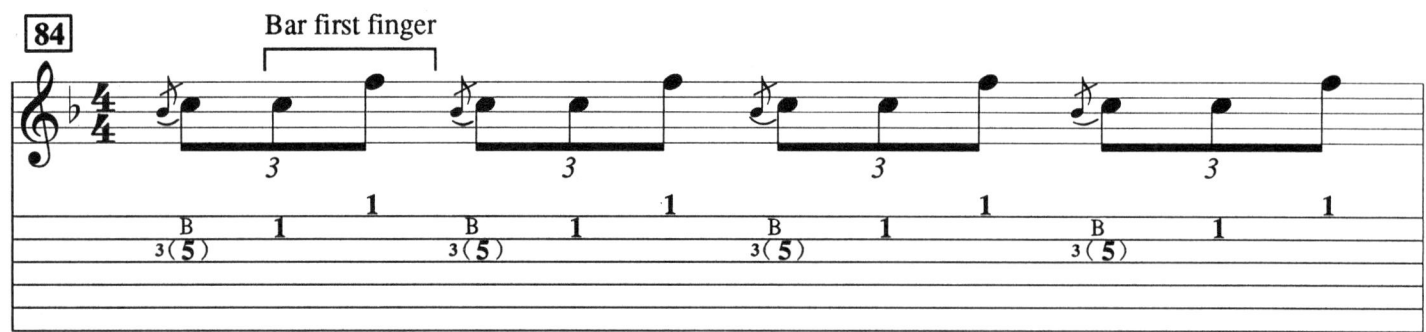

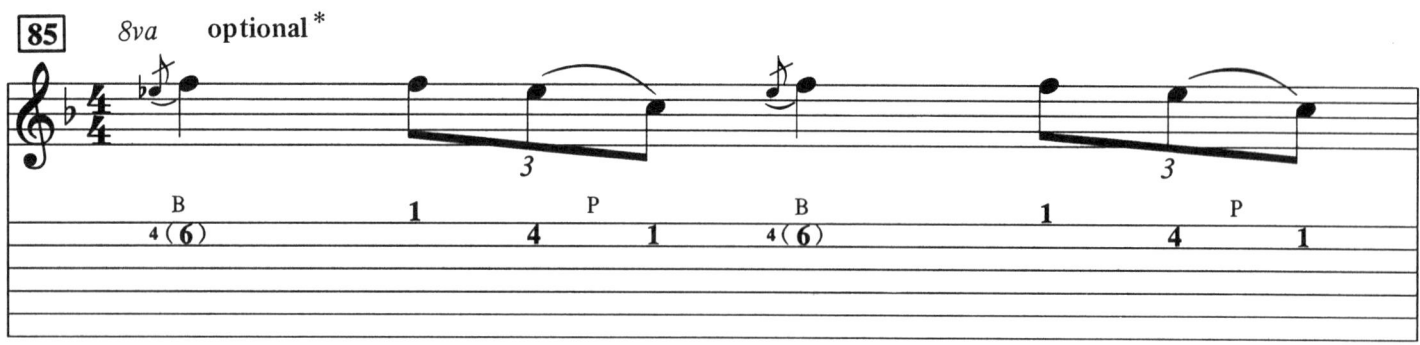

8va: **This means one octave above or 12 frets up the fretboard. In F, count 12 frets from the 1st fret to the 13th fret.**

F

In the style of Robert Johnson

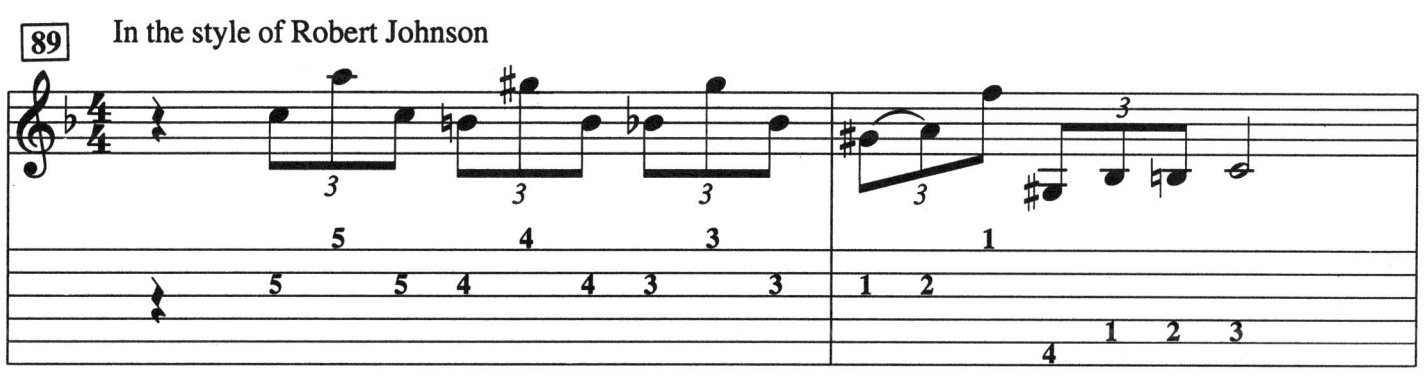

F

Funky Blues

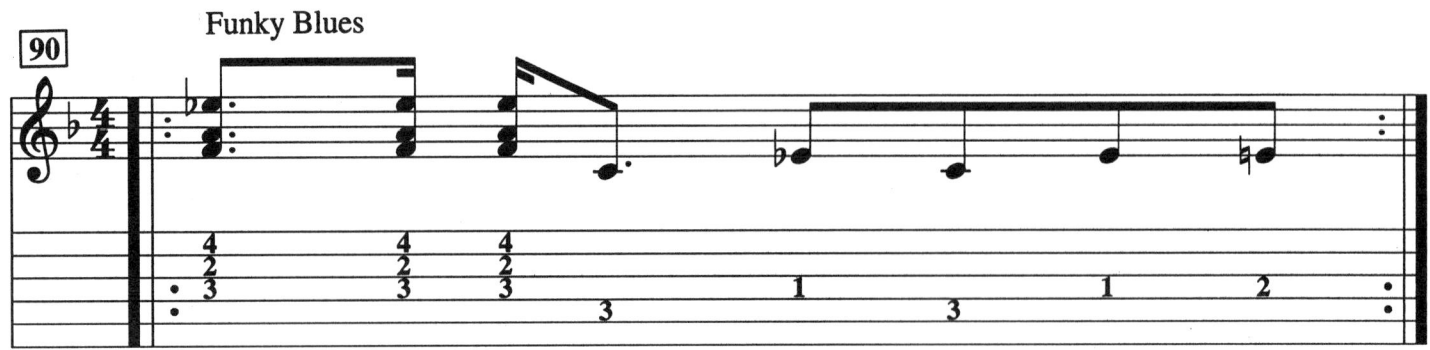

In the style of Stevie Ray Vaughan

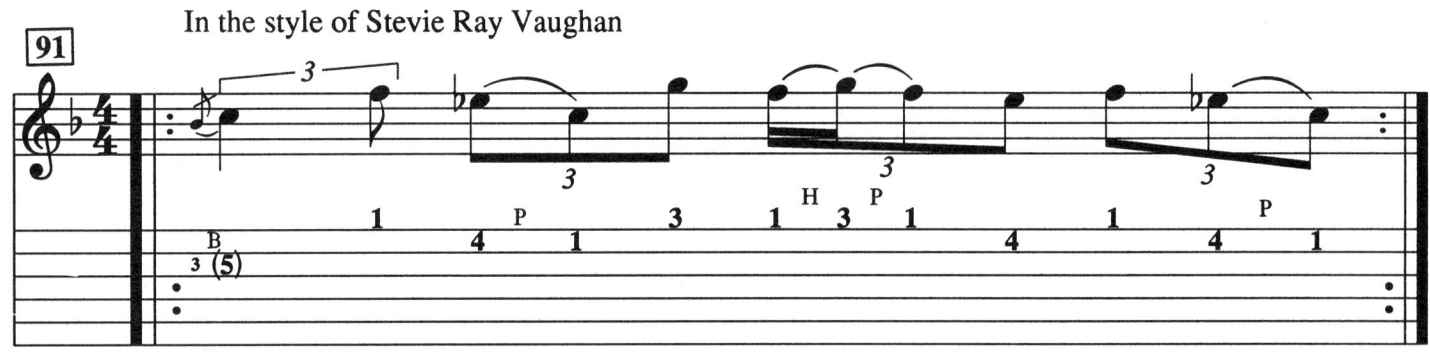

Section 3
Licks and Phrases
in the Key of F Sharp (F♯)

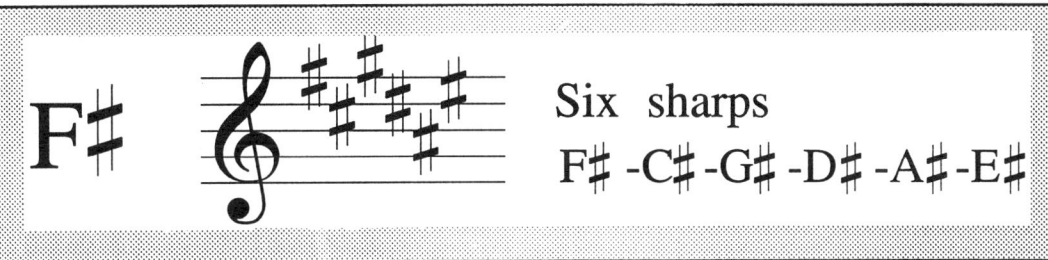

F♯   Six sharps
F♯ -C♯ -G♯ -D♯ -A♯ -E♯

Solos used in this section are based on the blues minor scale below.

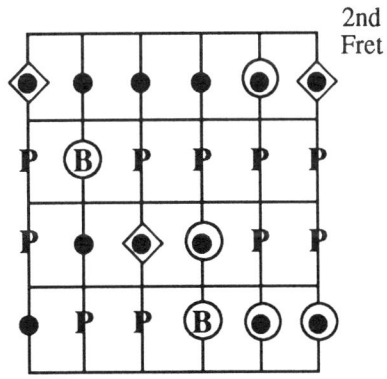

2nd
Fret

◈ = **Root (key) notes**
F

⦿ = **Popular notes to bend**

Ⓑ = **Blue notes (flat 5th tones)**

P = **Passing tones (see explanation in Section 1)**

F#

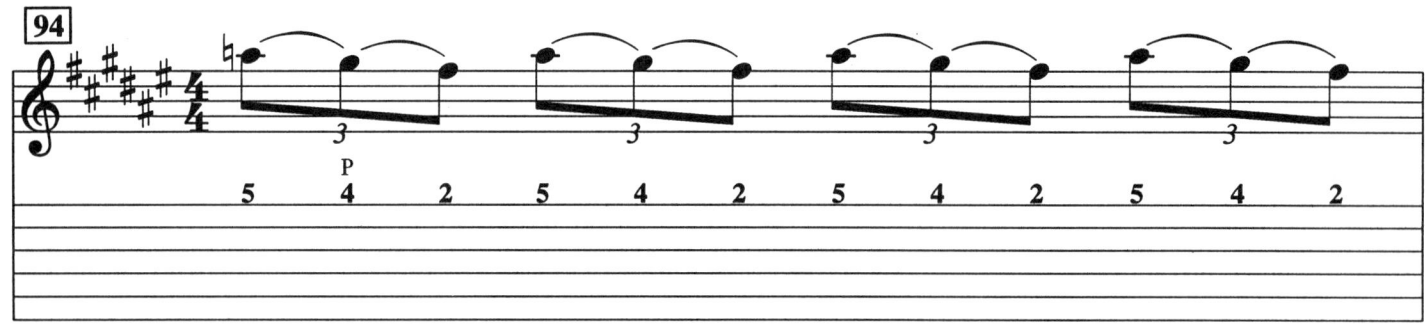

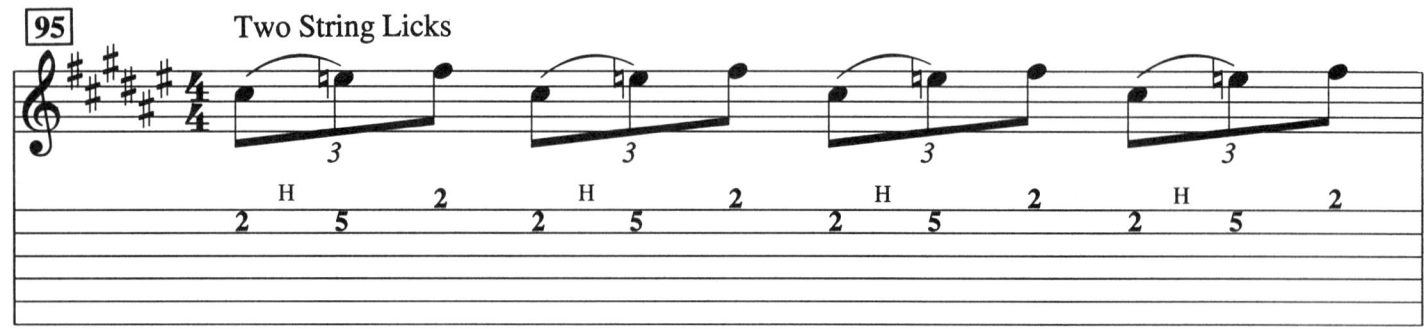

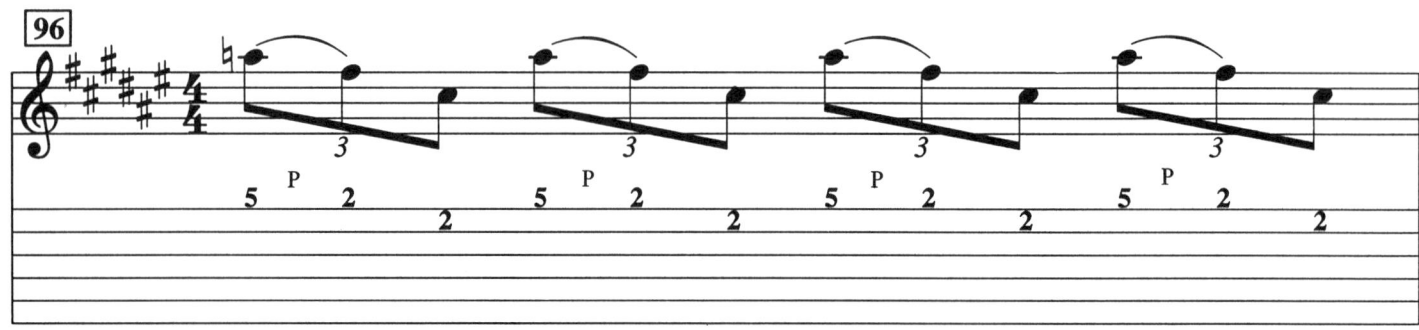

F#

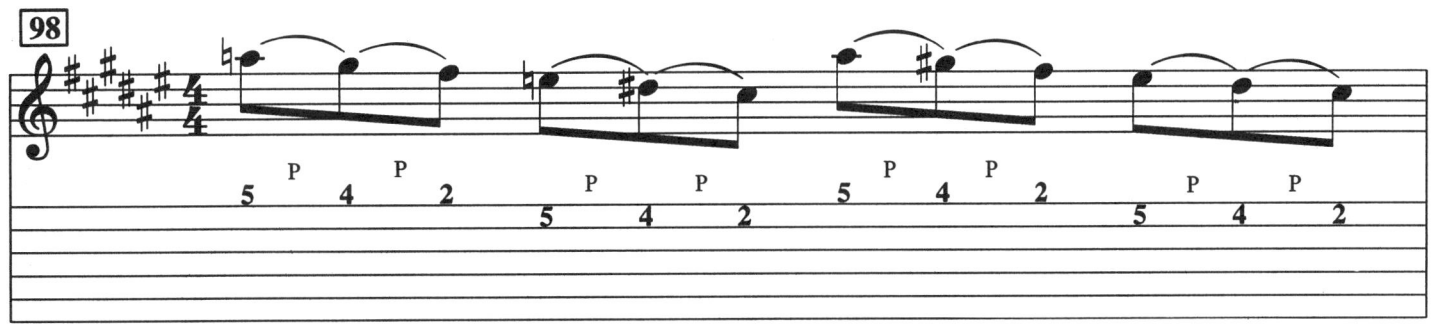

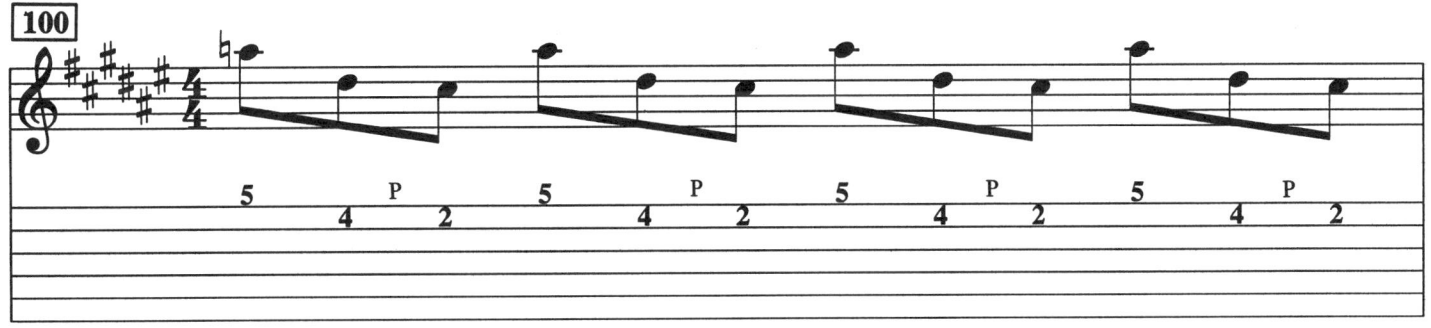

F♯

102

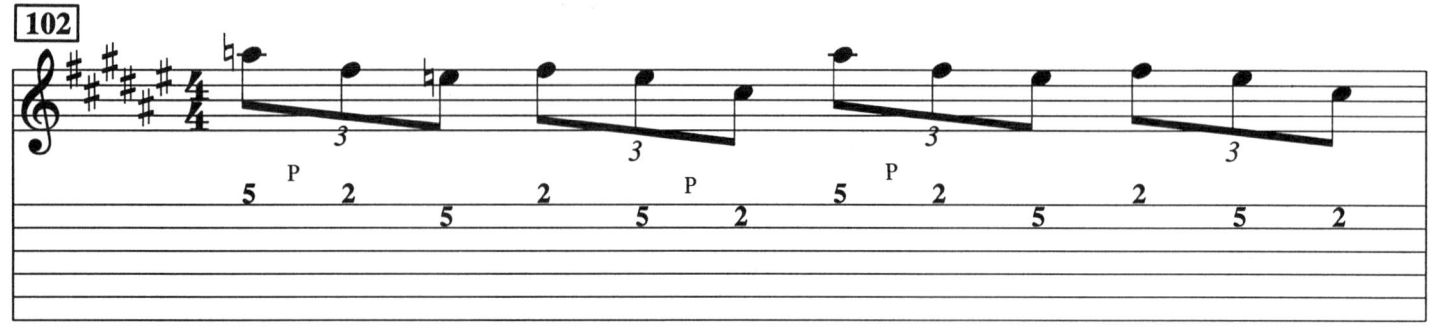

Style of Austin   **String Bending Licks**

103

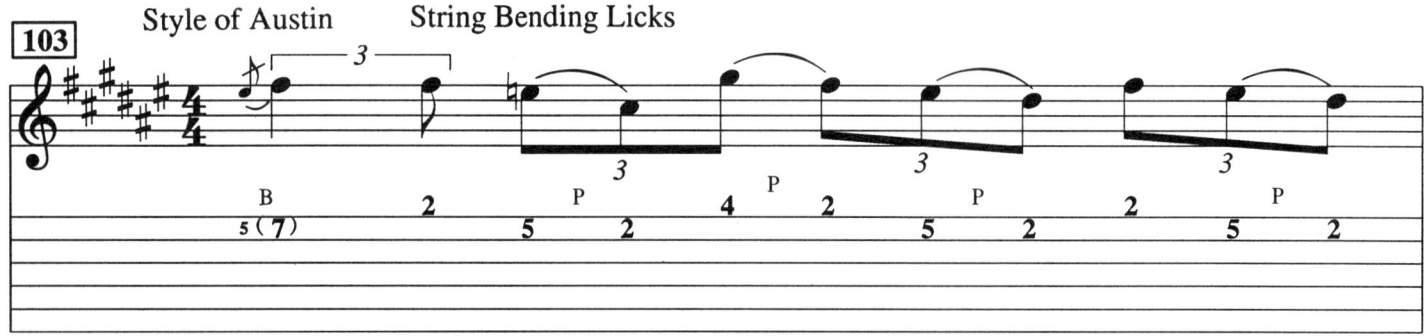

Style of Austin

104

Style of Austin

105

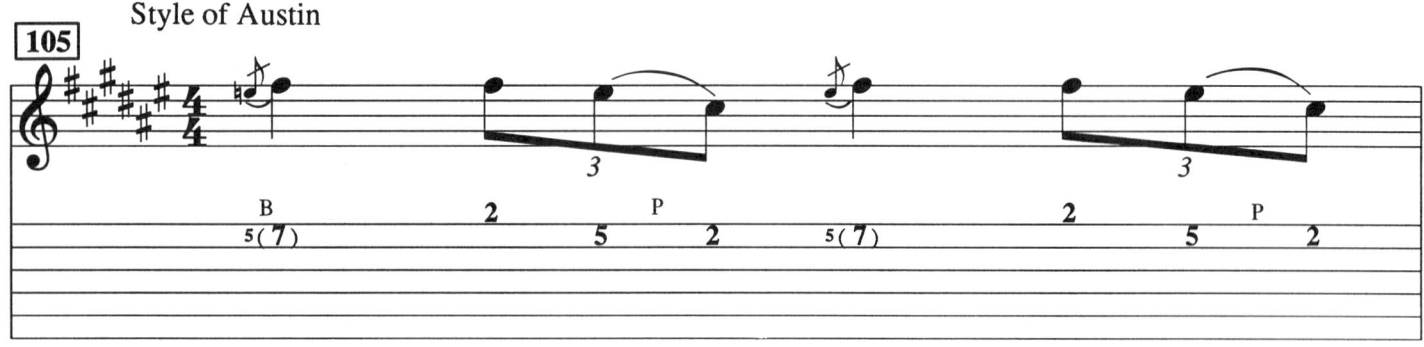

In the style of Jimmy Vaughan

106

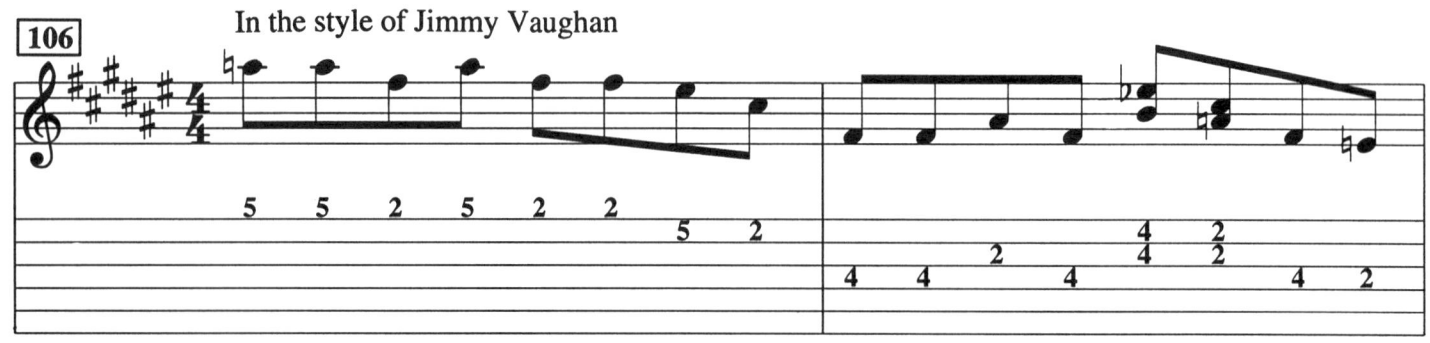

F♯

In the style of Jimmy Vaughan

107

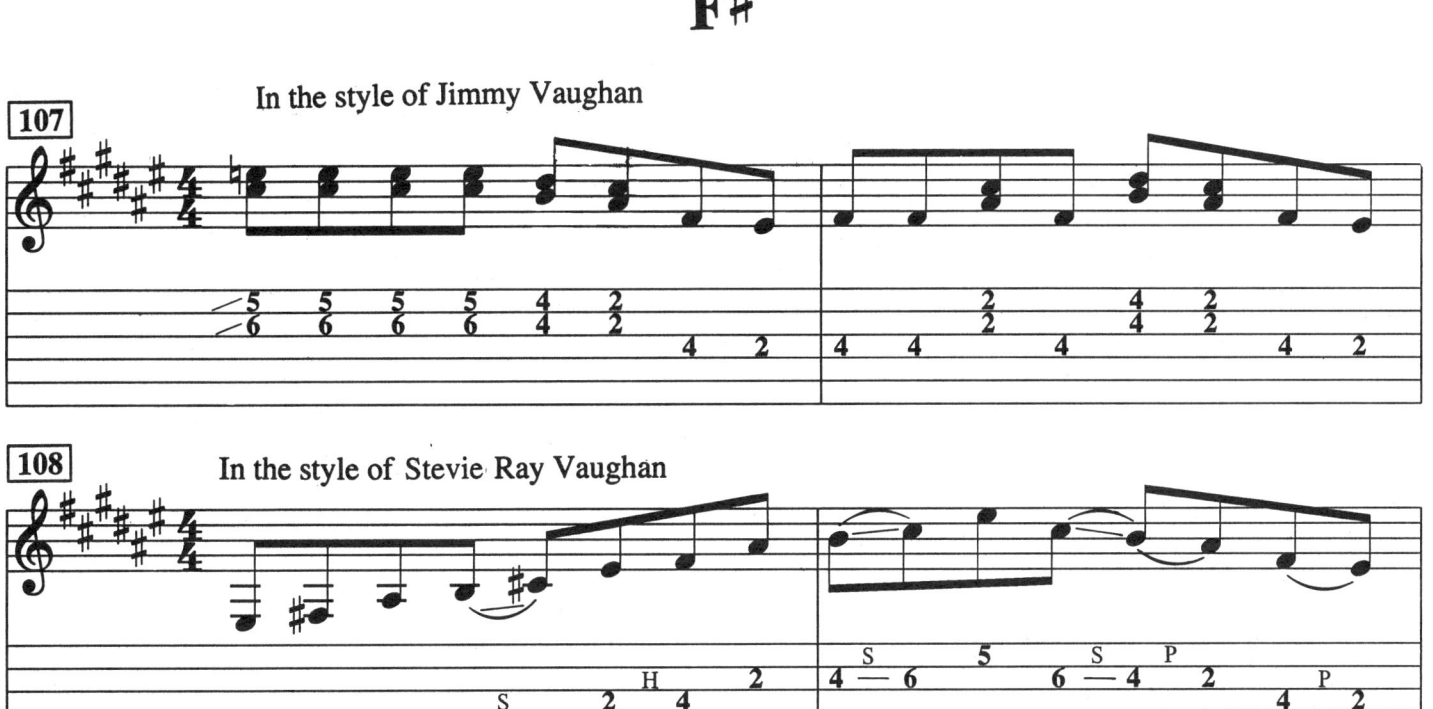

In the style of Stevie Ray Vaughan

108

In the style of Robert Johnson

109

Funky Blues

110

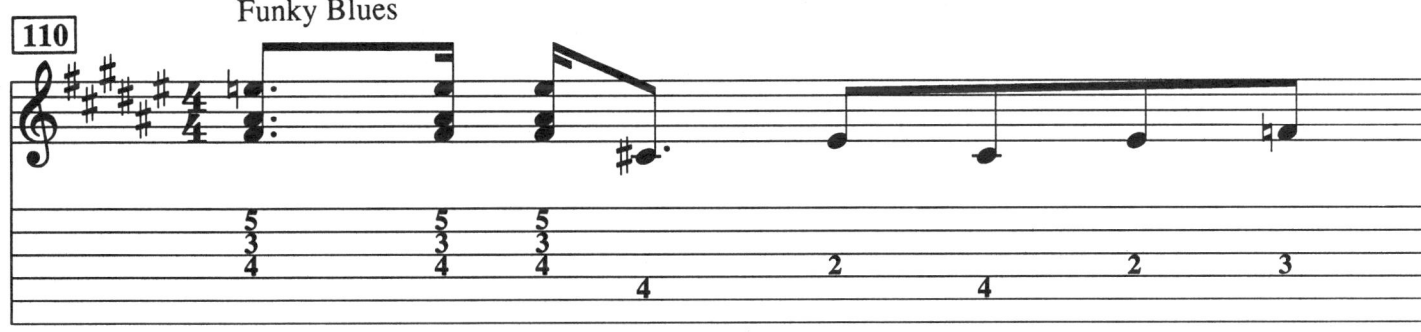

In the style of Stevie Ray Vaughan and Buddy Guy

111

Eighth Note and Quarter Note Triplet Licks

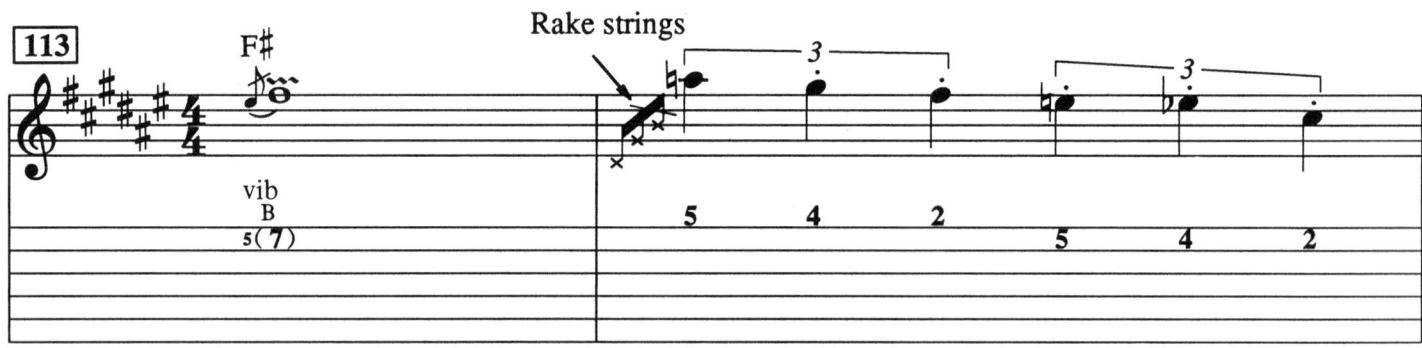

Section 4
Licks and Phrases
in the Key of G

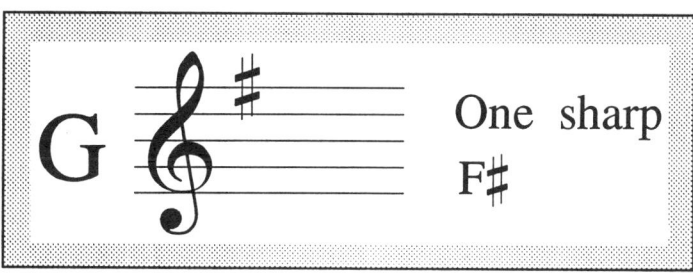

G — One sharp F♯

Solos used in this section are based on the blues minor scale below.

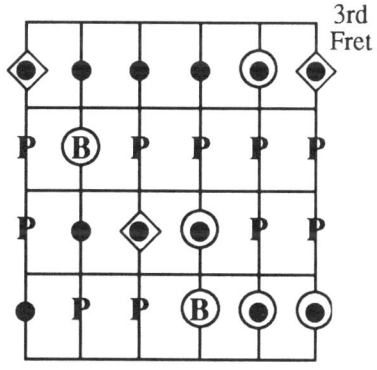

3rd
Fret

◆ = **Root (key) notes**
G

◉ = **Popular notes to bend**

Ⓑ = **Blue notes**
(flat 5th tones)

P = **Passing tones**
(see explanation in Section 1)

Standard Triplets in G

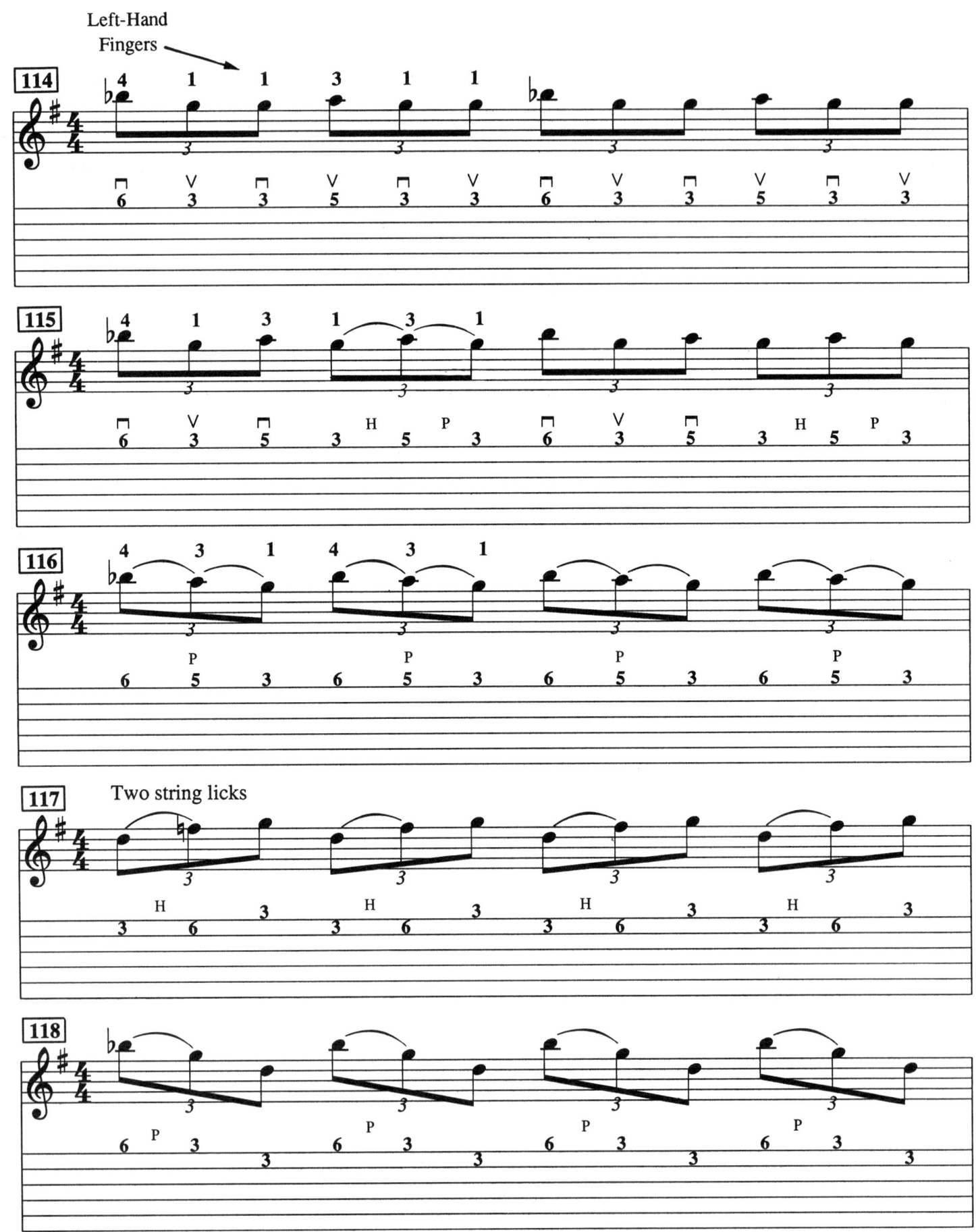

Note: Bar first finger over first and second strings for Solos 117, 118, 119, 120, 122, and 123.

More Triplets in G

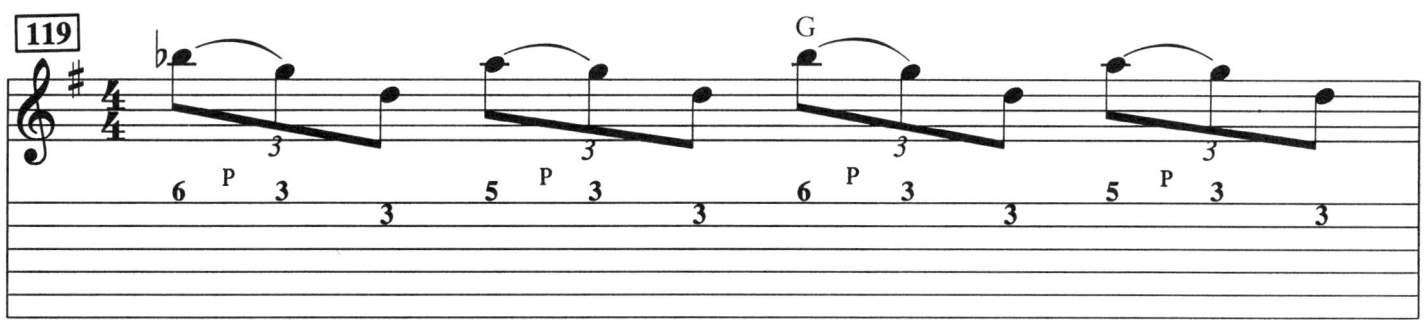

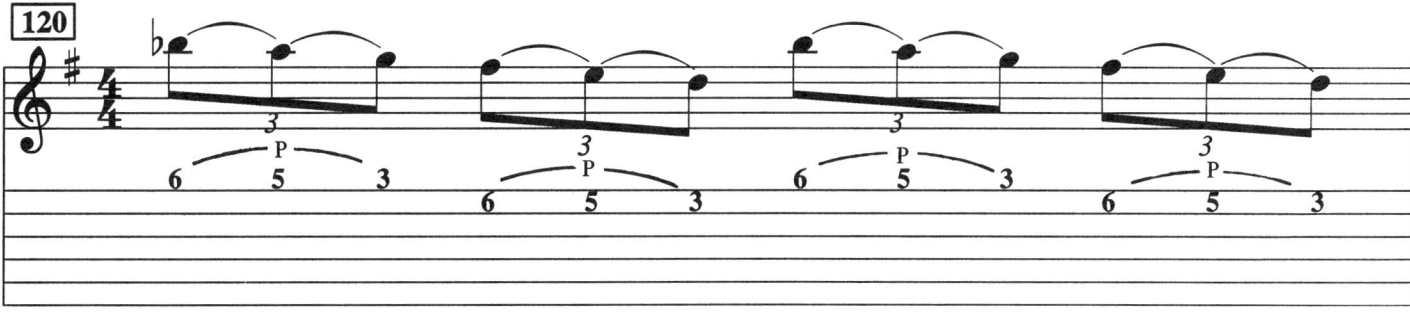

In the style of Jimmy Page (Blues Rock)

First finger bar over first and second strings.

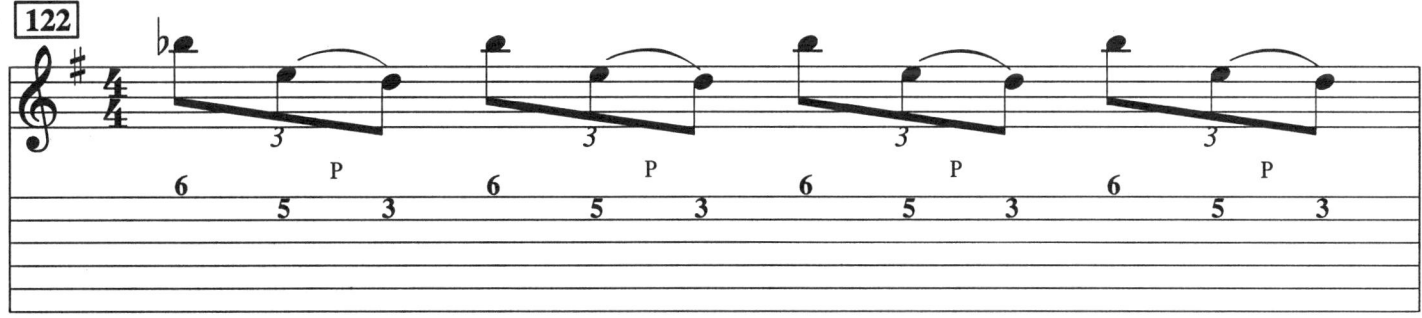

In the Style of Freddie King

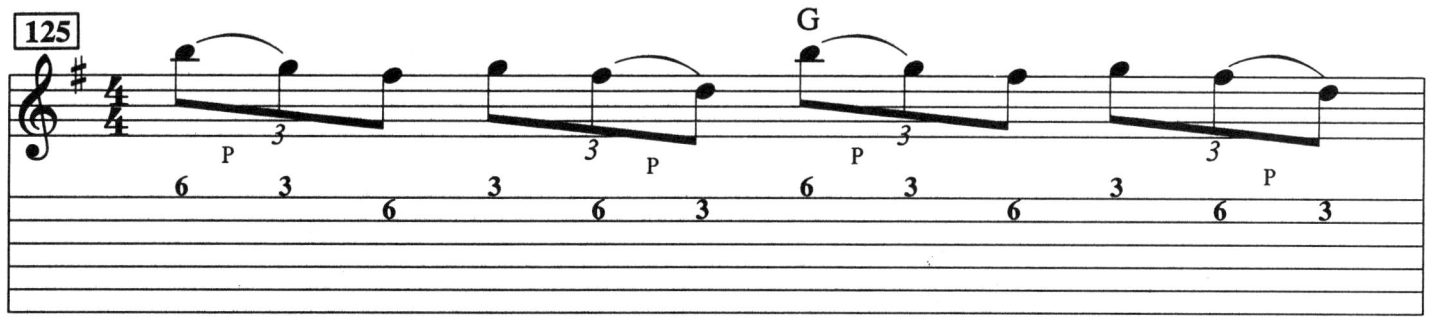

Standard Bending Licks & Phrases

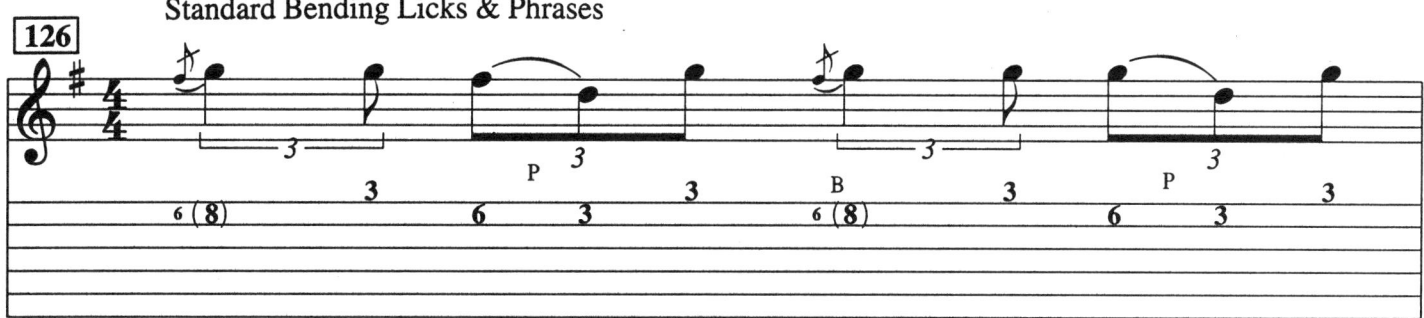

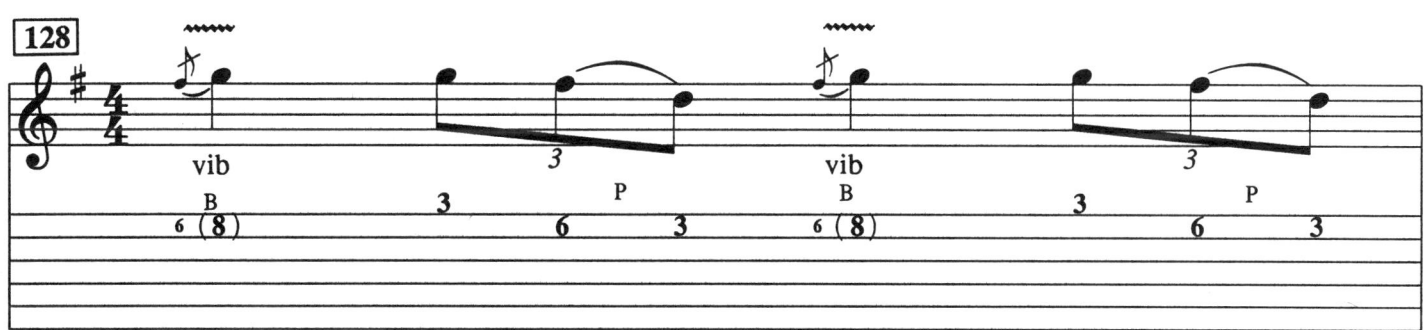

G

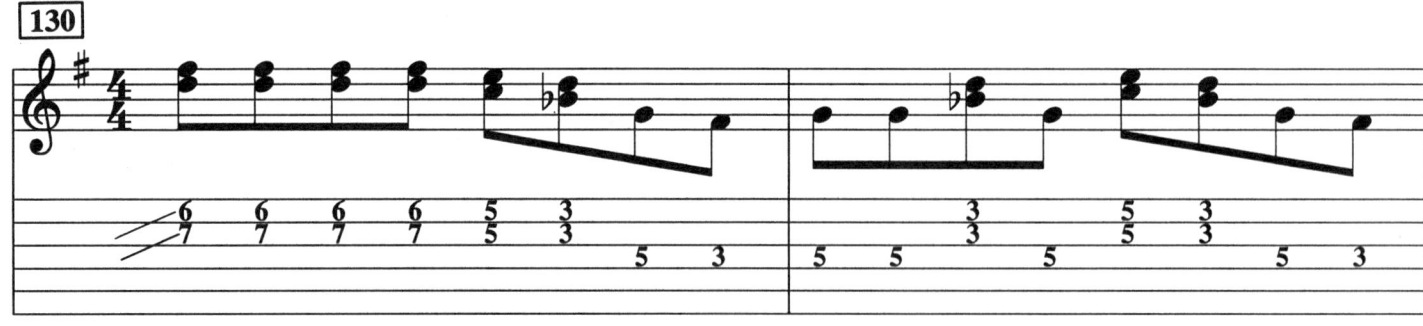

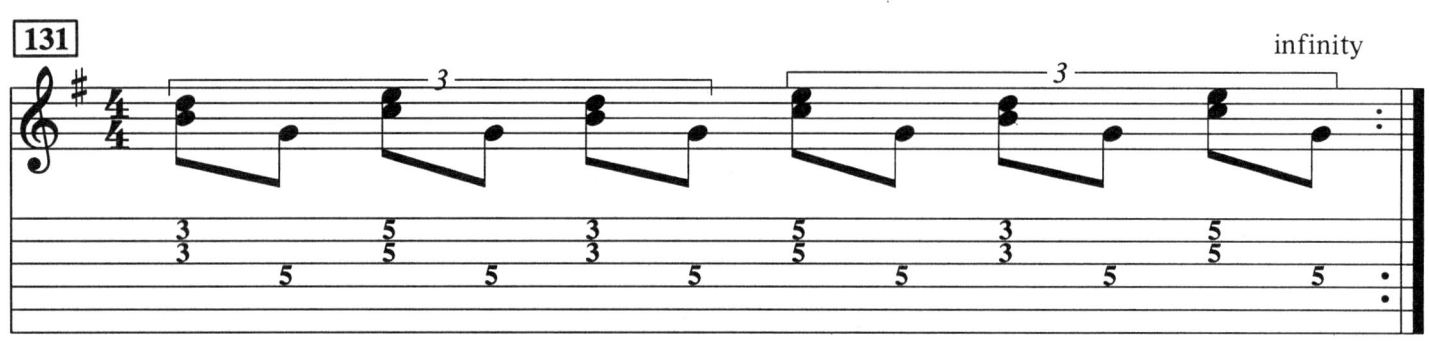

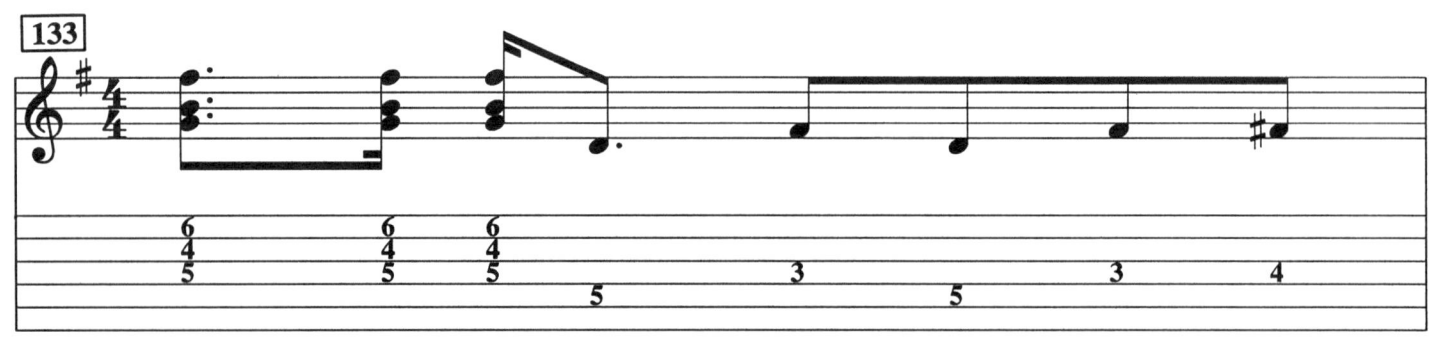

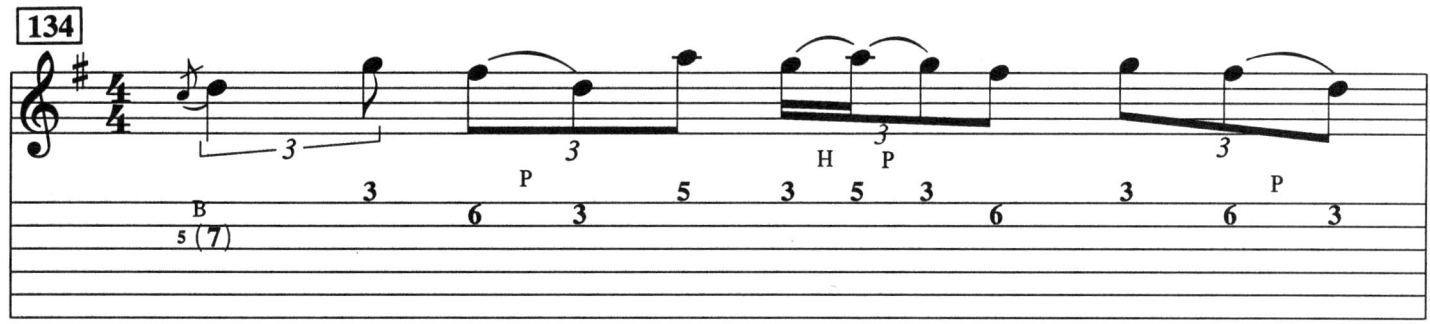

Rock and hillbilly combined were given the term "rockabilly."

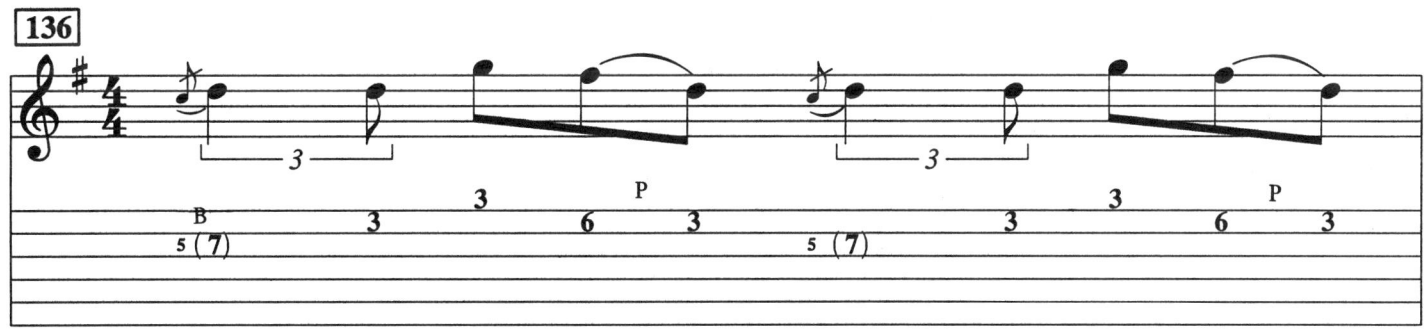

G

This solo is a high to low note movement using the slide of any left-hand finger.

RB = Reverse bend, a string bent from high note to low note.

RB = High note to low note bend. Without picking, ghost bend (pre-bend) second string up from fret 6 to fret 8, then pick the string, and release (8) string while maintaining sound back to fret 6.

Shuffle in G

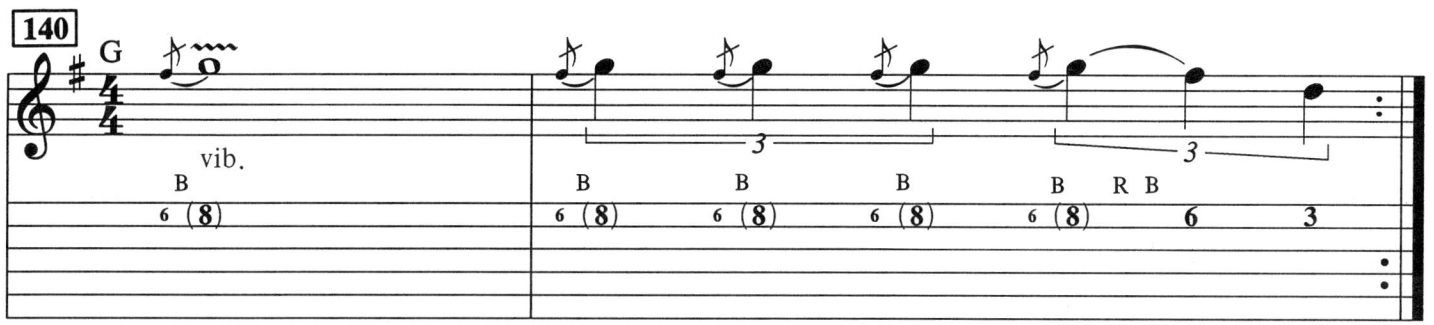

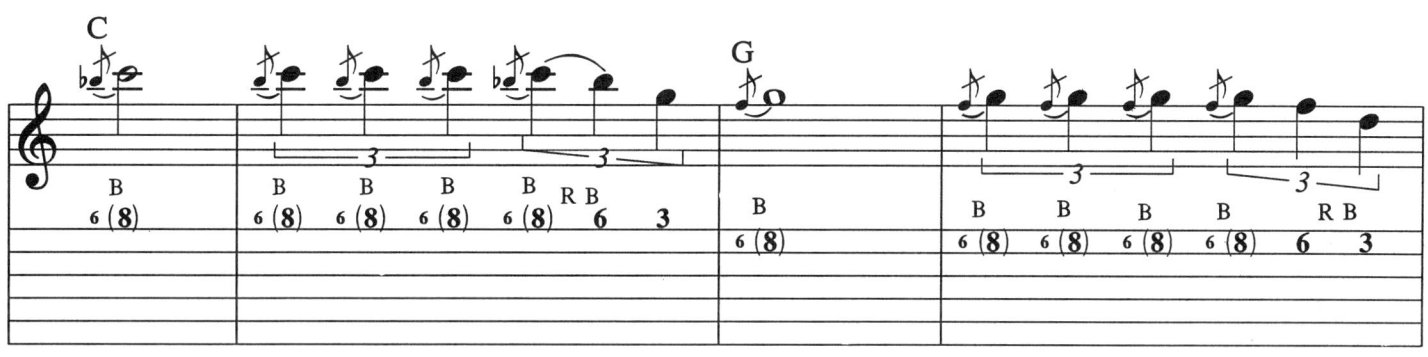

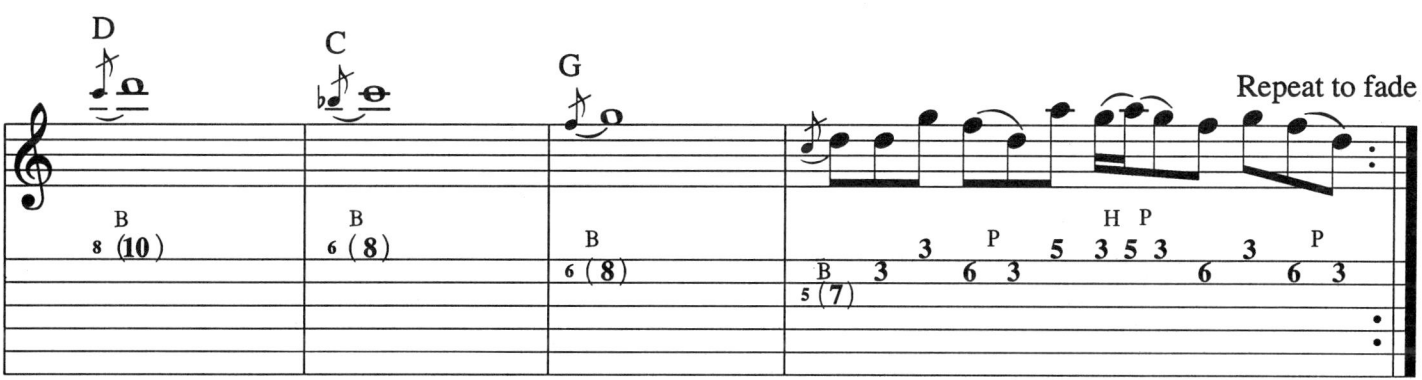

Country Blues Licks in G

141   Country Funk

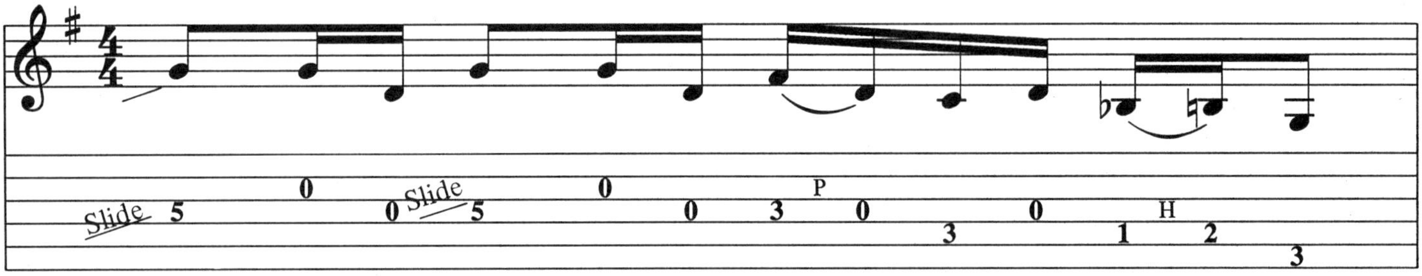

142   Country Blues (triplets)

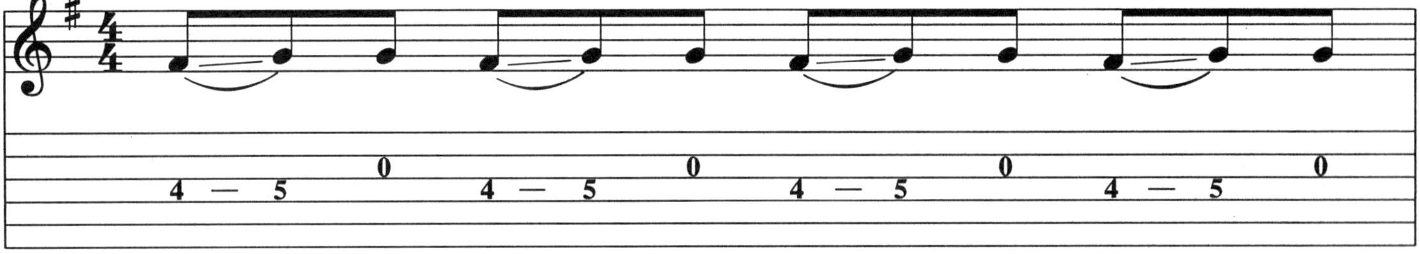

143   Country Rock

In the style of Eric Clapton

144   G

X = Lightly touch (mute) strings with left hand and strum with right hand (using a pick) to create a scratchy, percussive sound.

58

Section 5
Licks and Phrases
in the Key of A Flat (A♭)

A♭   Four flats
B♭ -E♭ -A♭ -D♭

Solos used in this section are based on the blues minor scale below.

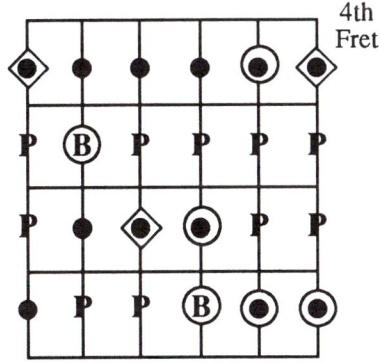

4th
Fret

◈ = **Root (key) notes**
A♭

◉ = **Popular notes to**
Bend

Ⓑ = **Blue notes**
(flat 5th tones)

P = **Passing tones**
(see explanation
in Section 1)

Standard Triplet Licks in A♭

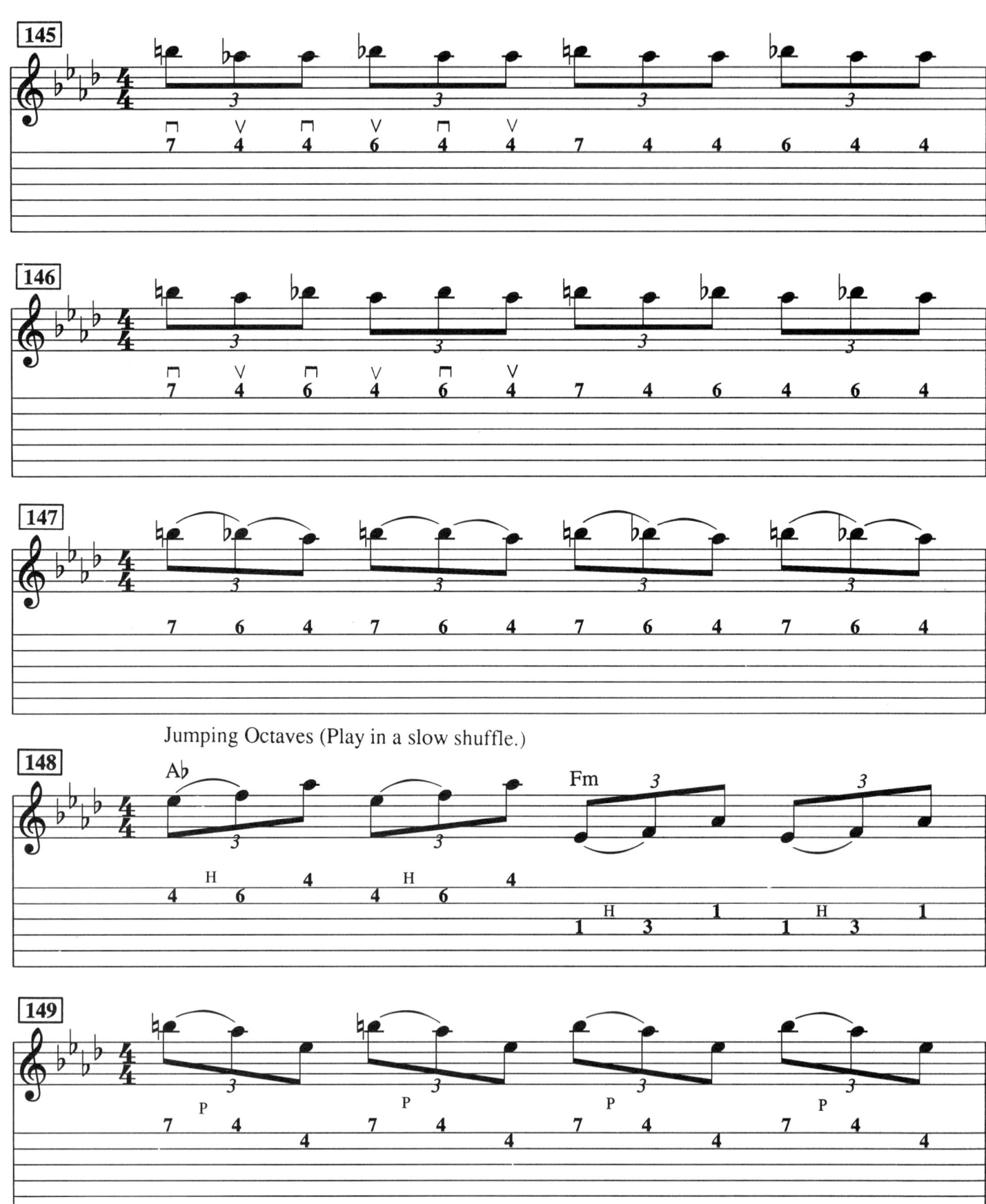

A♭

A♭

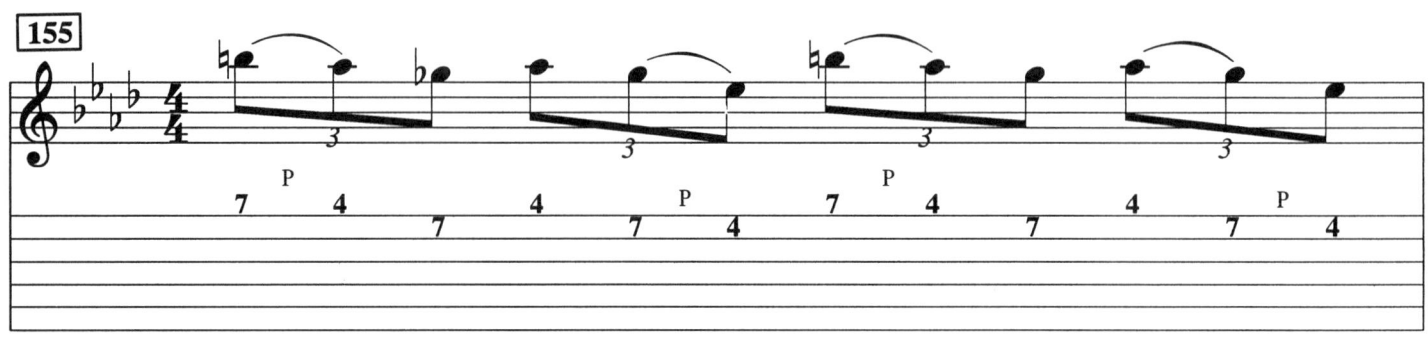

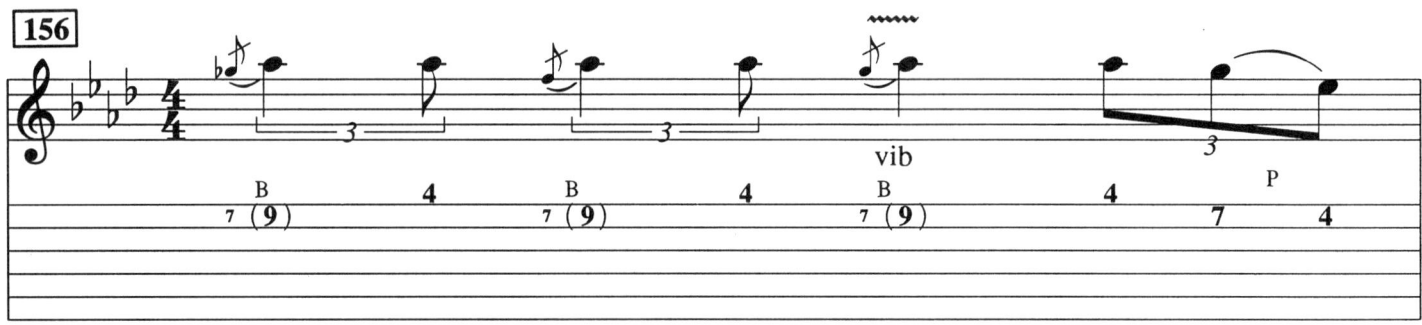

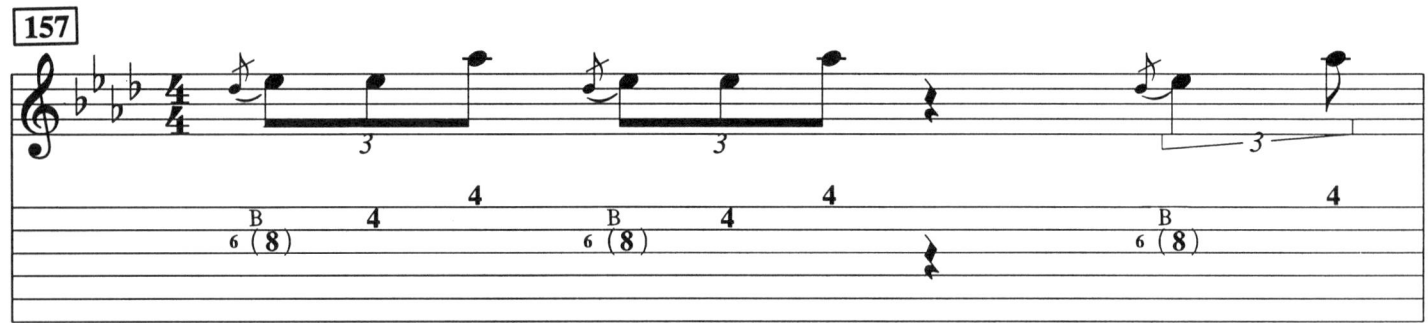

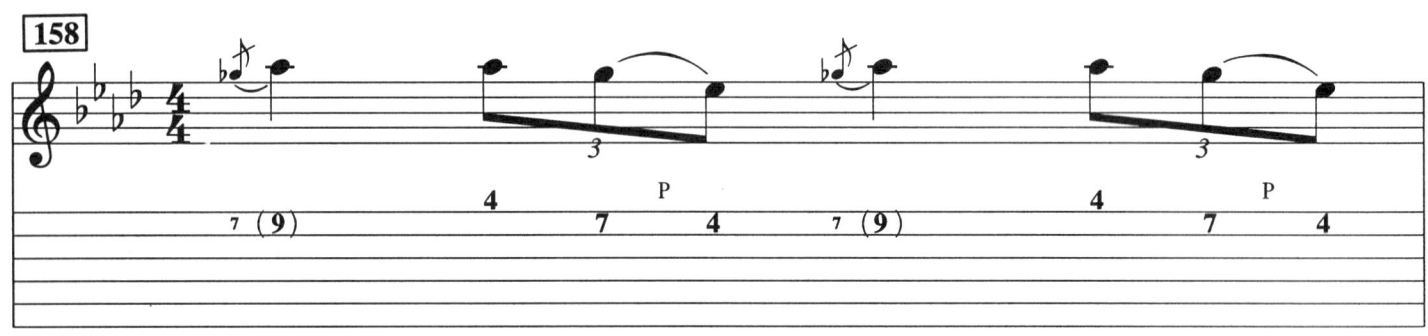

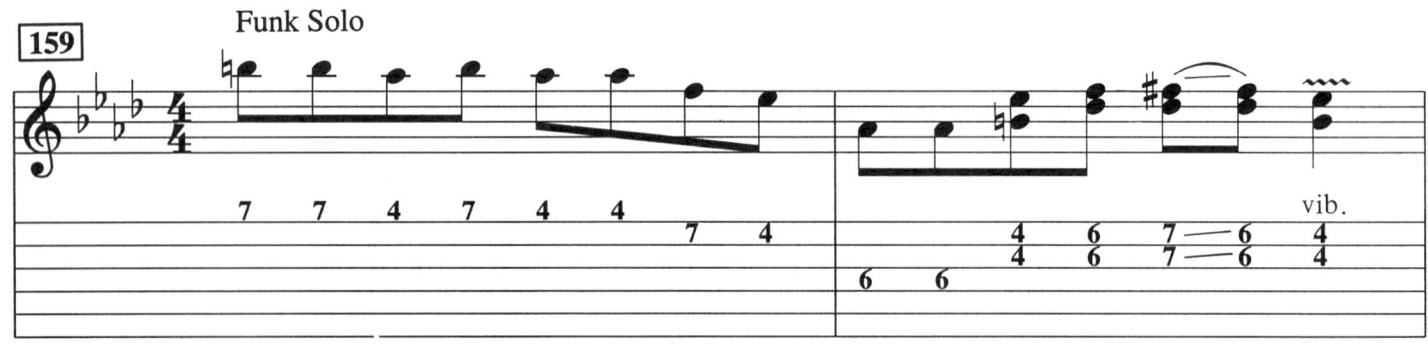

Triplet Licks in A♭

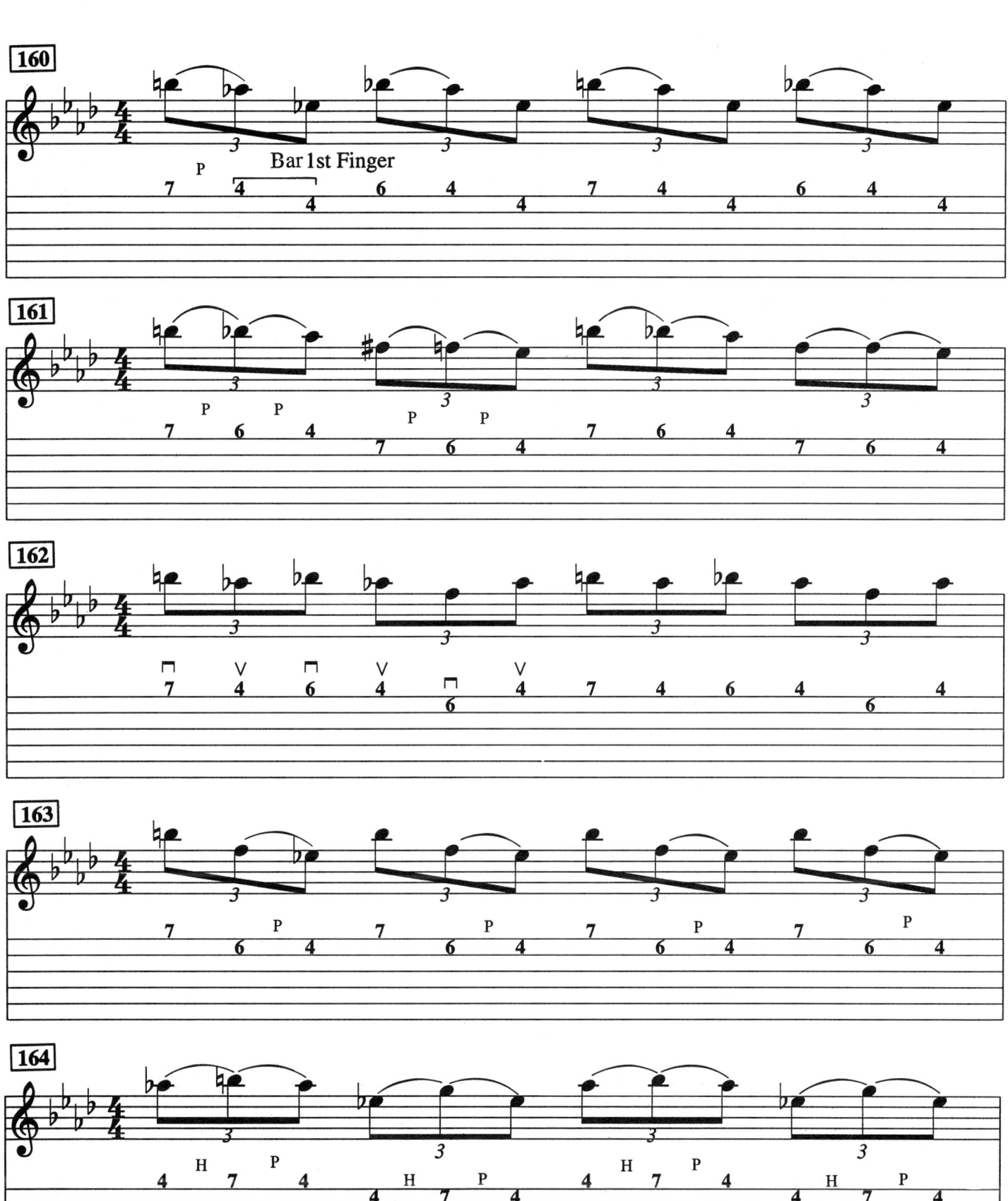

Section 6
Licks and Phrases
in the Key of A

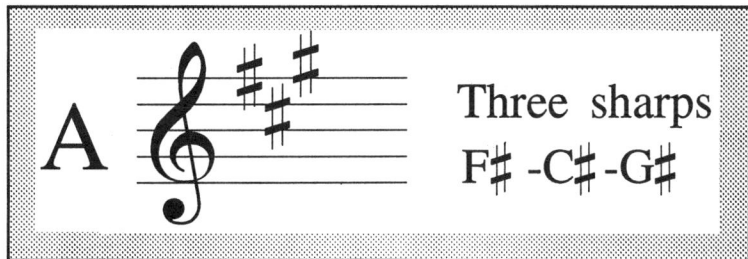

A   Three sharps
F♯ -C♯ -G♯

Solos used in this section are based on the blues minor scale below.

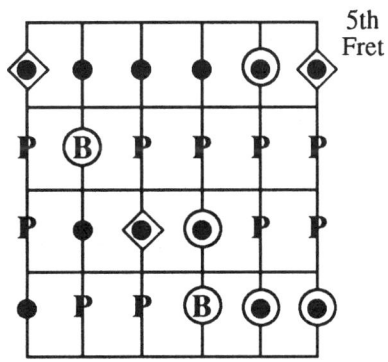

5th
Fret

◆ = Root (key) notes
    A

◉ = Popular notes to
    bend

Ⓑ = Blue notes
    (flat 5th tones)

P = Passing tones
    (see explanation
    in Section 1)

Single Play in A

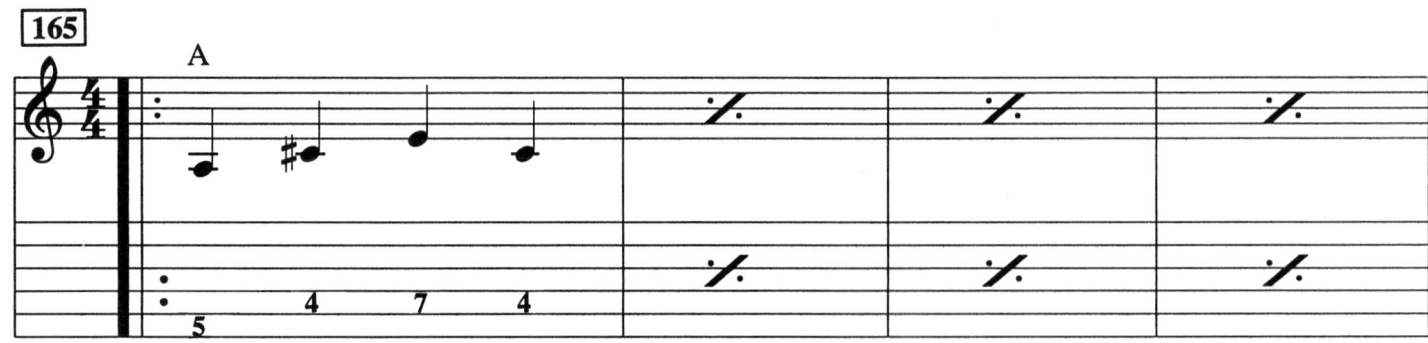

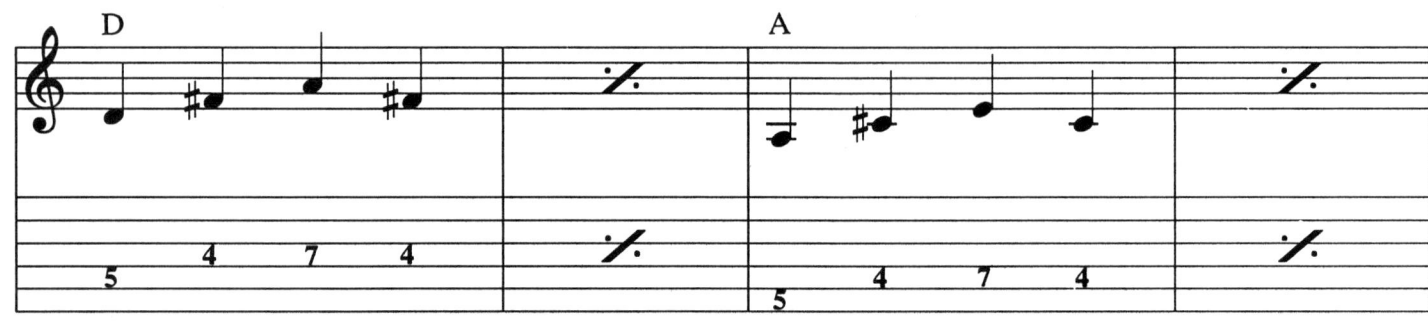

Double Play in A

A

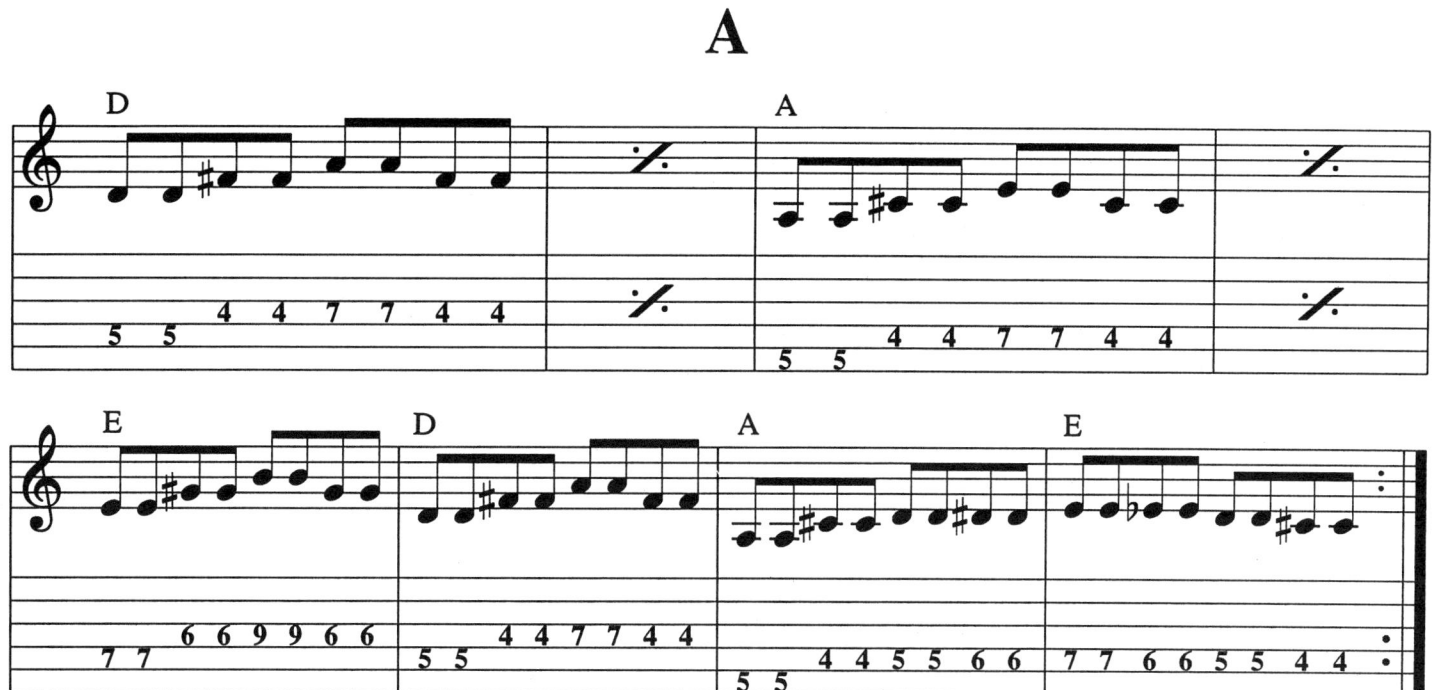

Raddle N Roll

167

A
Bed Rock Stomp

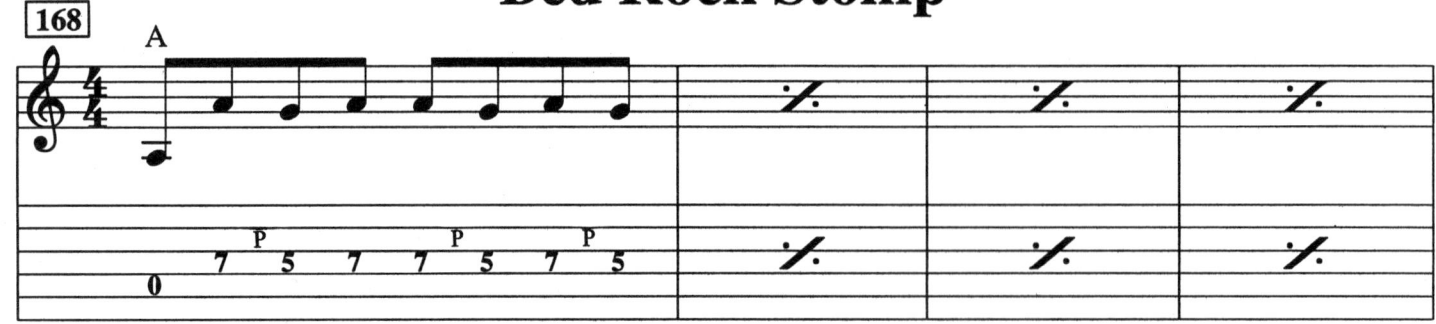

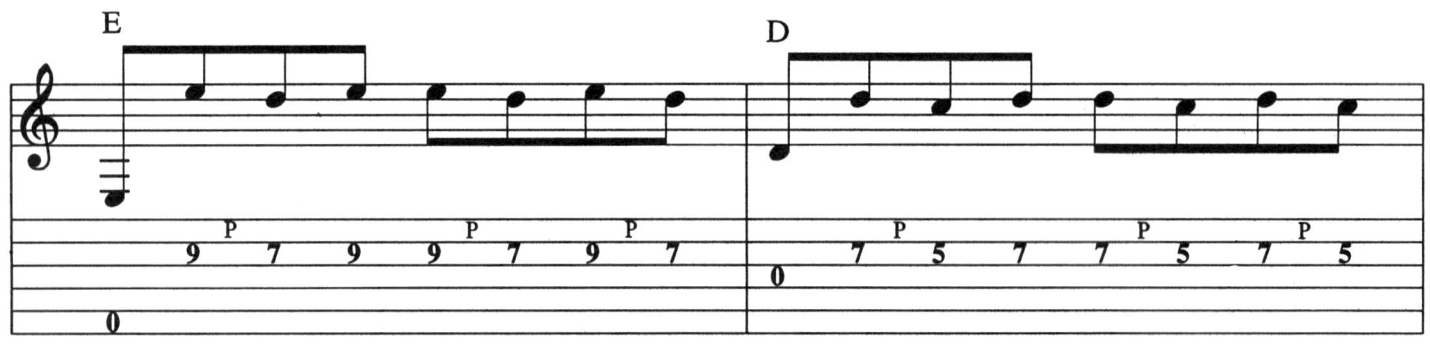

"A" Student

Key-of-A Standard Triplet Licks

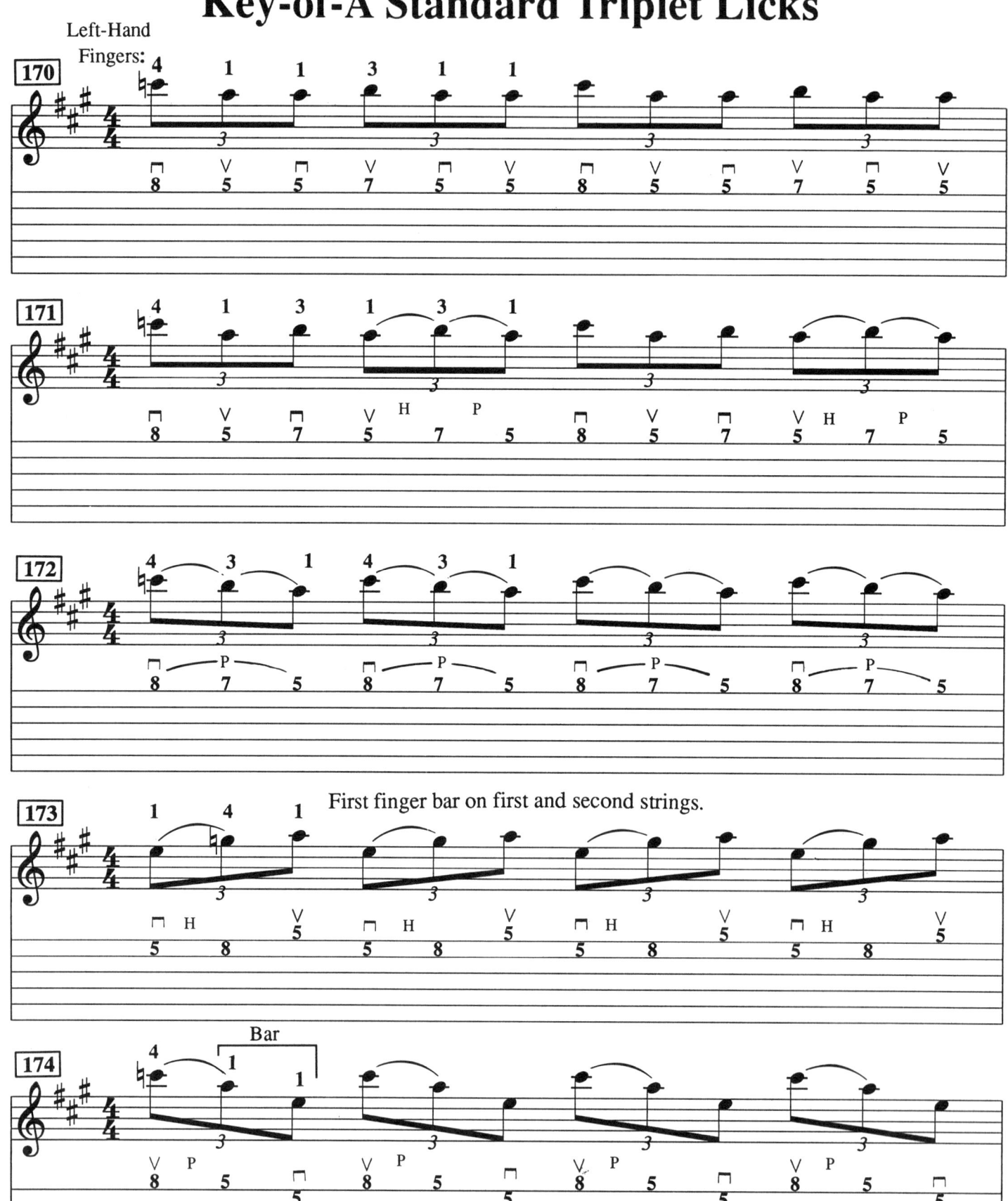

Standard Triplet Licks in A

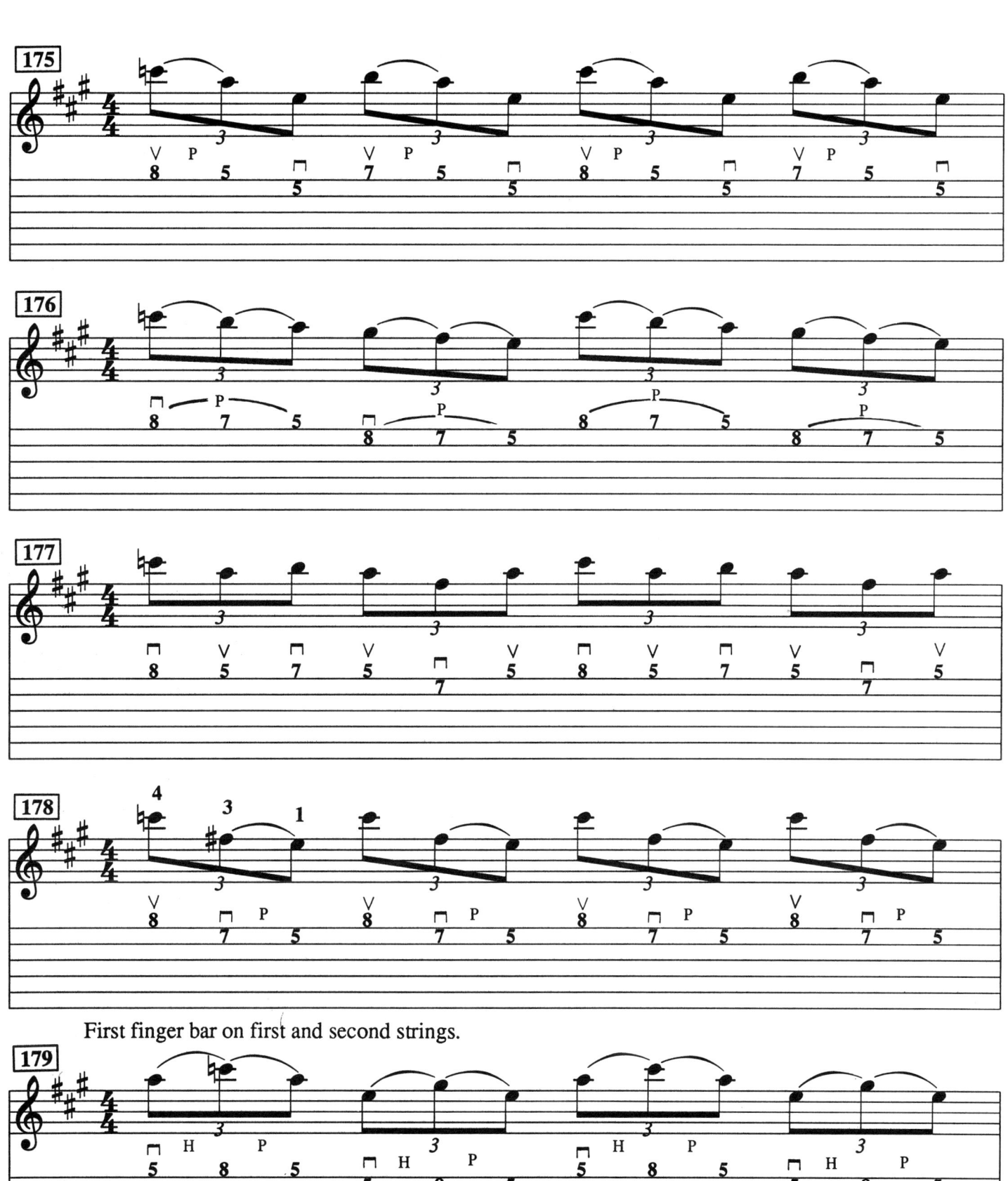

First finger bar on first and second strings.

Standard Clichés in A

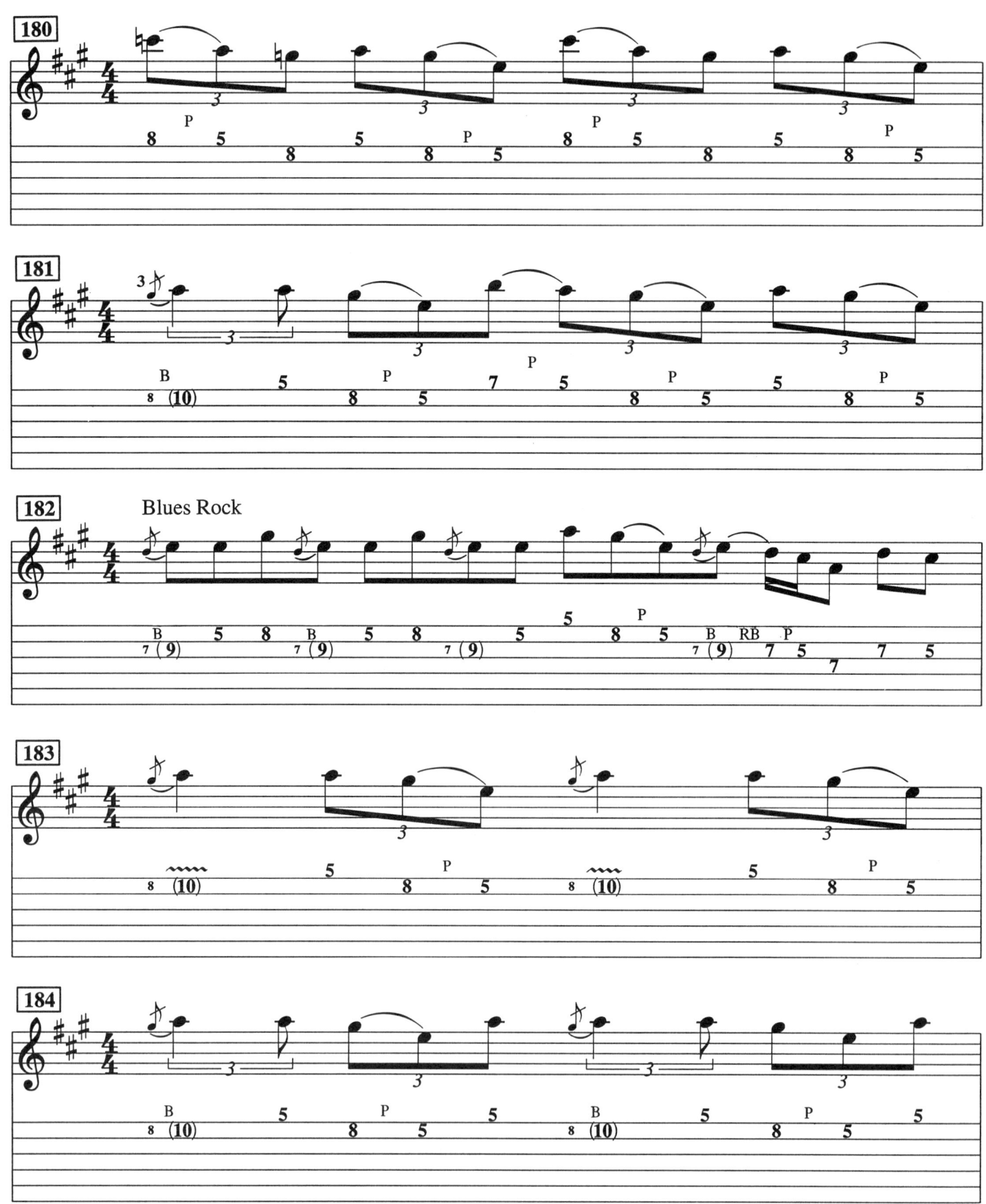

Personality Licks in A

*Note: For smoother picking, keep edge of pick at an angle instead of parallel to string.

More Personality Licks in A

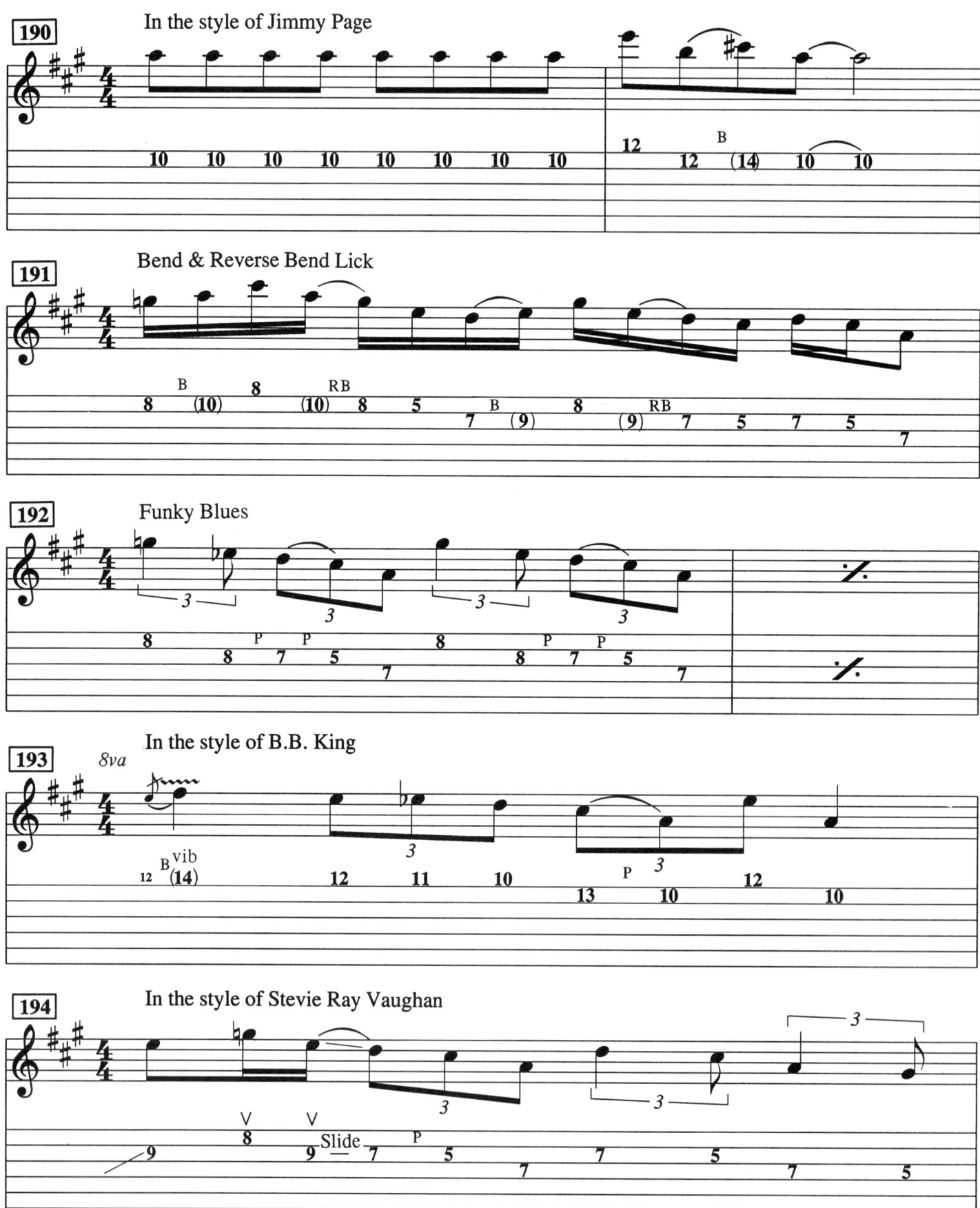

Personality Licks in A

In the style of Austin

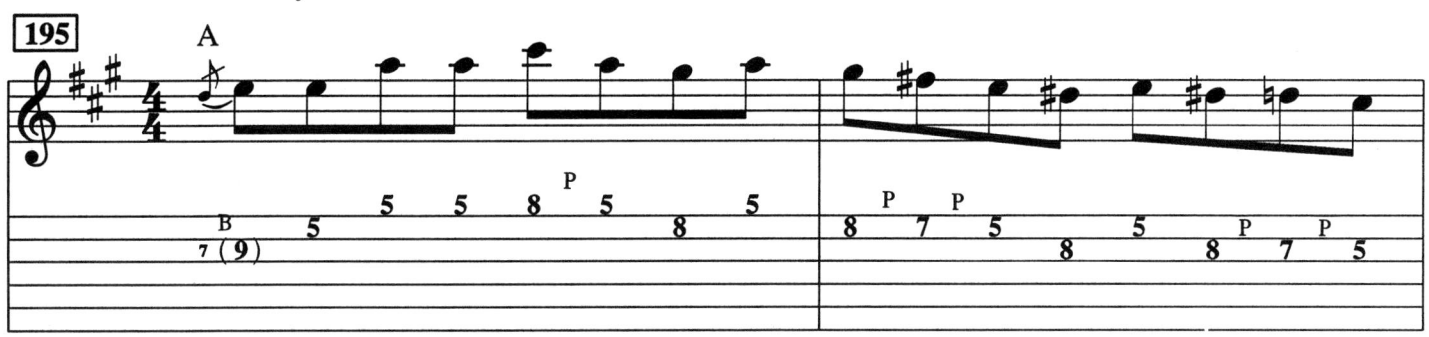

In the style of Austin

In the style of Jimmy Page

In the style of Albert King

Funky Blues Section in A

Speedy Licks in A

Triplet Slides and Pull-Offs in A

More Solos in A

In the Style of Duanne Allman and Eric Clapton

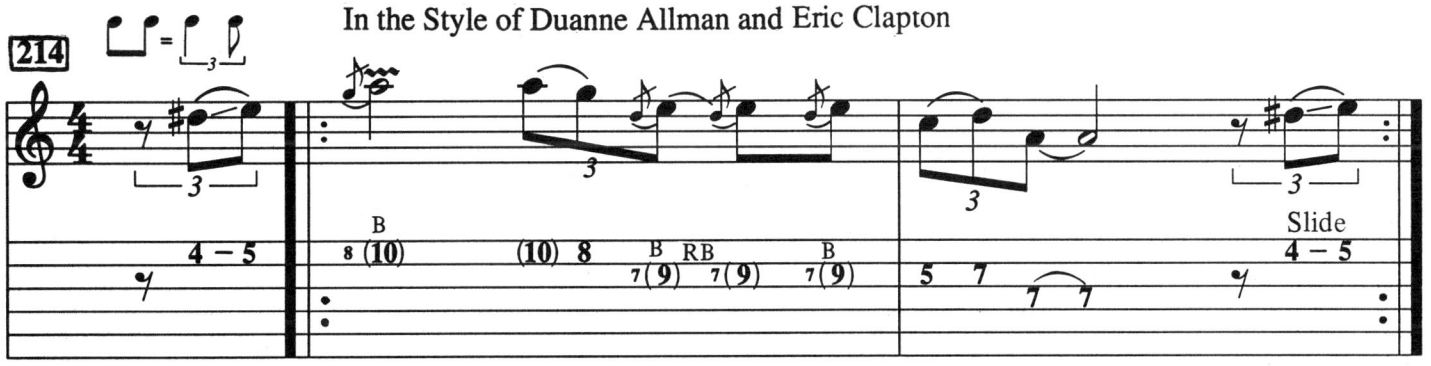

"A" Shuffle in the style of Eric Clapton

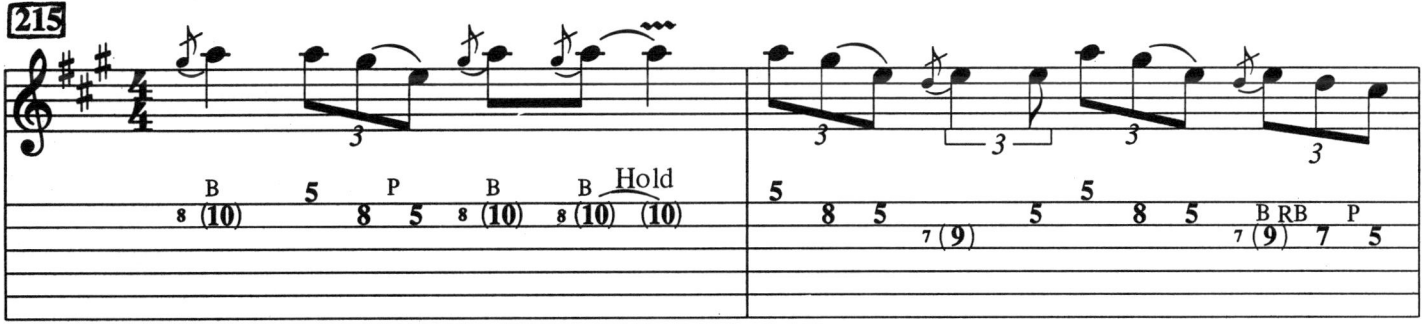

More Solos in A

In the style of Eric Clapton & Angus Young

"A" shuffle in the style of Eric Clapton

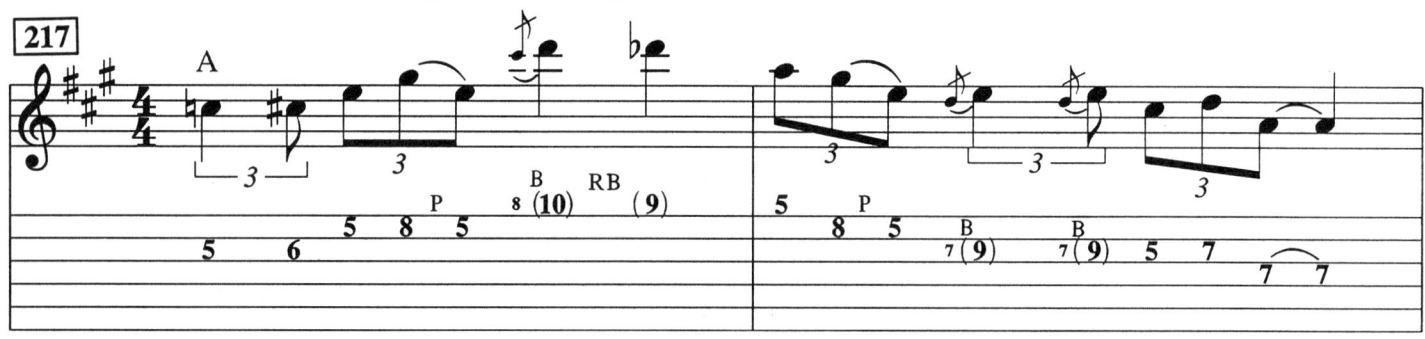

In the style of Eric Clapton

In the style of Eric Clapton

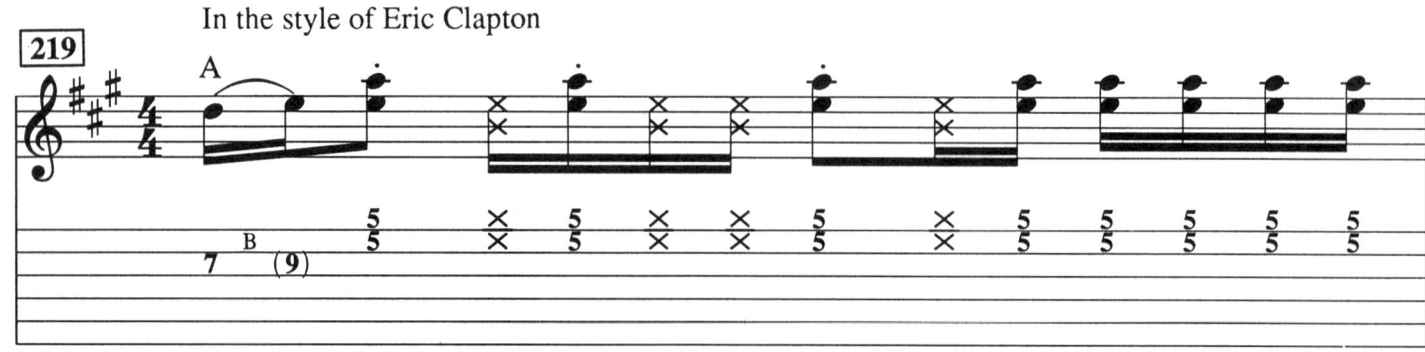

A

In Reverse

This solo demonstrates the reverse bend.*

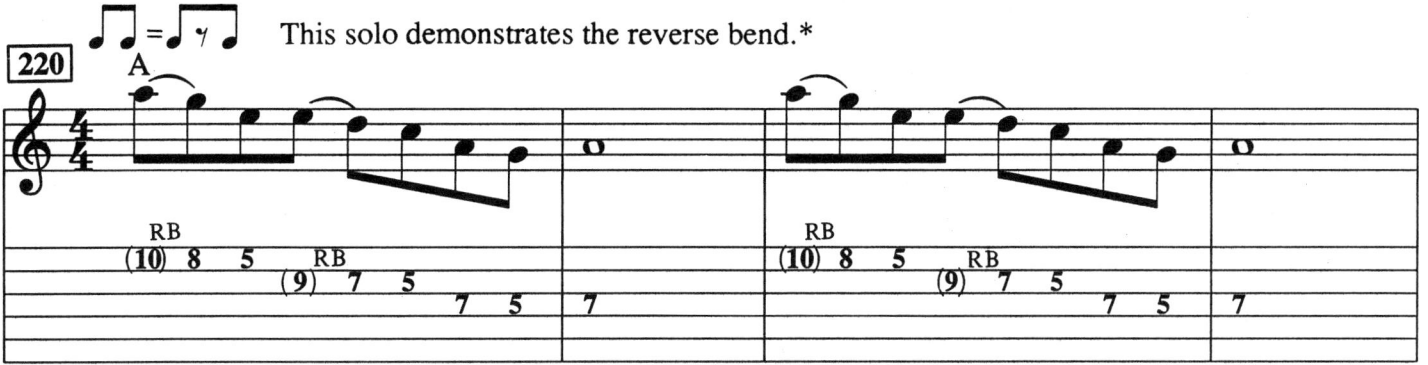

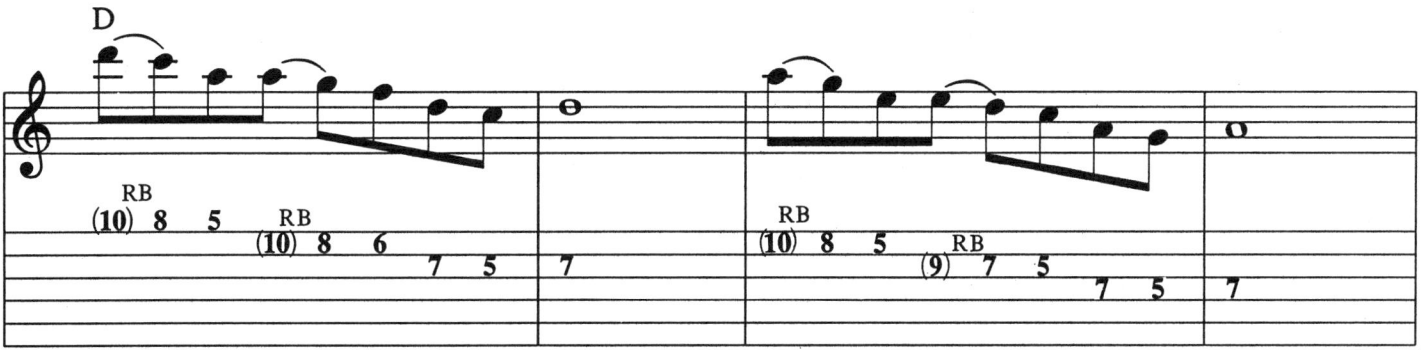

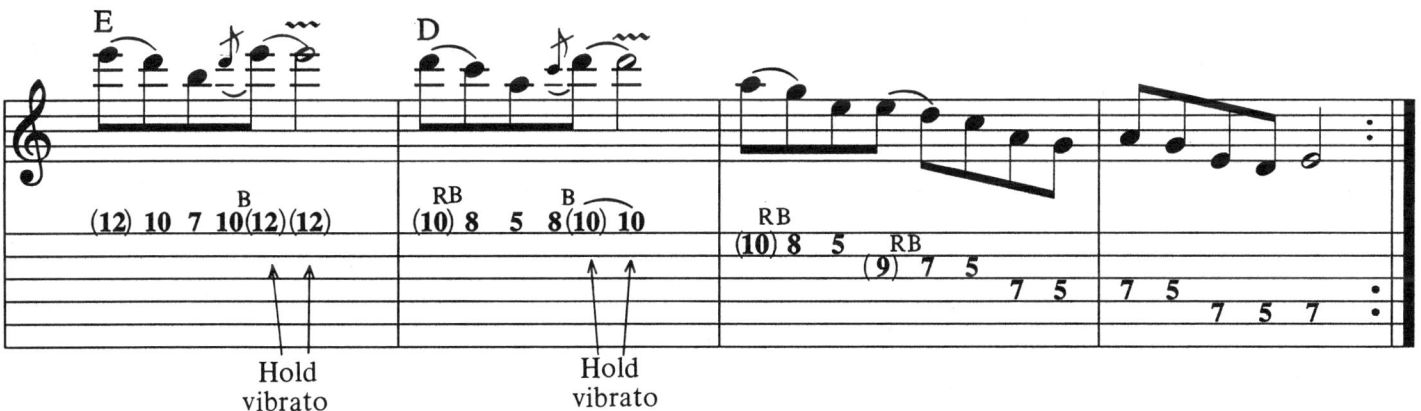

*RB = Pick an already bent string, then allow it to return to its straight string position. See page 8.

81

A
Double Stop Swap
(In the Style of Stevie Ray Vaughan)

A

In the Style of Stevie Ray Vaughan

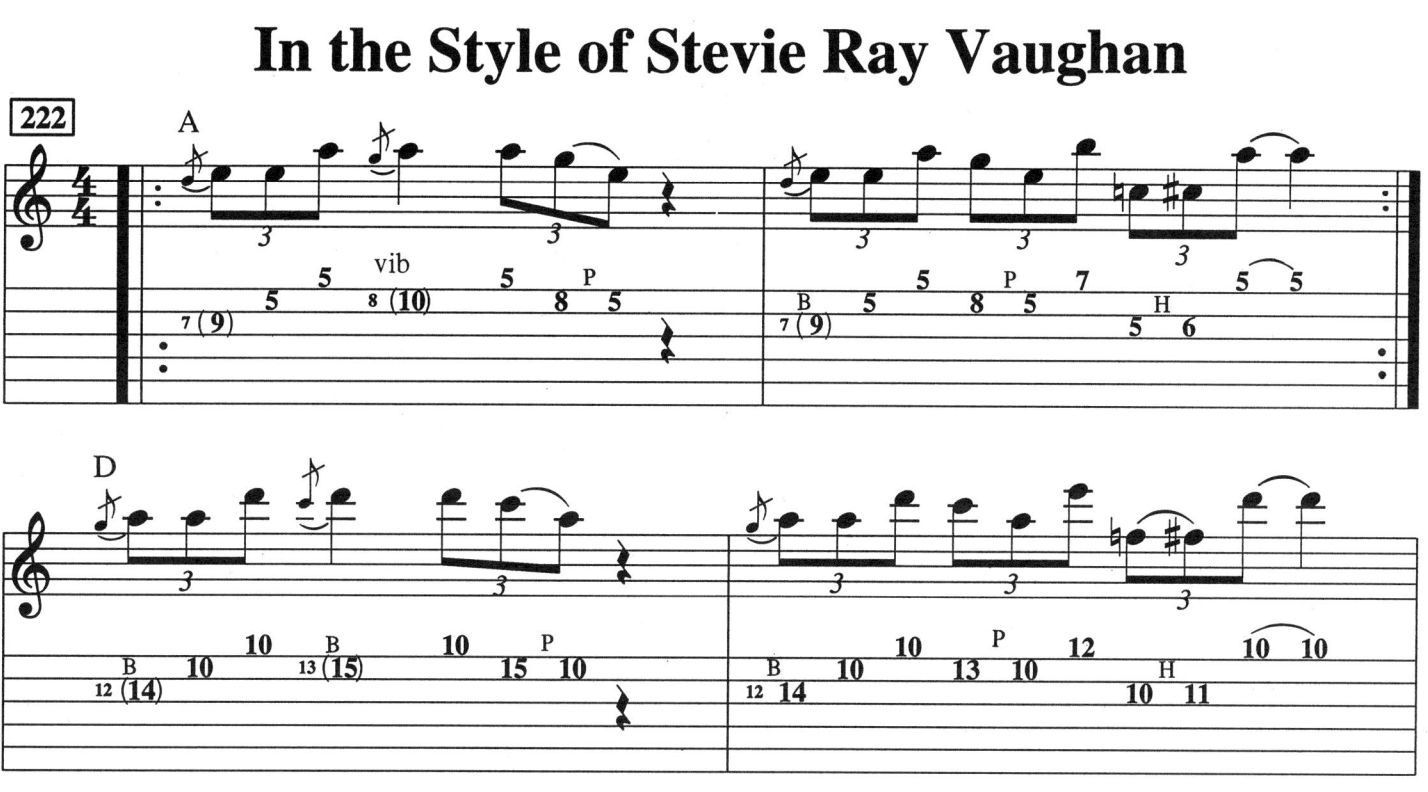

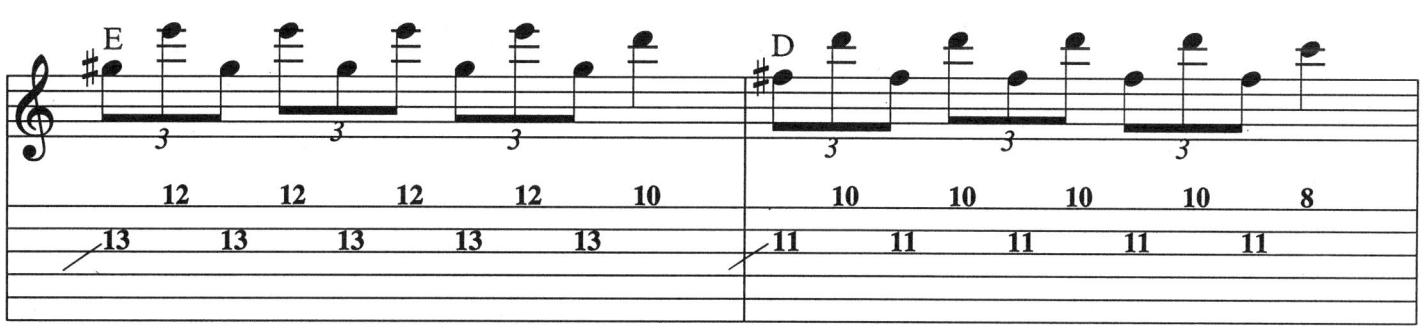

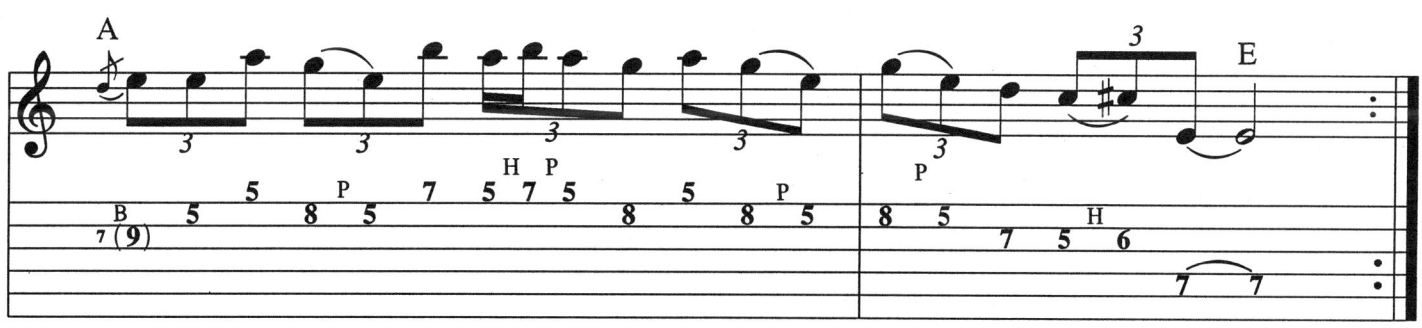

Blues Pentatonic Minor Scale in Triplet Form

Box Diagram of Blues Pentatonic Minor Scale

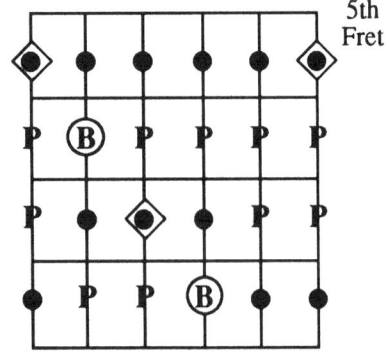

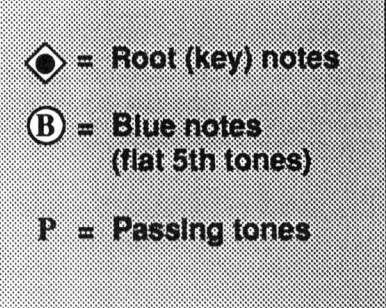

Section 7
Licks and Phrases
in the Key of B Flat (B♭)

B♭   Two flats
B♭ -E♭

Solos used in this section are based on the blues minor scale below.

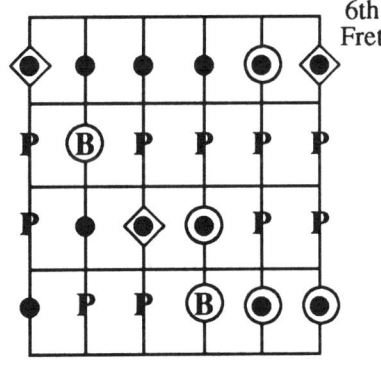

6th Fret

⬦ = **Root (key) notes**
B♭

⊙ = **Popular notes to bend**

Ⓑ = **Blue notes (flat 5th tones)**

P = **Passing tones (see explanation in Section 1)**

85

B♭

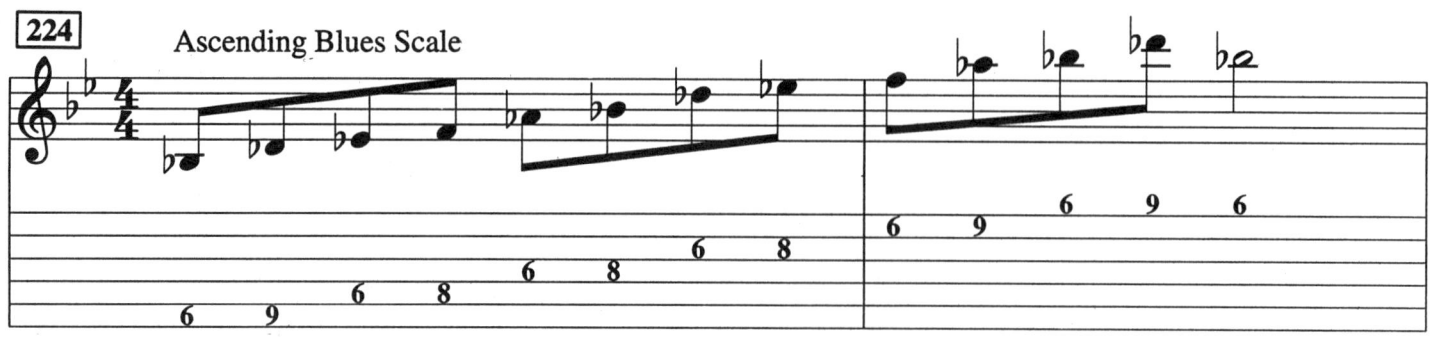

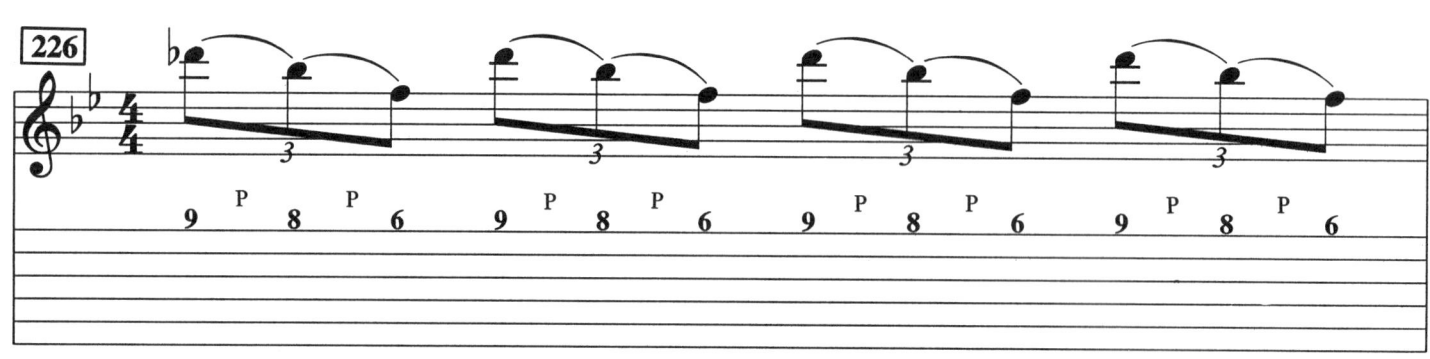

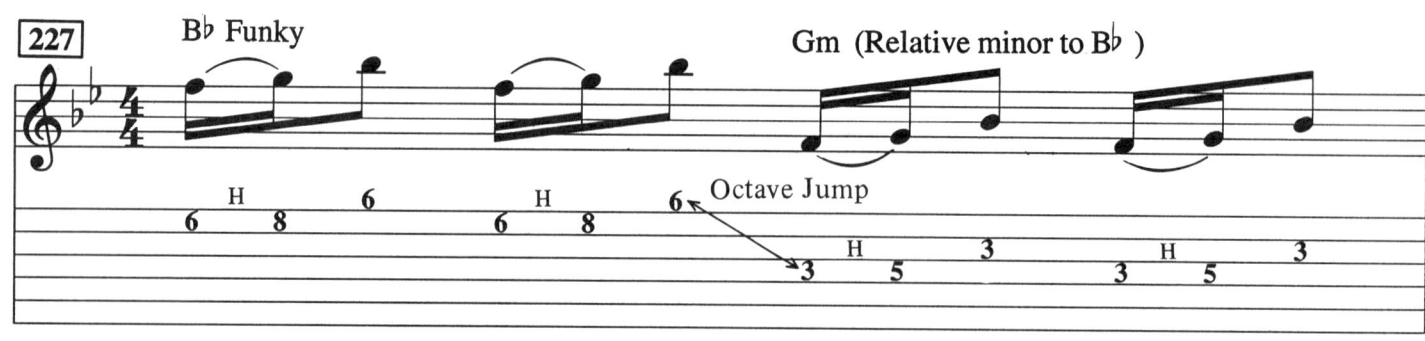

B♭

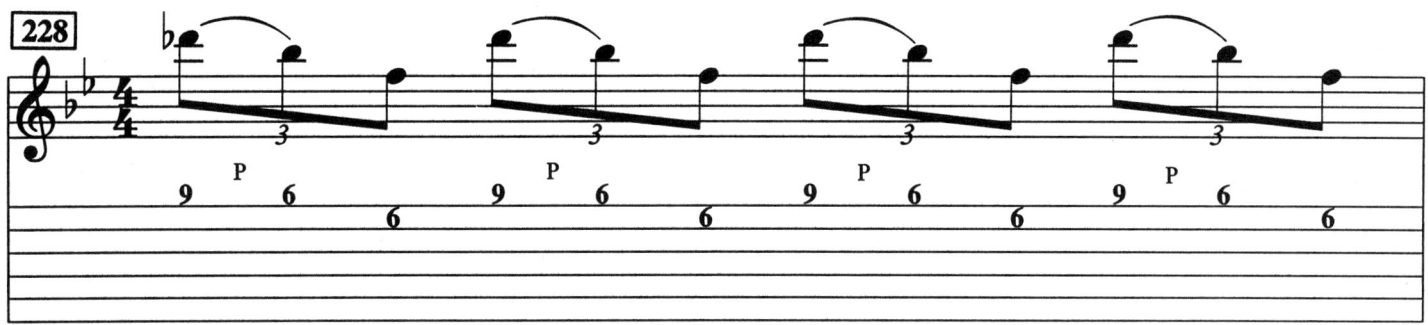

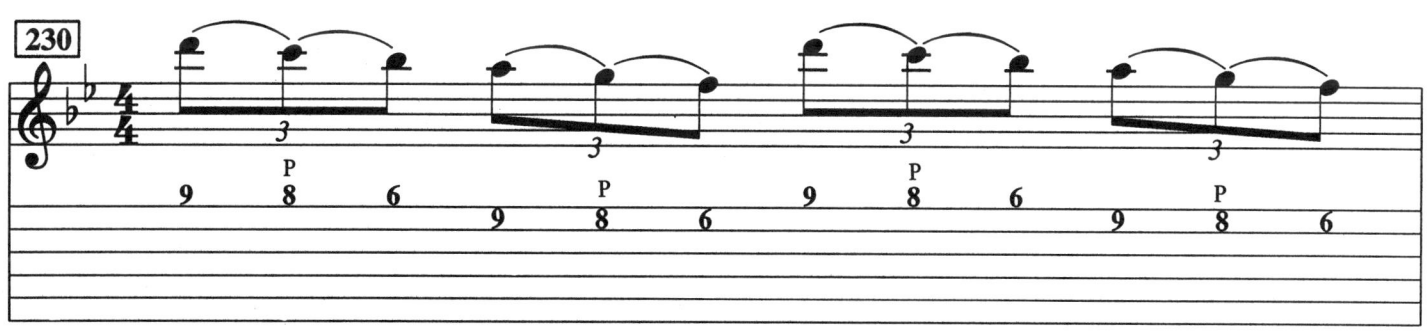

B♭

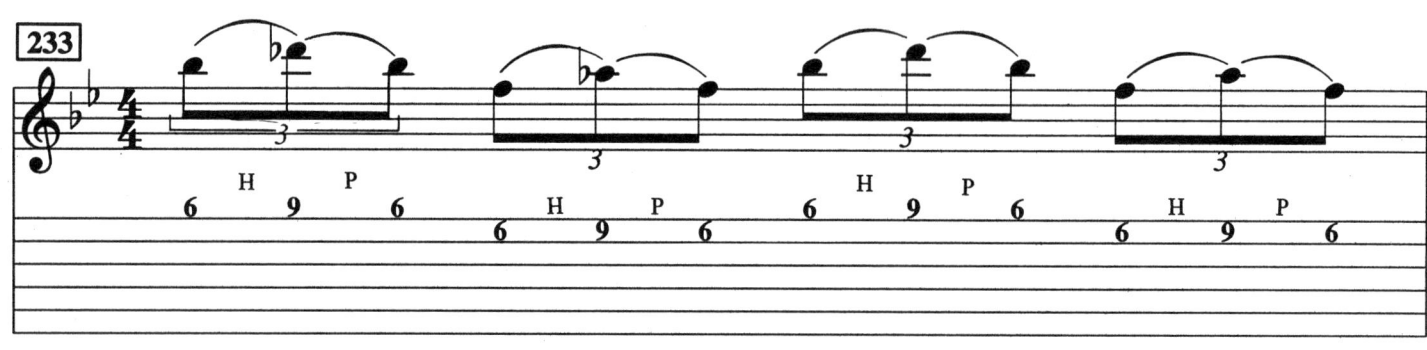

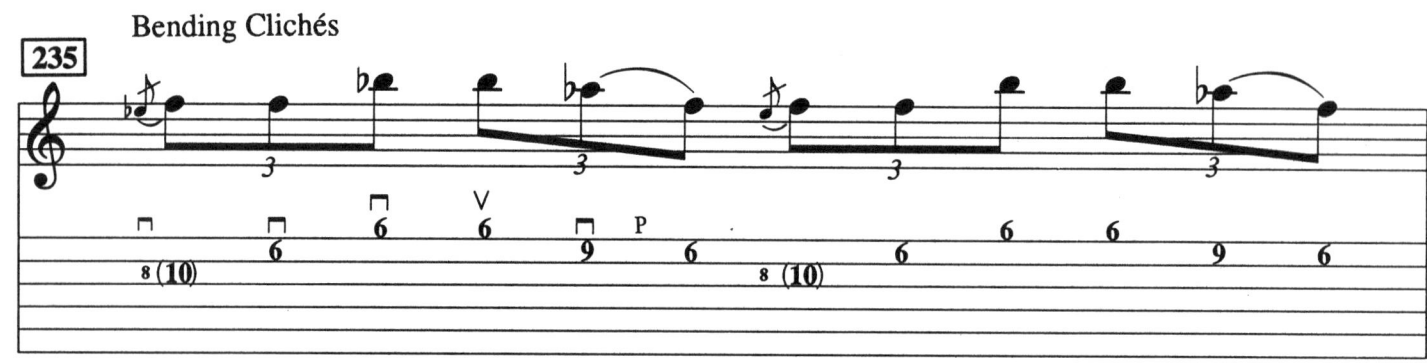

B♭

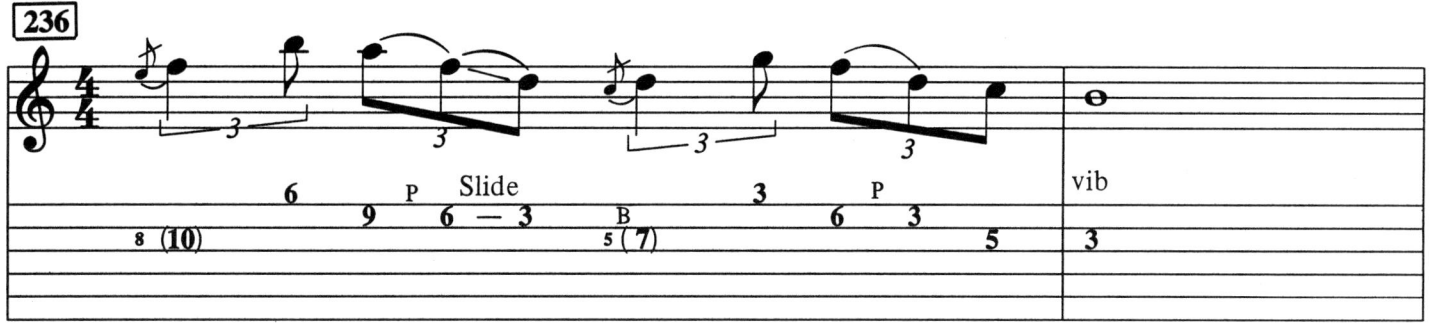

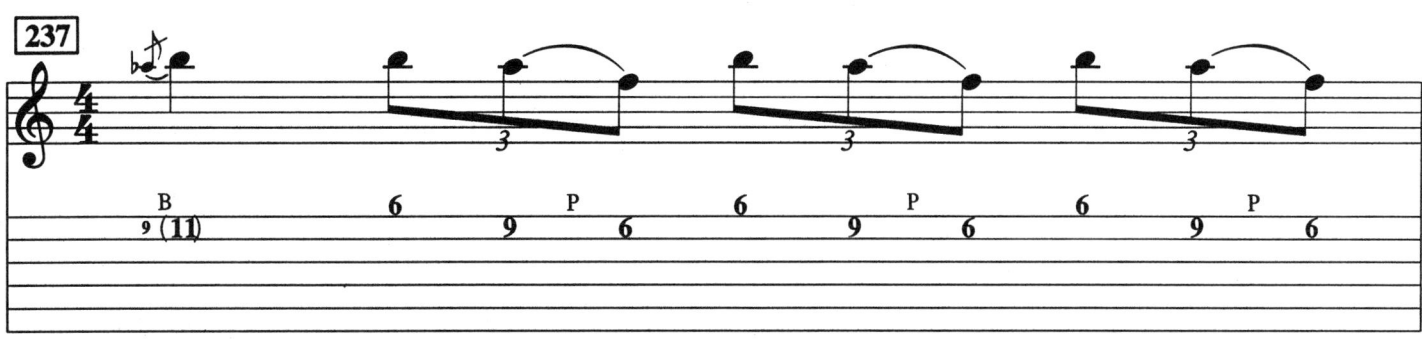

This is a string bending lick using quarter note triplets.

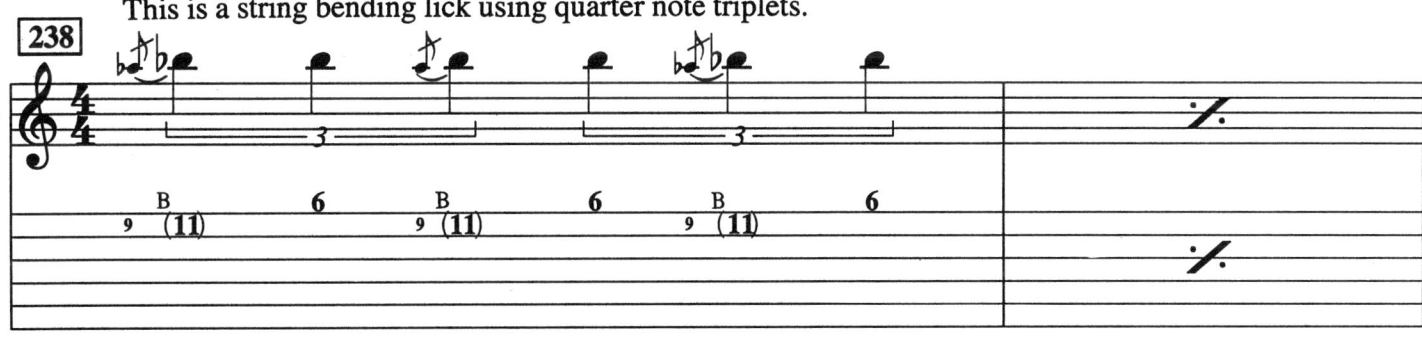

89

B♭

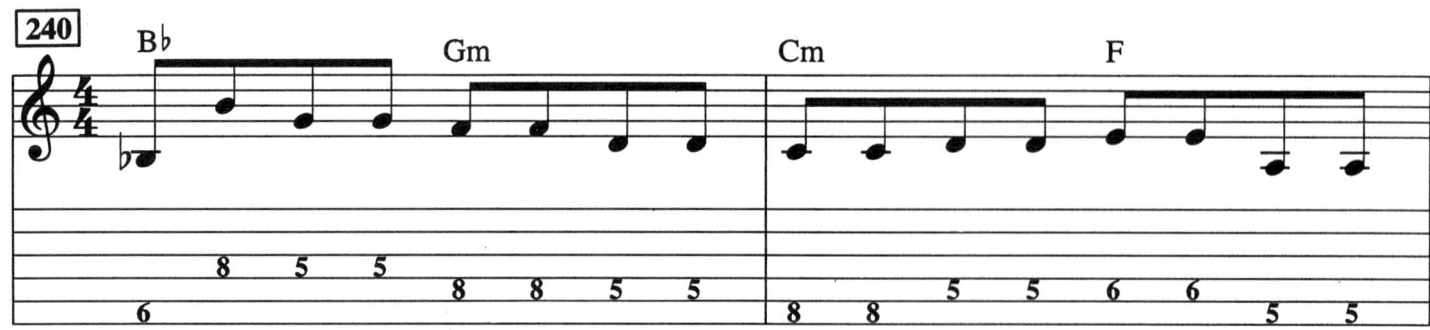

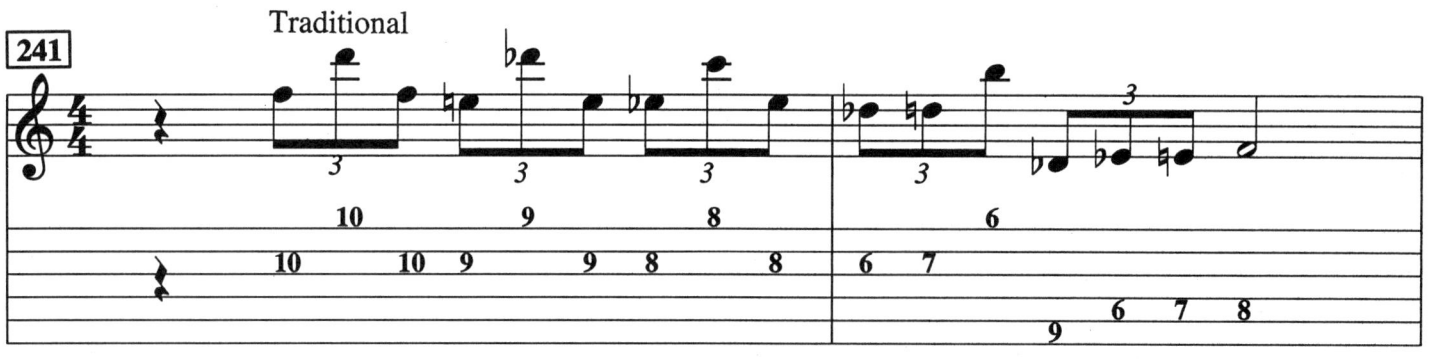

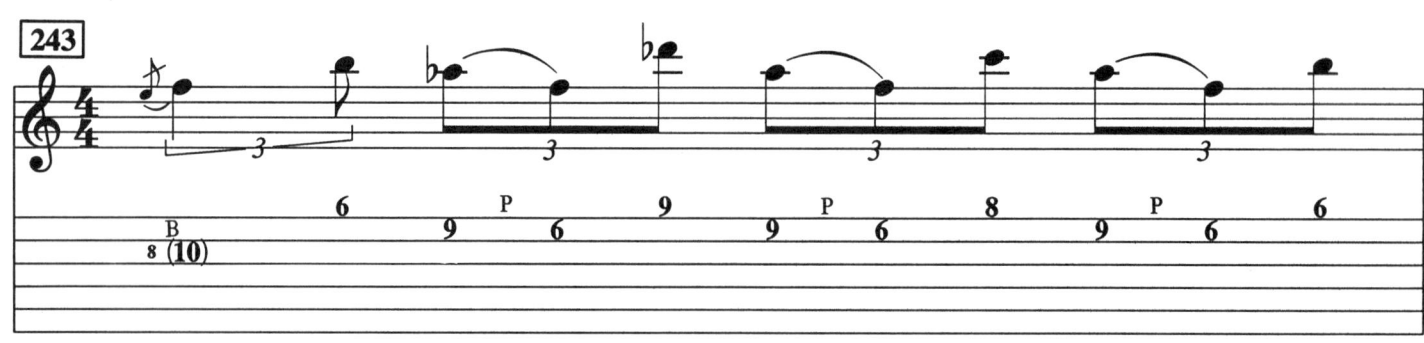

Section 8
Licks and Phrases
in the Key of B

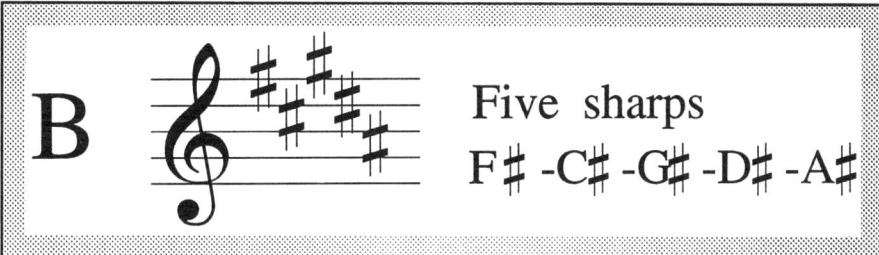

B — Five sharps
F♯ -C♯ -G♯ -D♯ -A♯

Solos used in this section are based on the blues minor scale below.

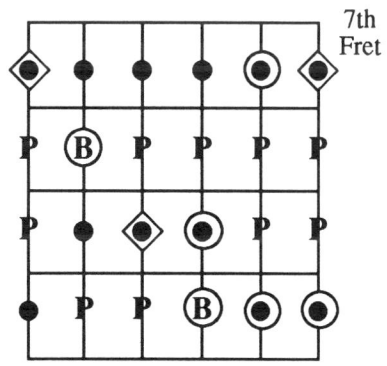

7th
Fret

◈ = Root (key) notes
B

◉ = Popular notes to
bend

Ⓑ = Blue notes
(flat 5th tones)

P = Passing tones
(see explanation
in Section 1)

Standard Triplet Licks in B

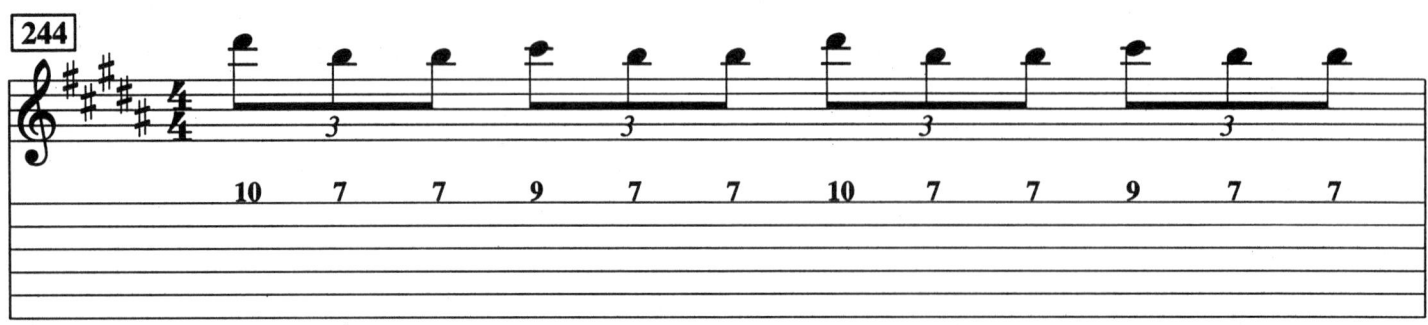

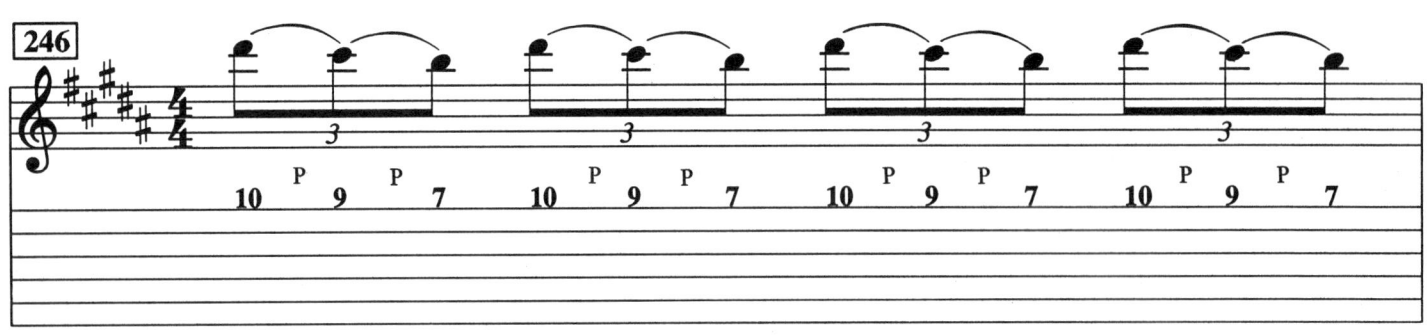

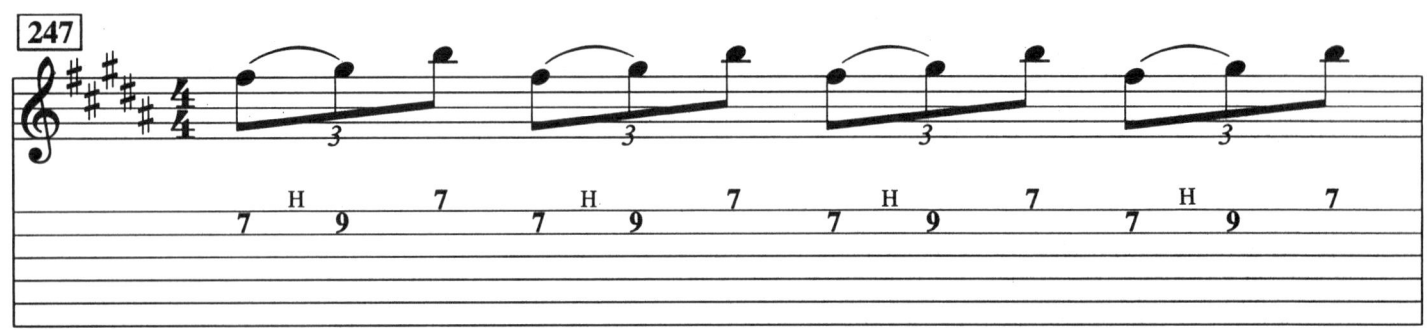

Standard Triplet Licks in B (Cont.)

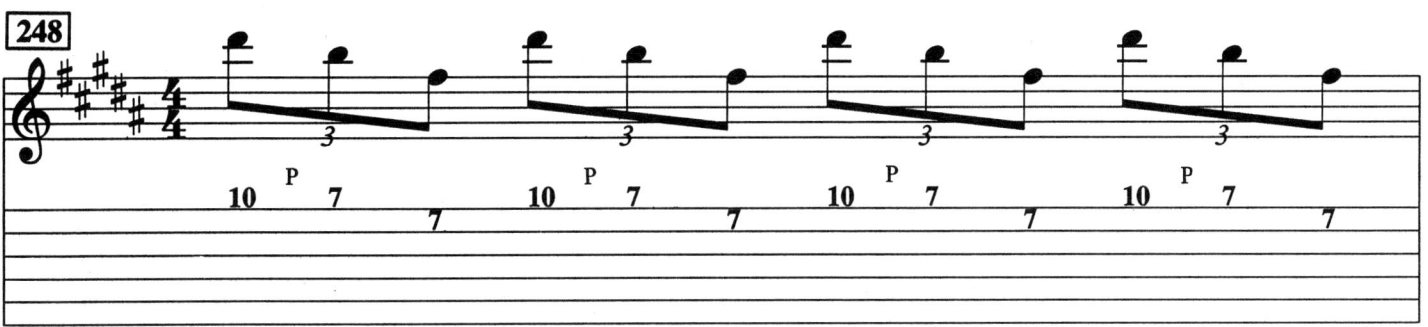

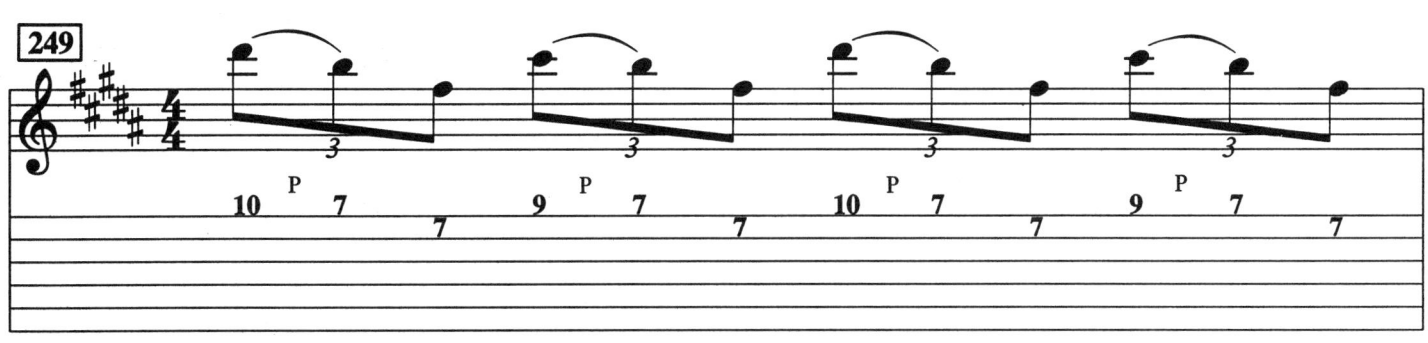

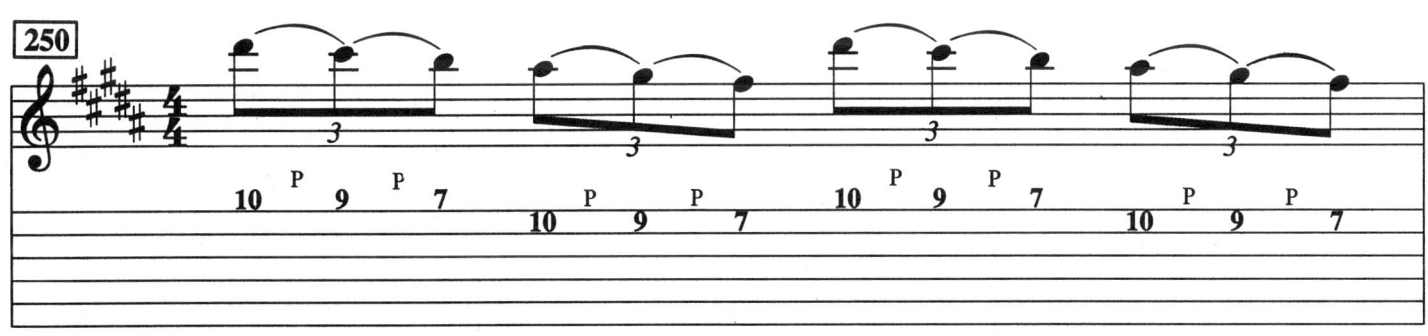

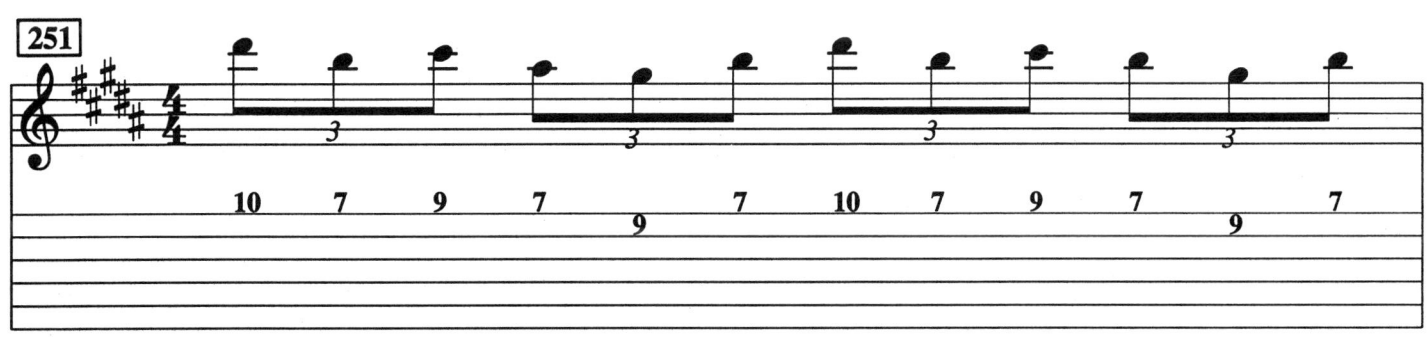

Standard Triplet Licks in B (Cont.)

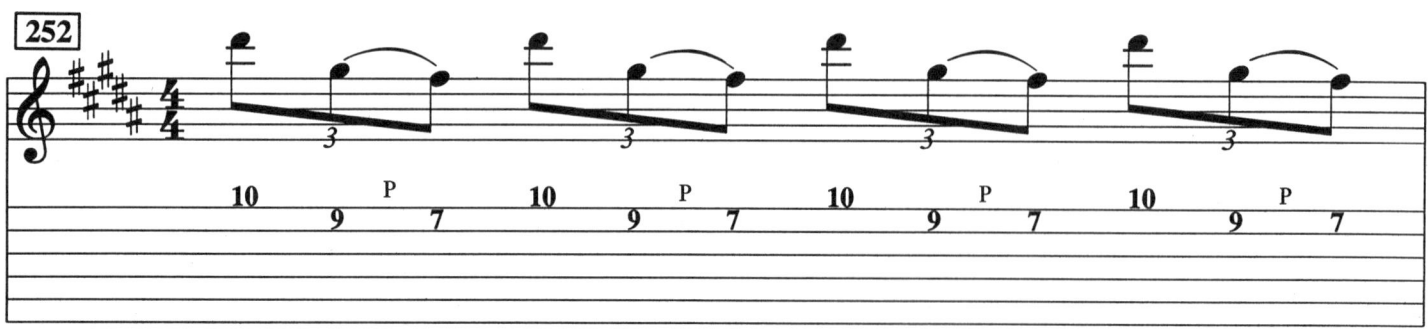

More Licks in B

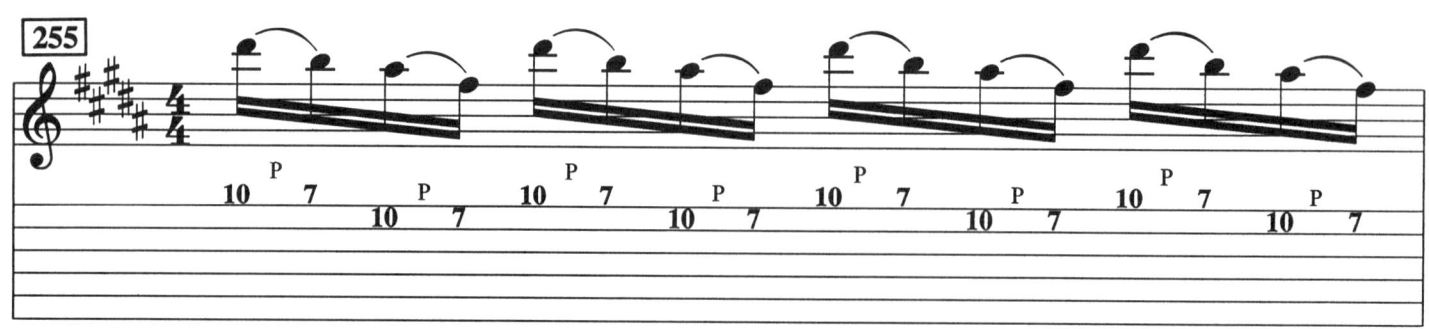

B

Funky Stuff

In the style of Jeff Beck

In the style of Billy Gibbons (Z Z Top)

Licks and Popular Clichés

B

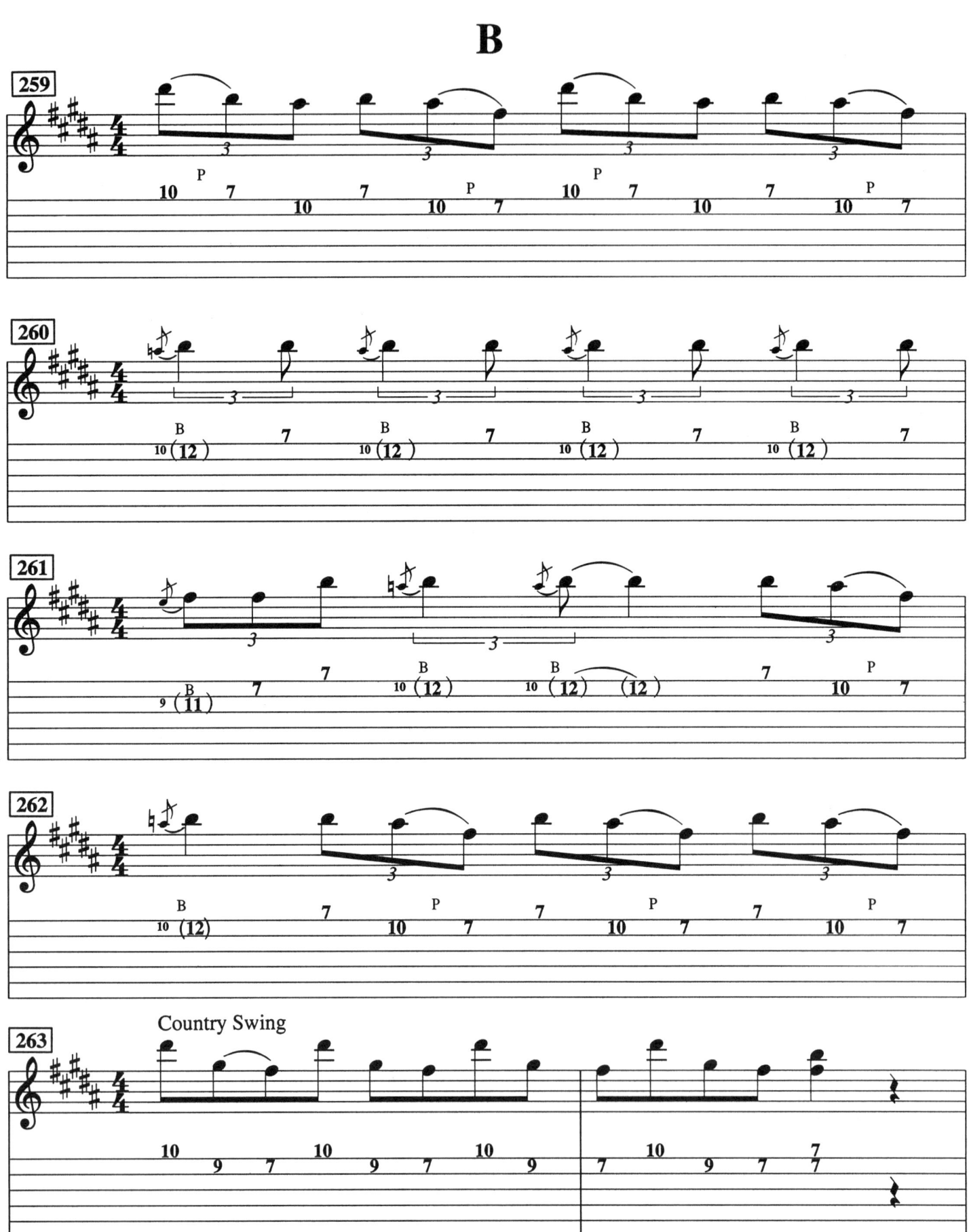

96

Section 9
Licks and Phrases
in the Key of C

C   No sharps
     or flats

Solos used in this section are based on the blues minor scale below.

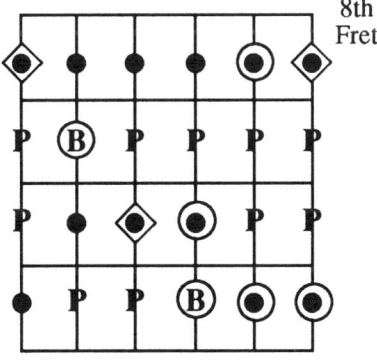

8th
Fret

◈ = Root (key) notes
    C

◉ = Popular notes to
    bend

Ⓑ = Blue notes
    (flat 5th tones)

P = Passing tones
    (see explanation
    in Section 1)

Standard Triplet Licks in C

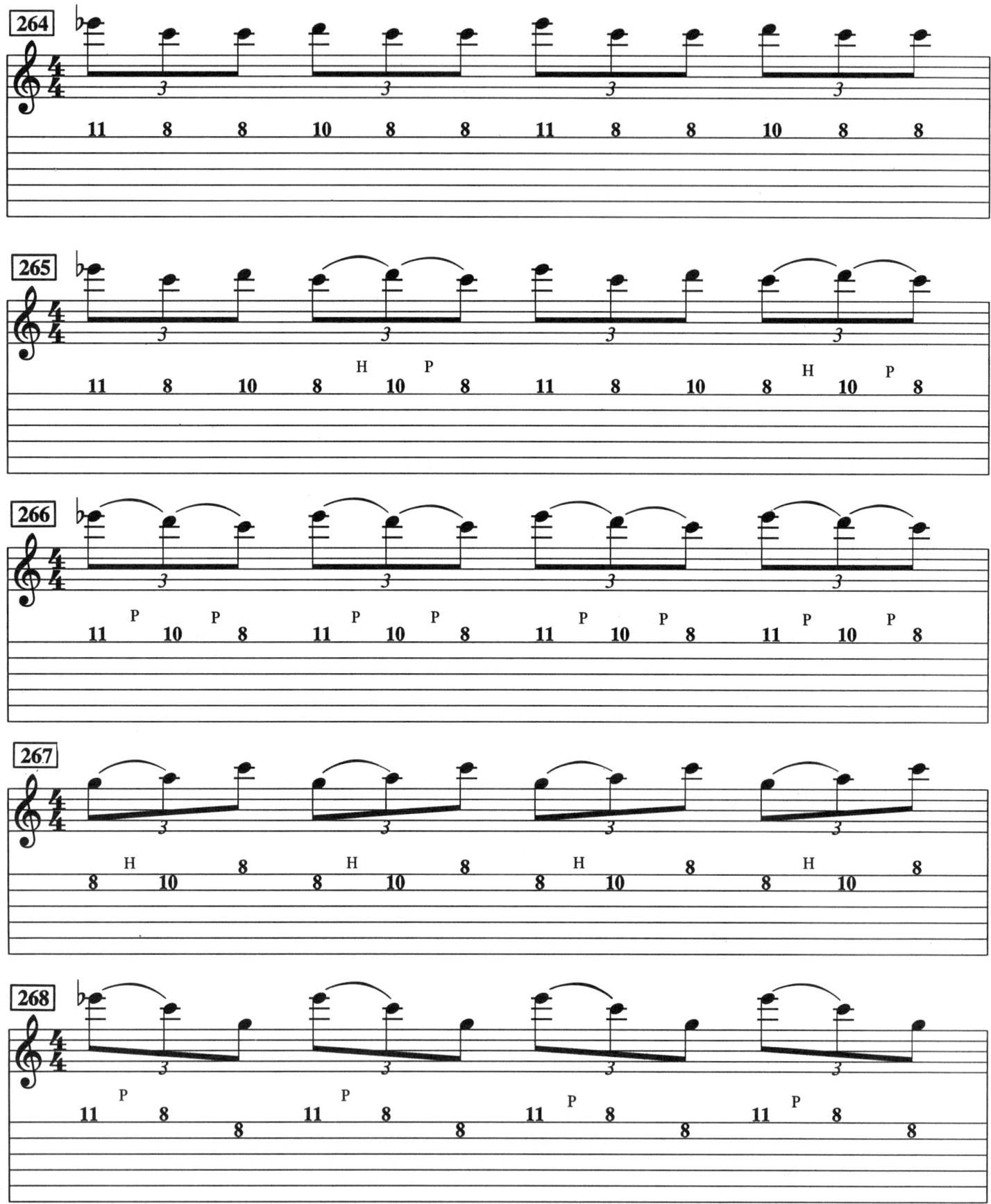

Standard Triplets in C

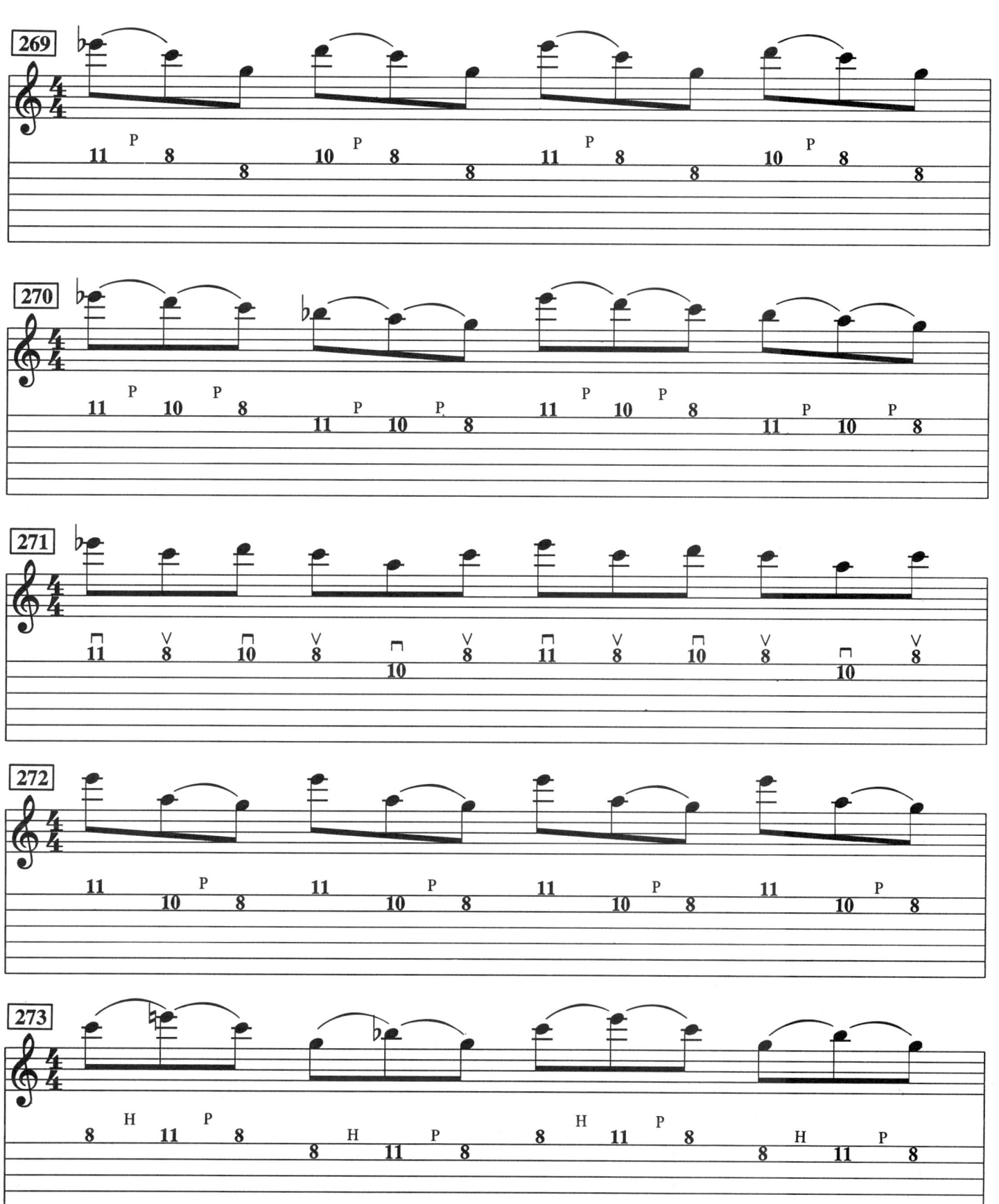

Cool Solo in C

(In the style of Freddie King)

Standard Clichés in C

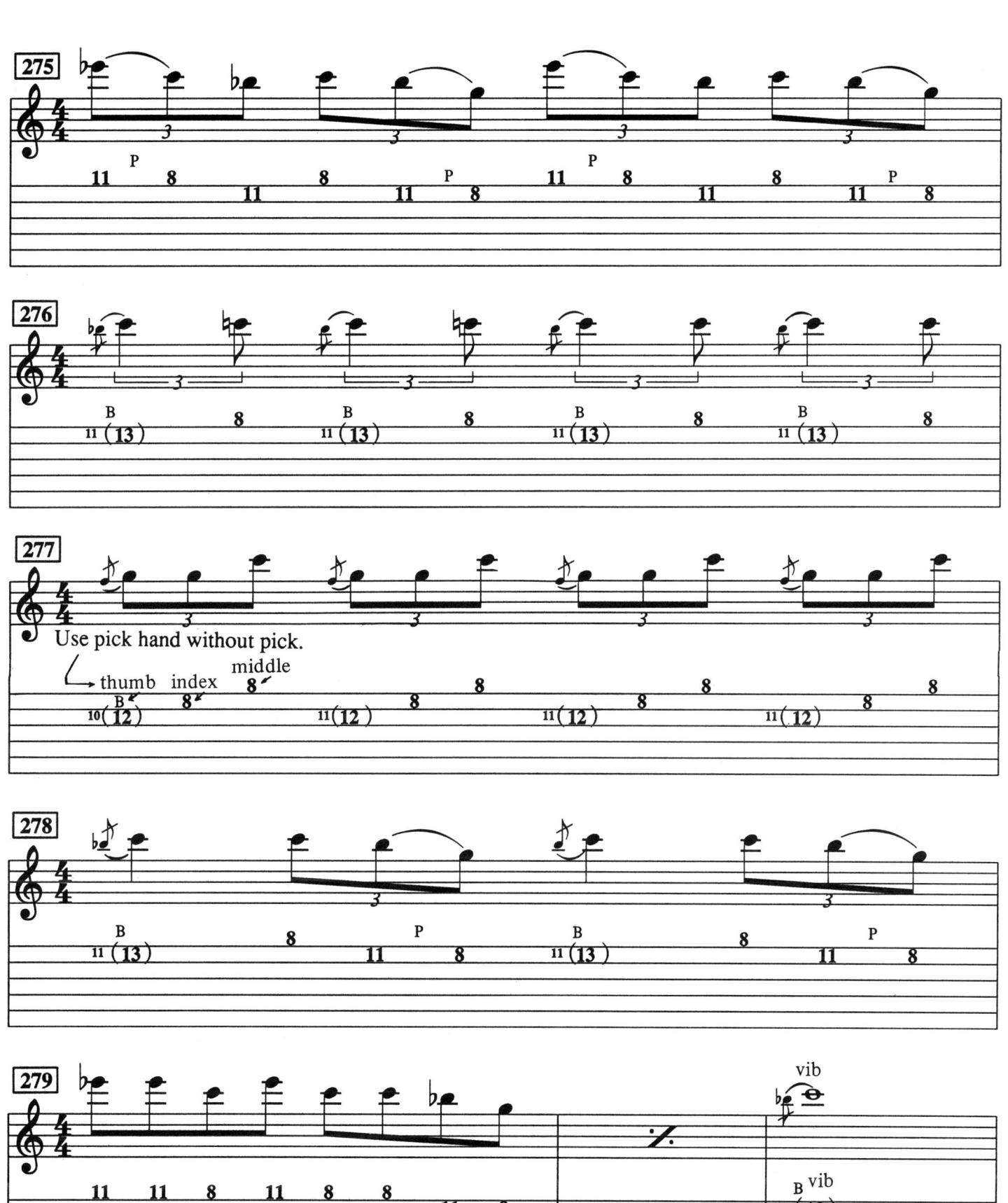

Boogie "C" Boogie Do

Rockin the "C" Saw

Personality Licks in C

Good Solo Introduction

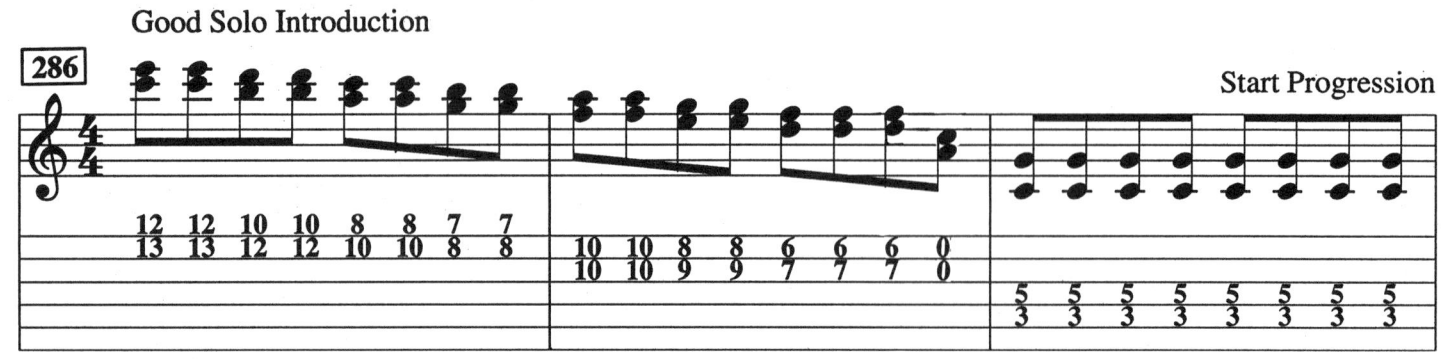

In the style of Buddy Guy

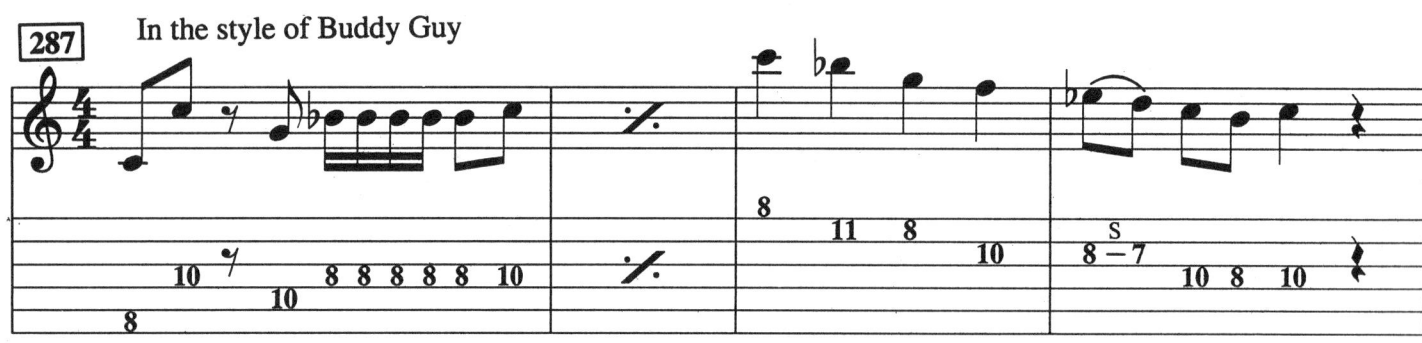

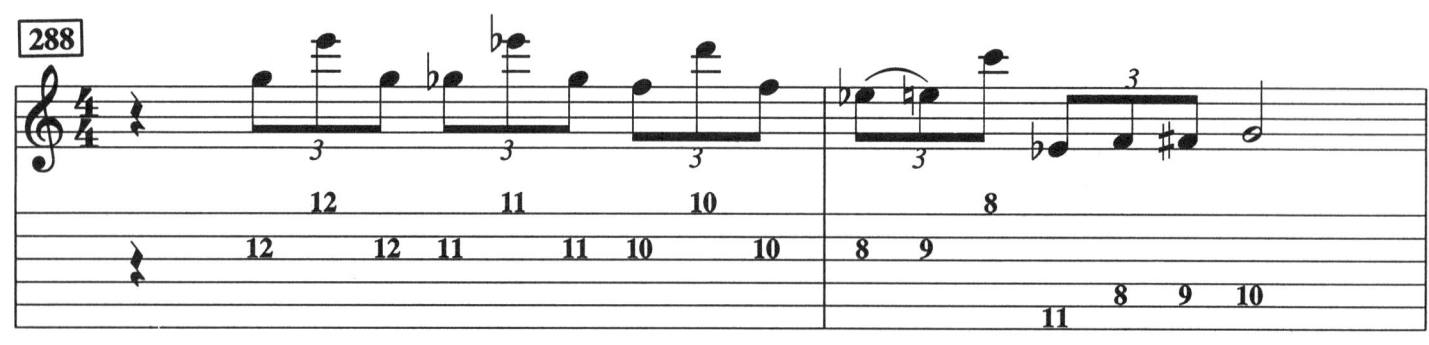

In the Style of Stevie Ray Vaughan

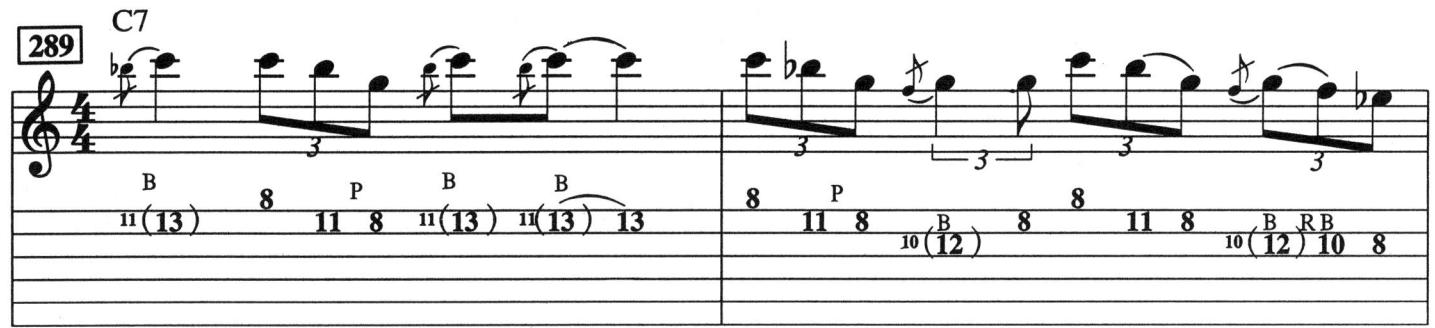

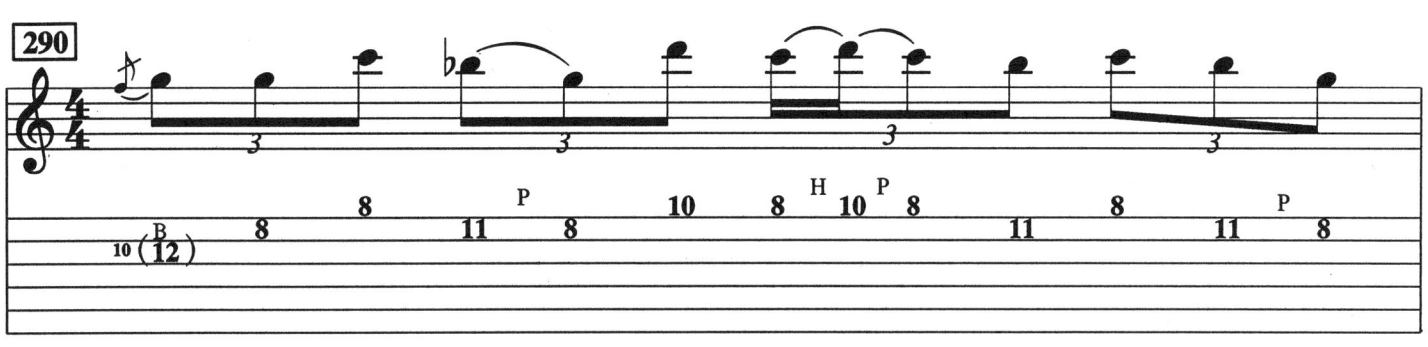

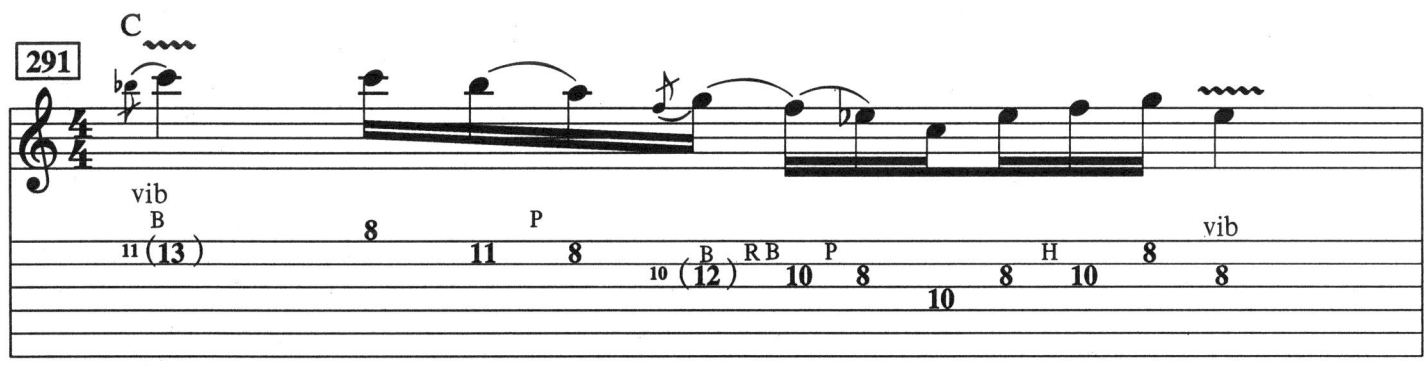

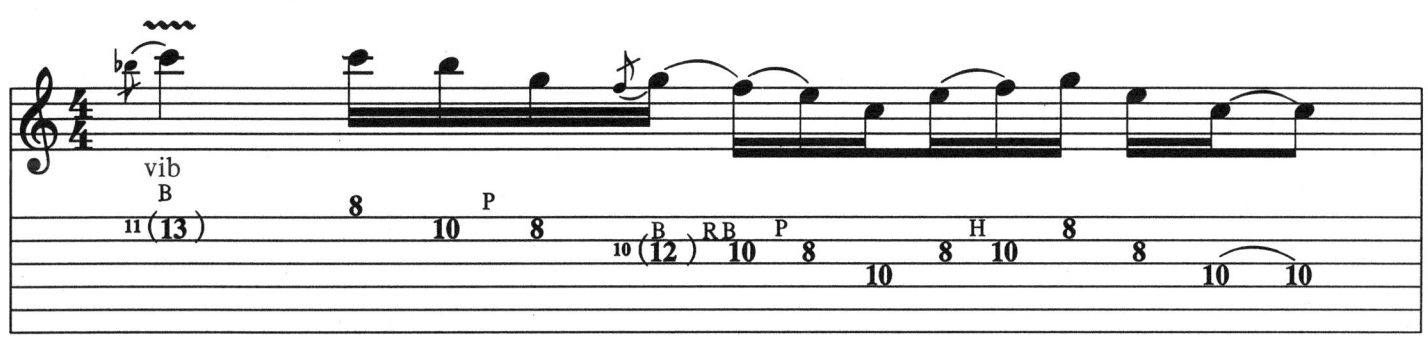

Section 10
Licks and Phrases
in the Key of D Flat (D♭)

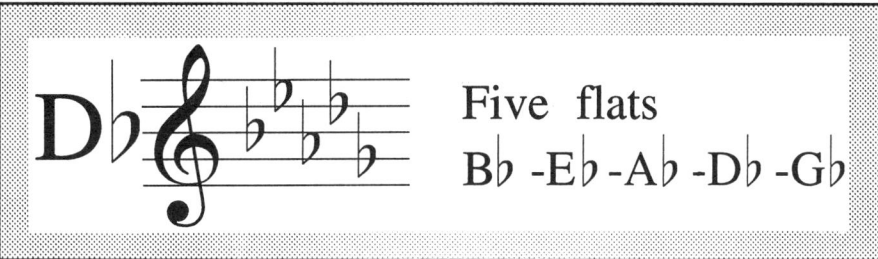

D♭   Five flats
B♭ -E♭ -A♭ -D♭ -G♭

Solos used in this section are based on the blues minor scale below.

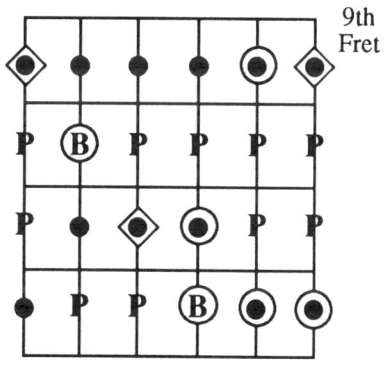

9th
Fret

◈ = **Root (key) notes**
D♭

◉ = **Popular notes to**
bend

Ⓑ = **Blue notes**
(flat 5th tones)

P = **Passing tones**
(see explanation
in Section 1)

107

Standard Licks in D♭

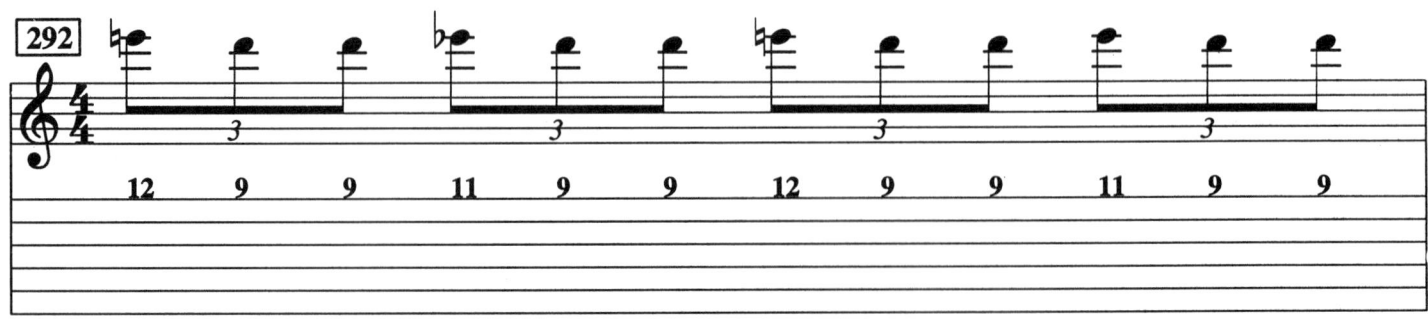

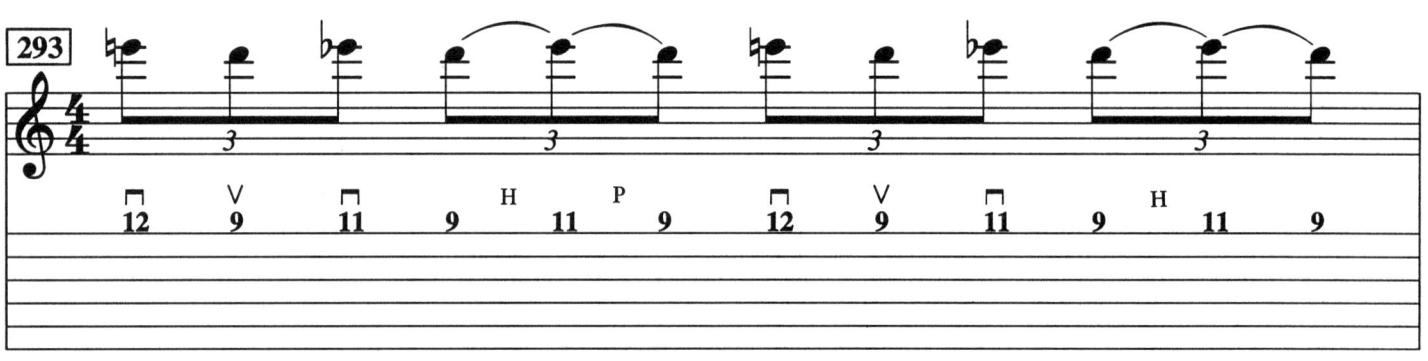

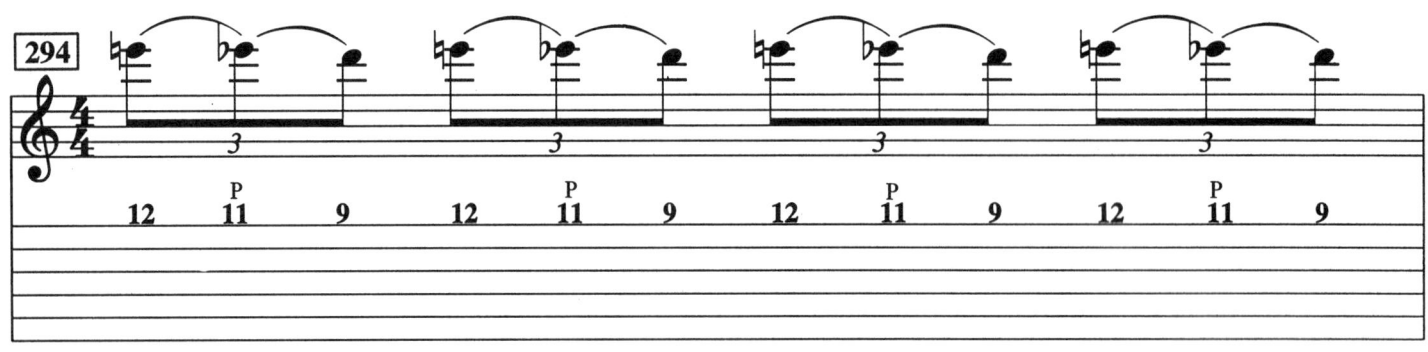

More Standard Licks in D♭

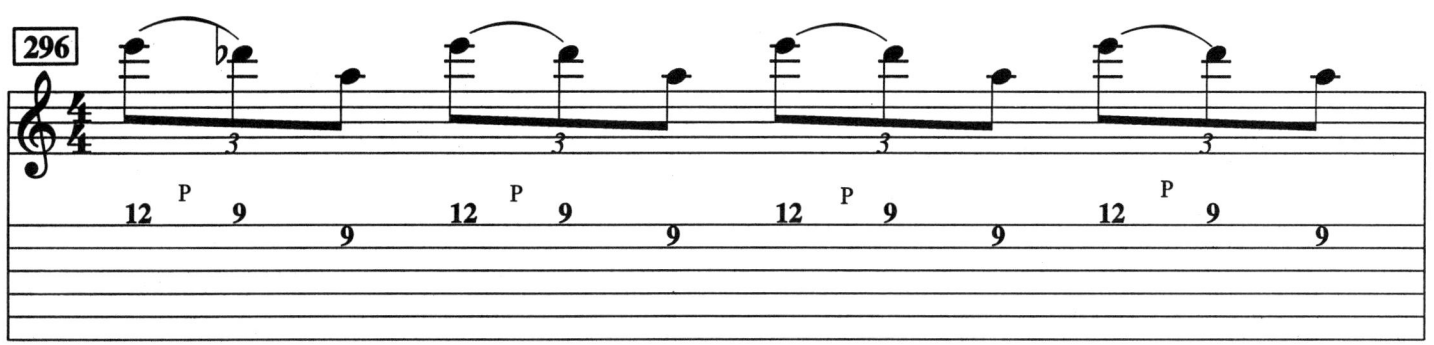

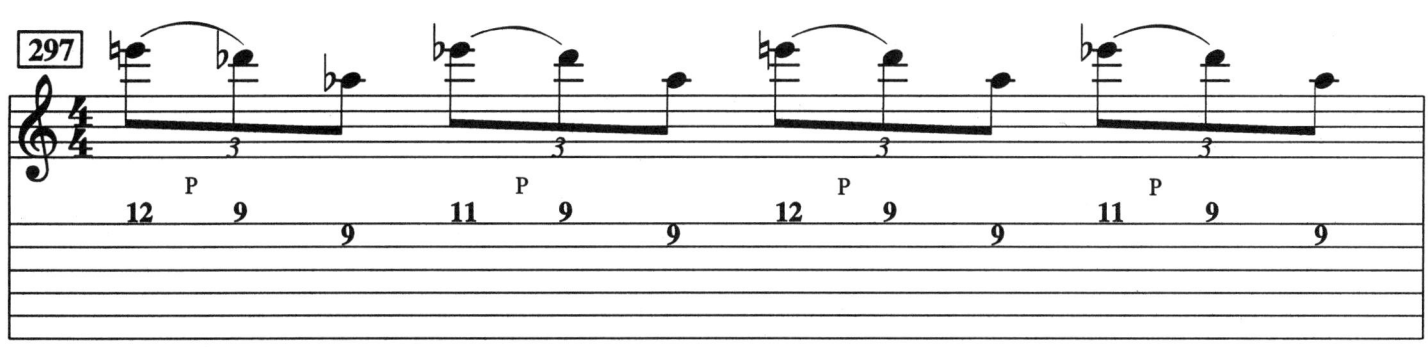

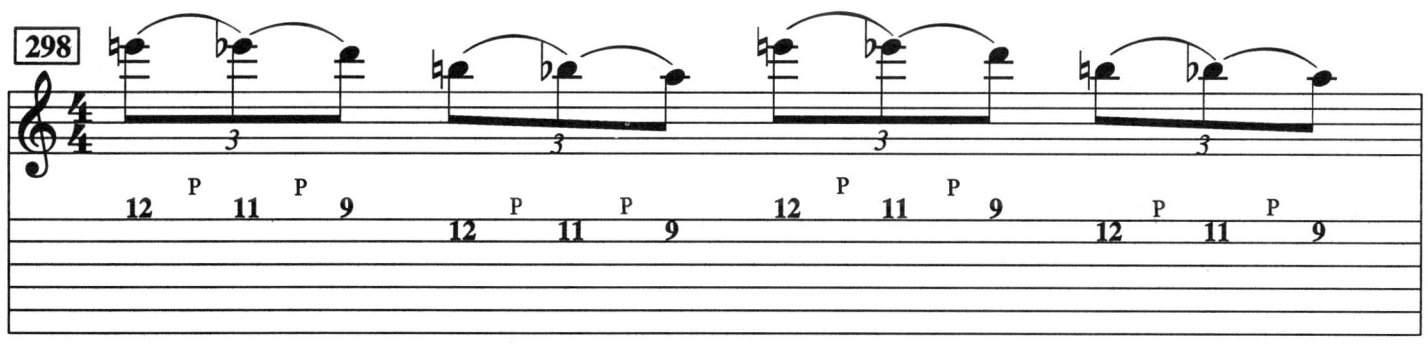

More Standard Licks in D♭ (Cont.)

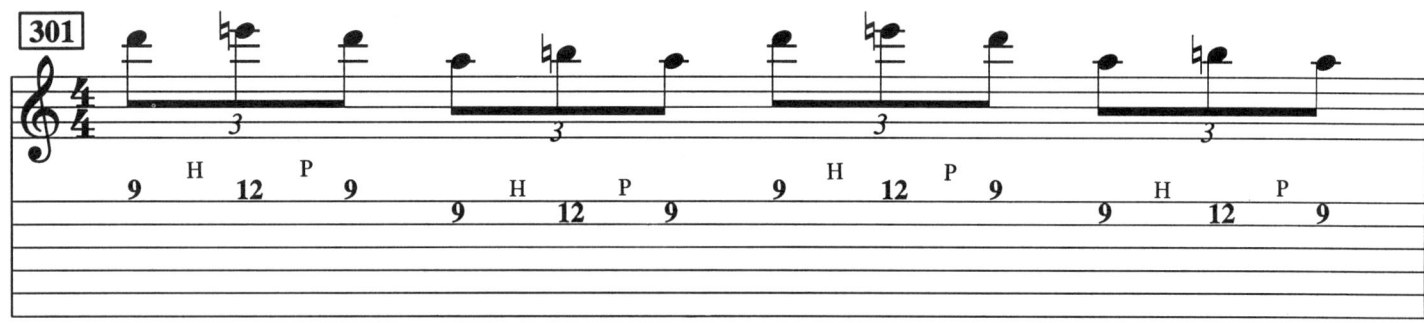

Standard Clichés in D♭

Bending Licks & Phrases

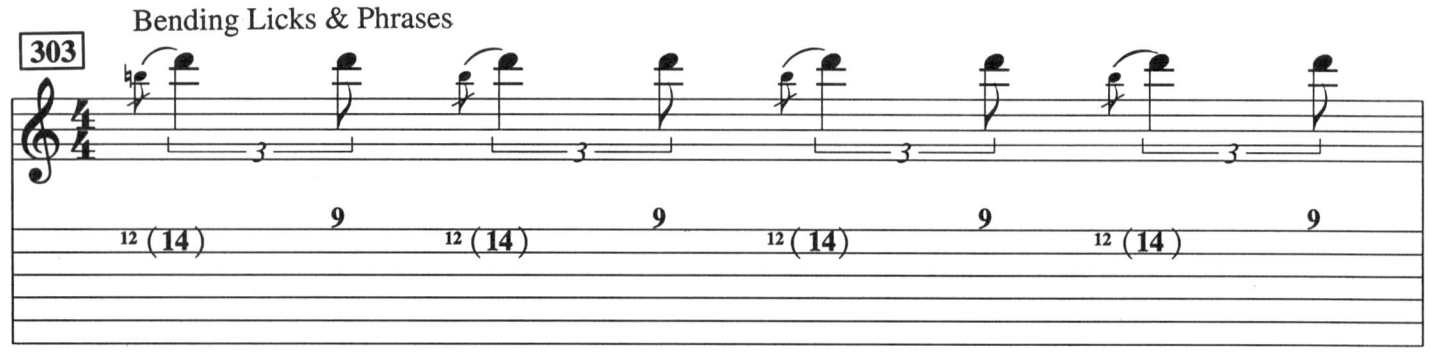

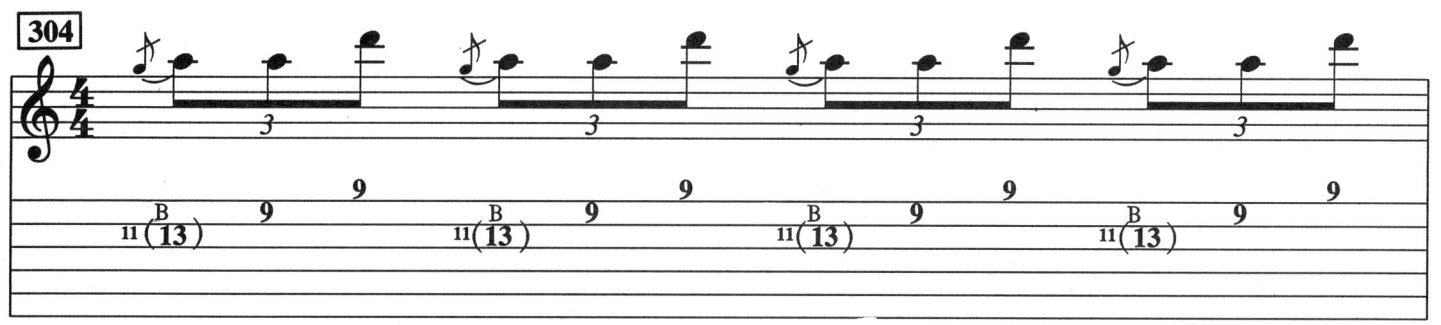

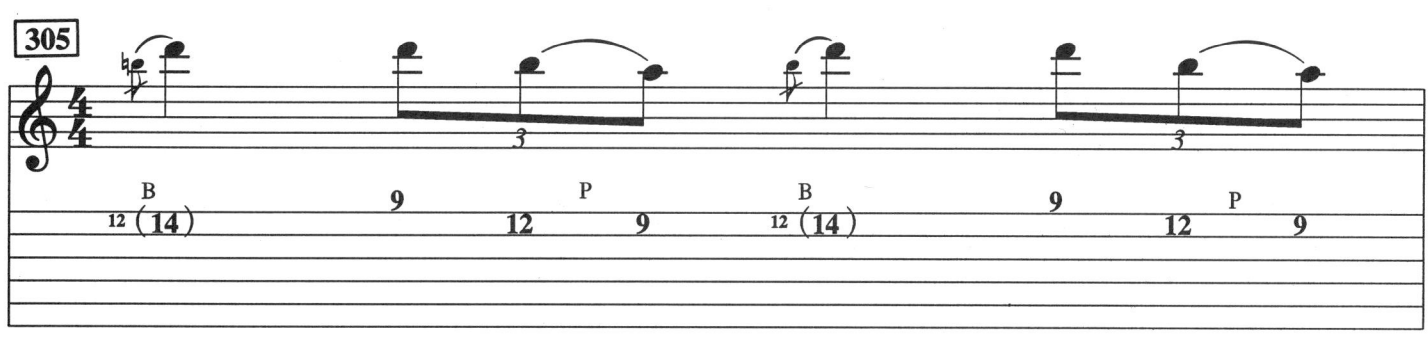

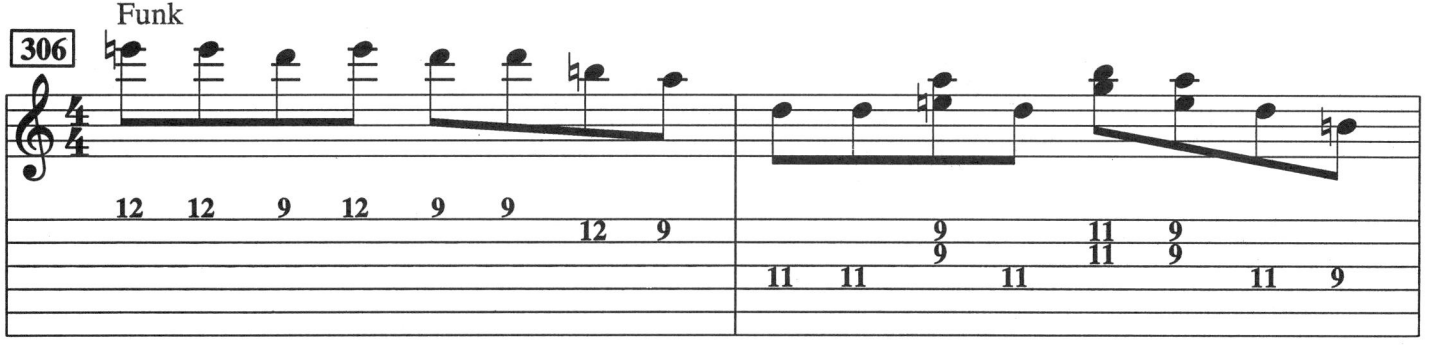

Personality Licks in D♭

B♭ minor is related to D♭ major. The first three solos are B♭ minor blues licks ending with a D♭ note.

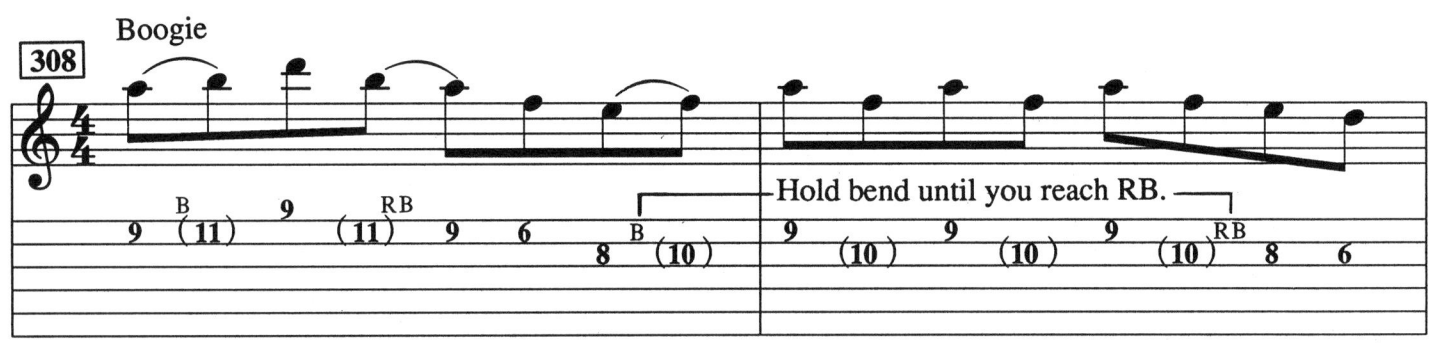

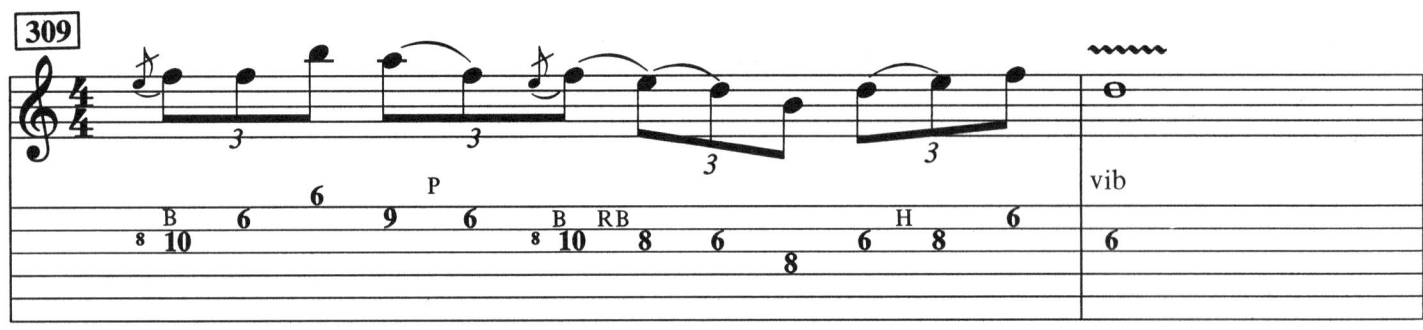

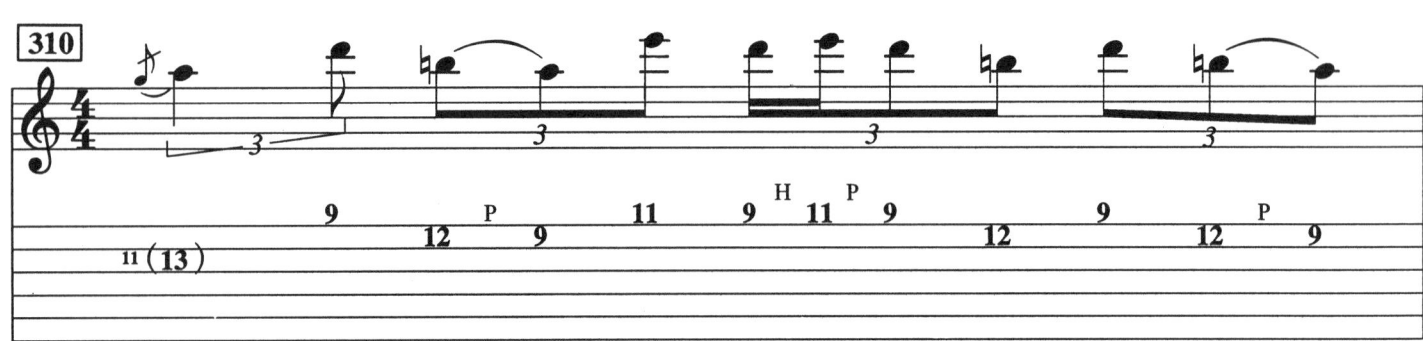

Section 11
Licks and Phrases
in the Key of D

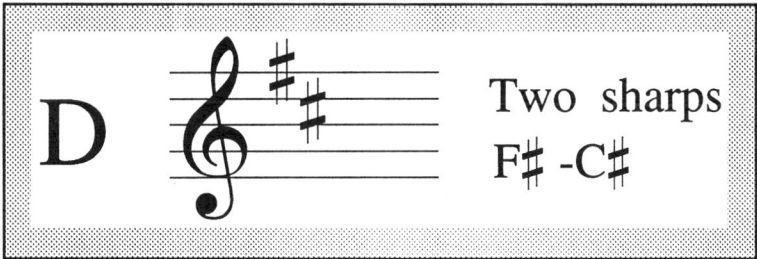

D — Two sharps F♯ -C♯

Solos used in this section are based on the blues minor scale below.

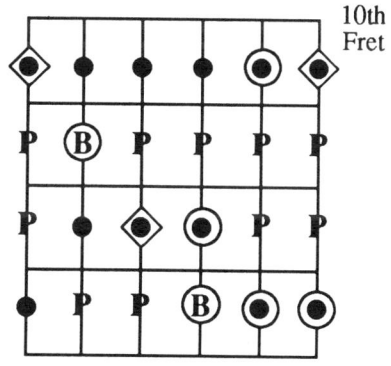

10th Fret

◈ = Root (key) notes
D

◉ = Popular notes to
bend

Ⓑ = Blue notes
(flat 5th tones)

P = Passing tones
(see explanation
in Section 1)

Triplet Licks in D

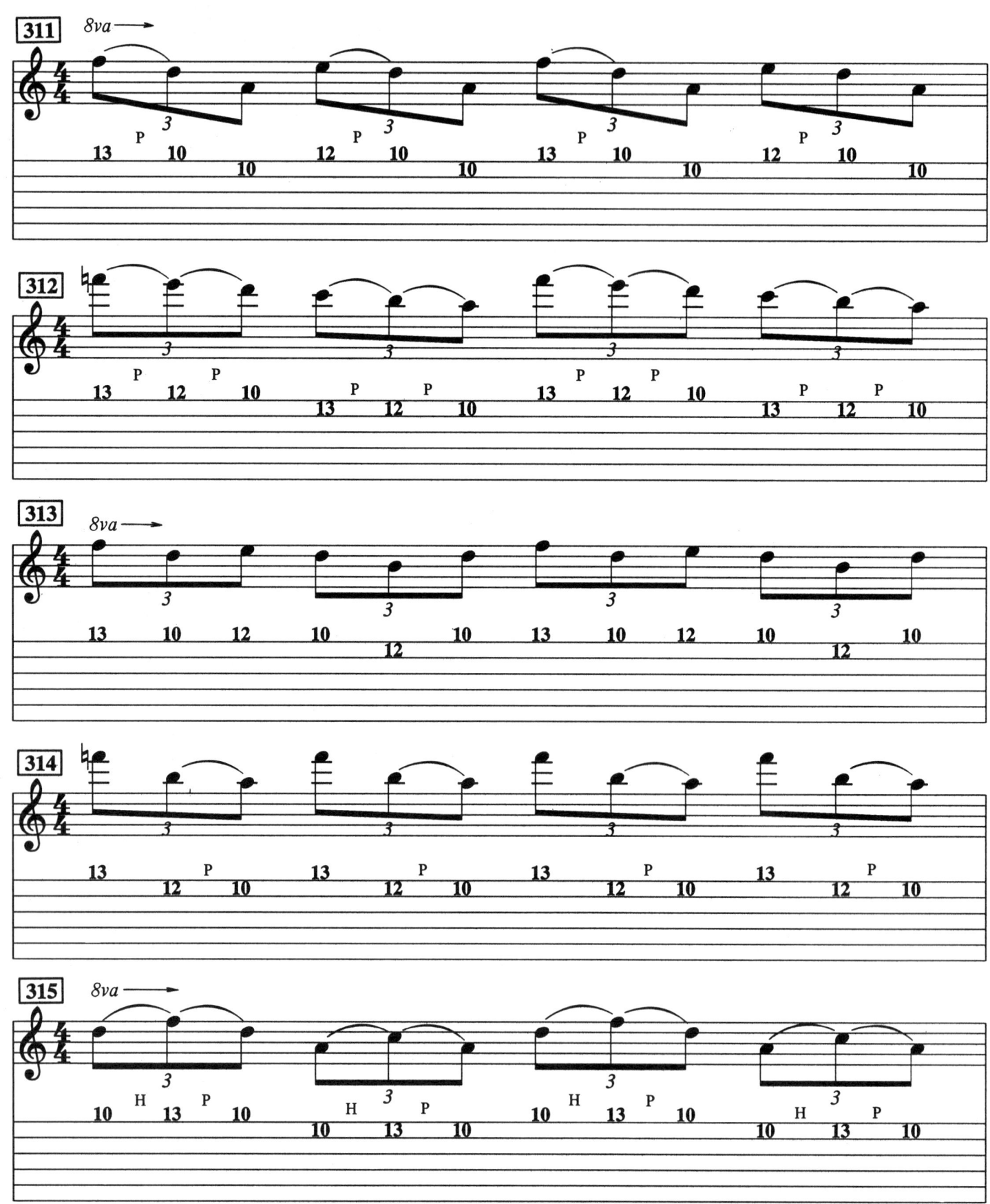

Standard Clichés and Phrases in D

Solo in D

B minor licks are related to the key of D, so all blues licks in B can be used in D. Remember to use the D note as the root when playing the B minor licks.

Solo Licks in D

In the style of Eric Clapton

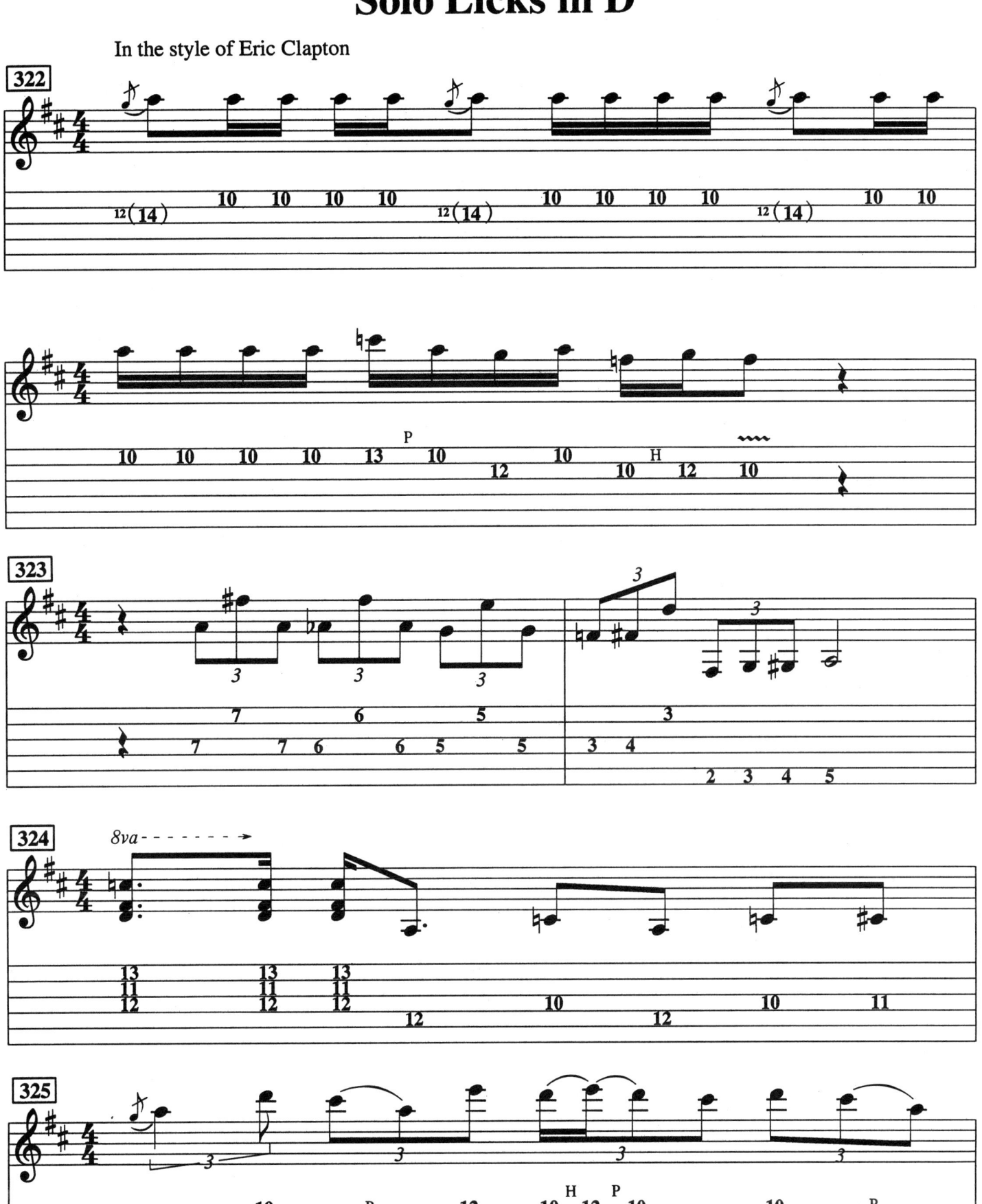

Traditional Blues Solo in D

D

Play to a 12-bar "Tobacco Road"-type rhythm.

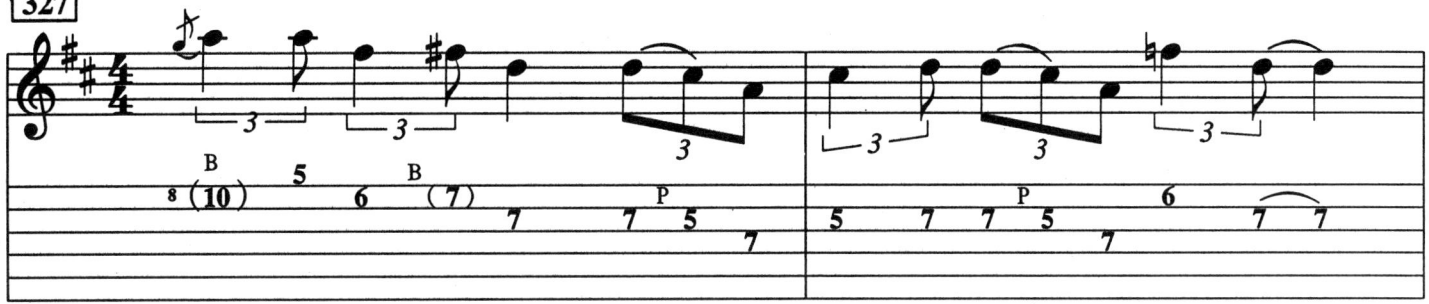

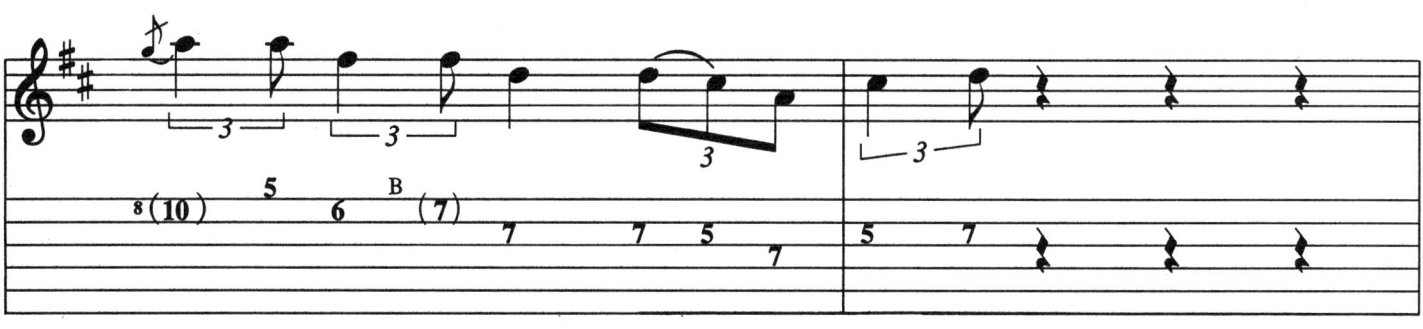

Swing Solo in D

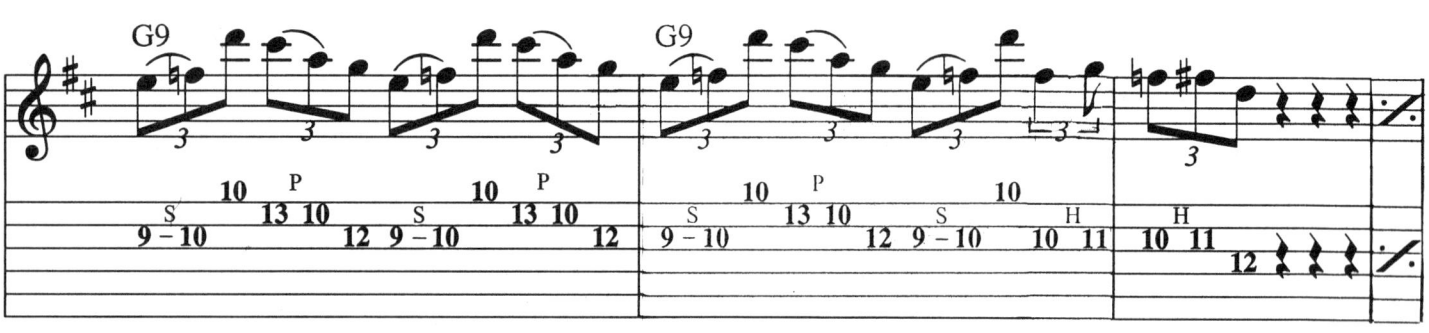

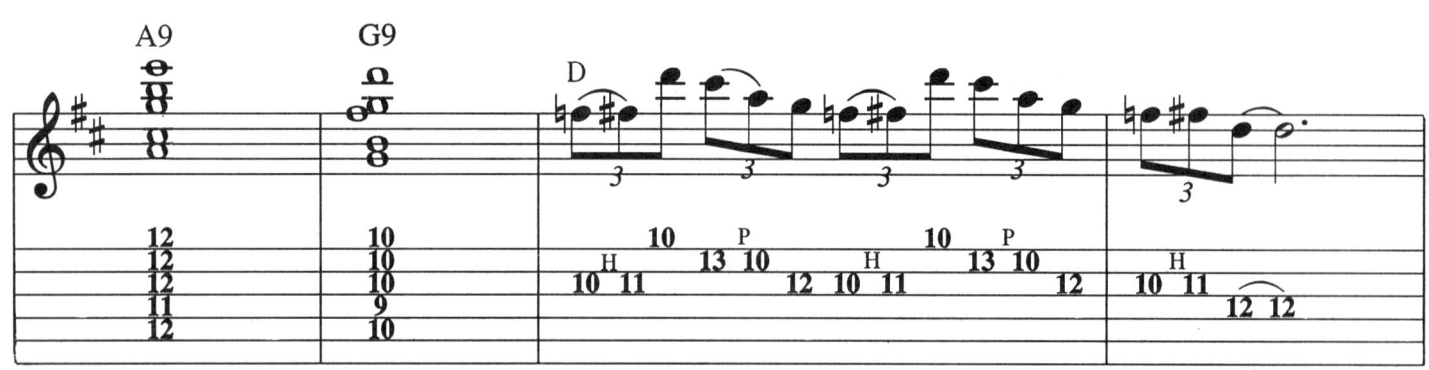

Section 12
Licks and Phrases in the Key of E Flat (E♭)

E♭ Three flats
B♭ -E♭ -A♭

Solos used in this section are based on the blues minor scale below.

11th
Fret

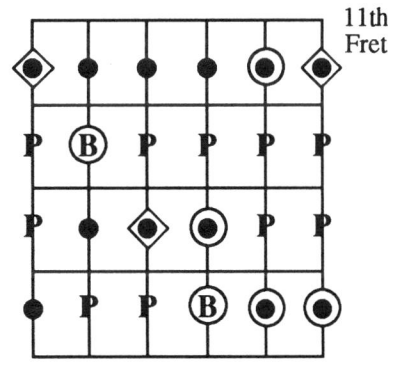

◈ = Root (key) notes
E♭

◉ = Popular notes to bend

Ⓑ = Blue notes
(flat 5th tones)

P = Passing tones
(see explanation in Section 1)

Standard Triplet Licks in E♭

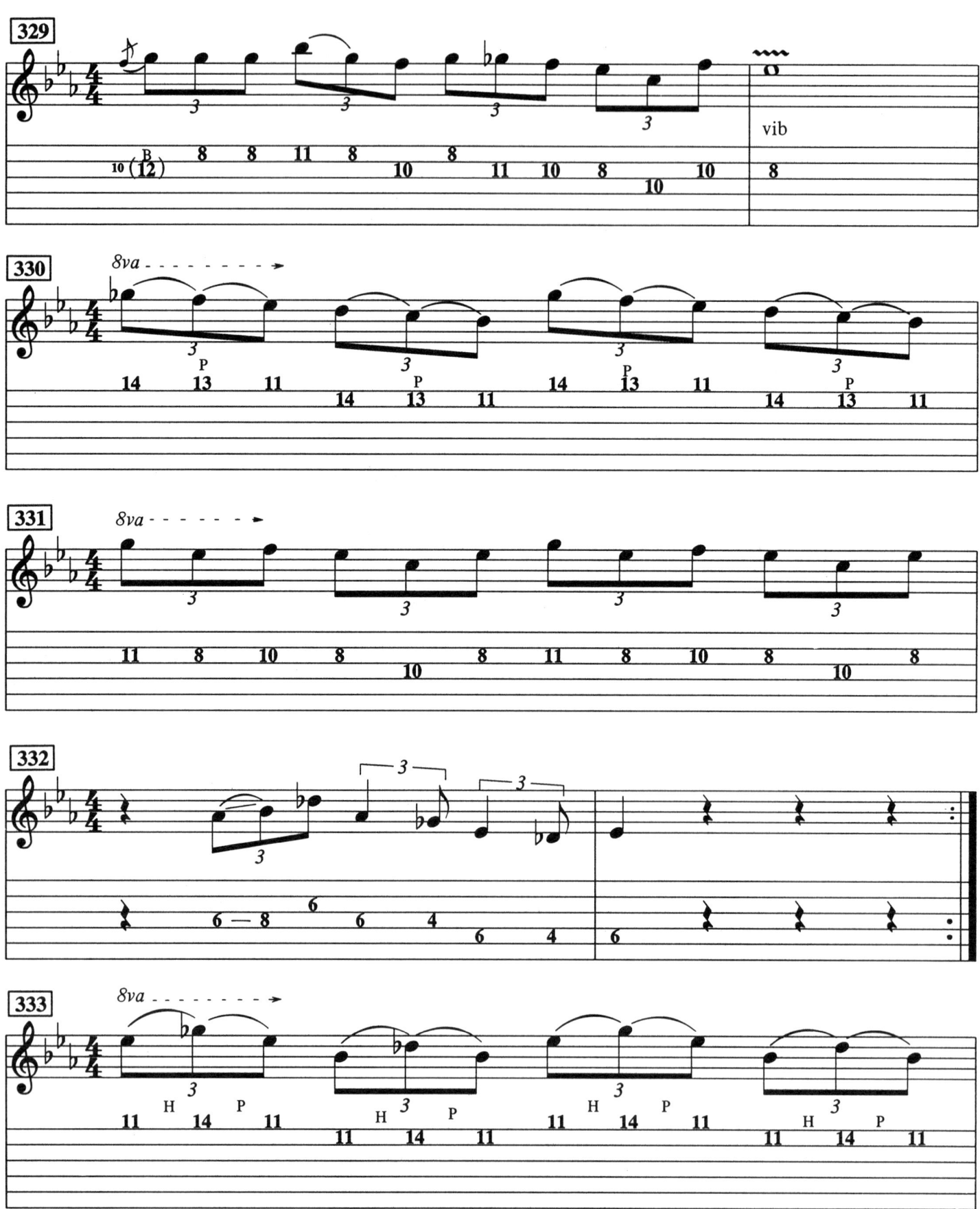

Standard Clichés in E♭

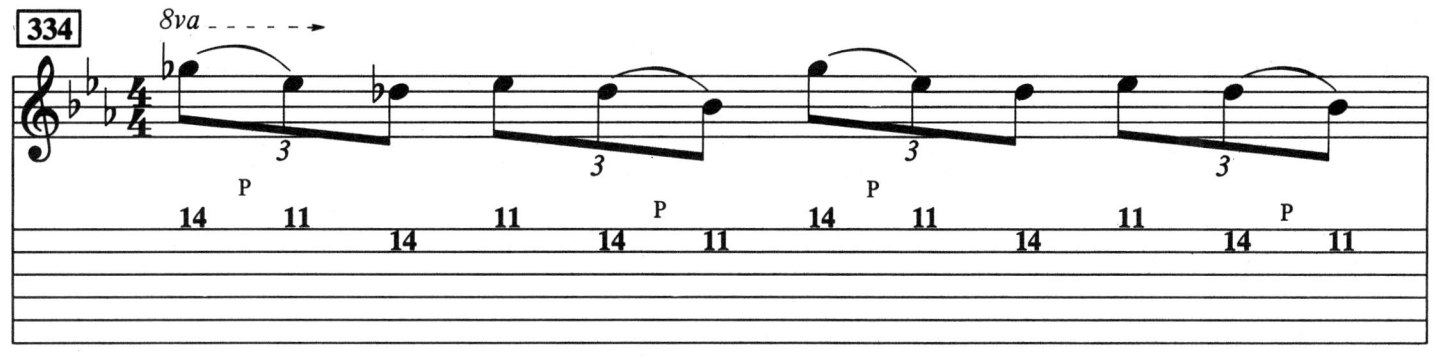

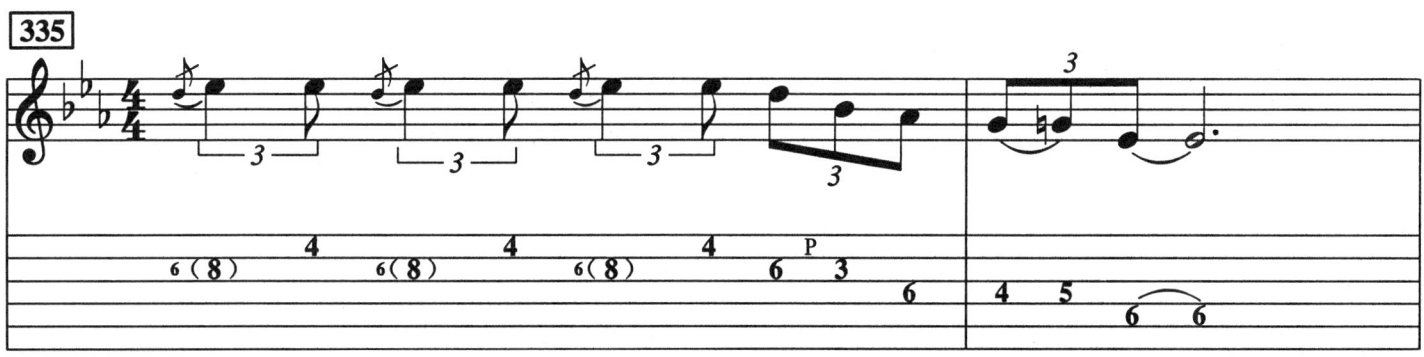

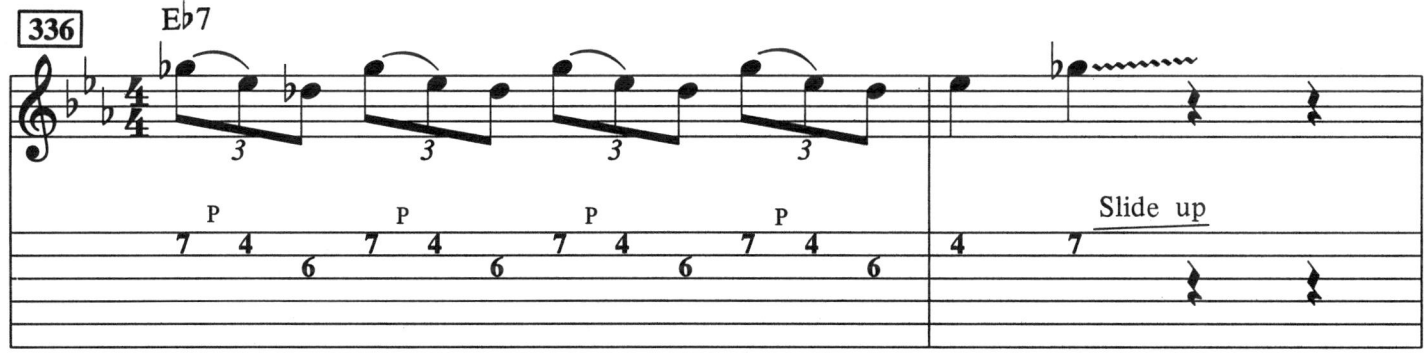

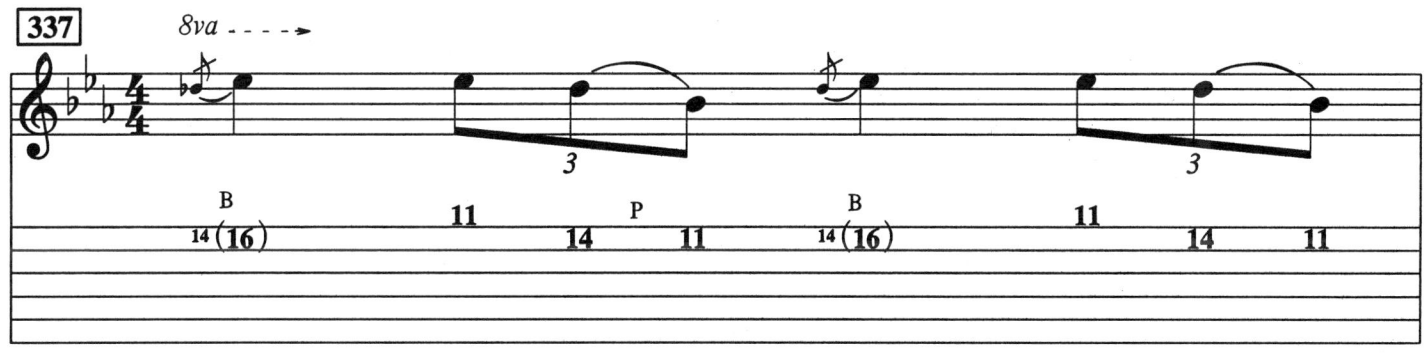

123

Licks in E♭

C minor is related to E♭. The first two solos (Solos 338 and 339) are C minor pentatonic.*

*When relative minor licks are played to their relative major key, the sound is more country music oriented. Ex.: C minor licks can be played in the key of E♭. Make sure E♭ is the key (target) note, not C.

Section 13
Solo Examples Using Each Blues Scale (Pattern) Extension

In this section, each box scale diagram is an extension of the home base scale. An example solo has been written to the right of each of these scale diagrams.

Blues Solos for Each Box Scale Diagram
in the Key of E

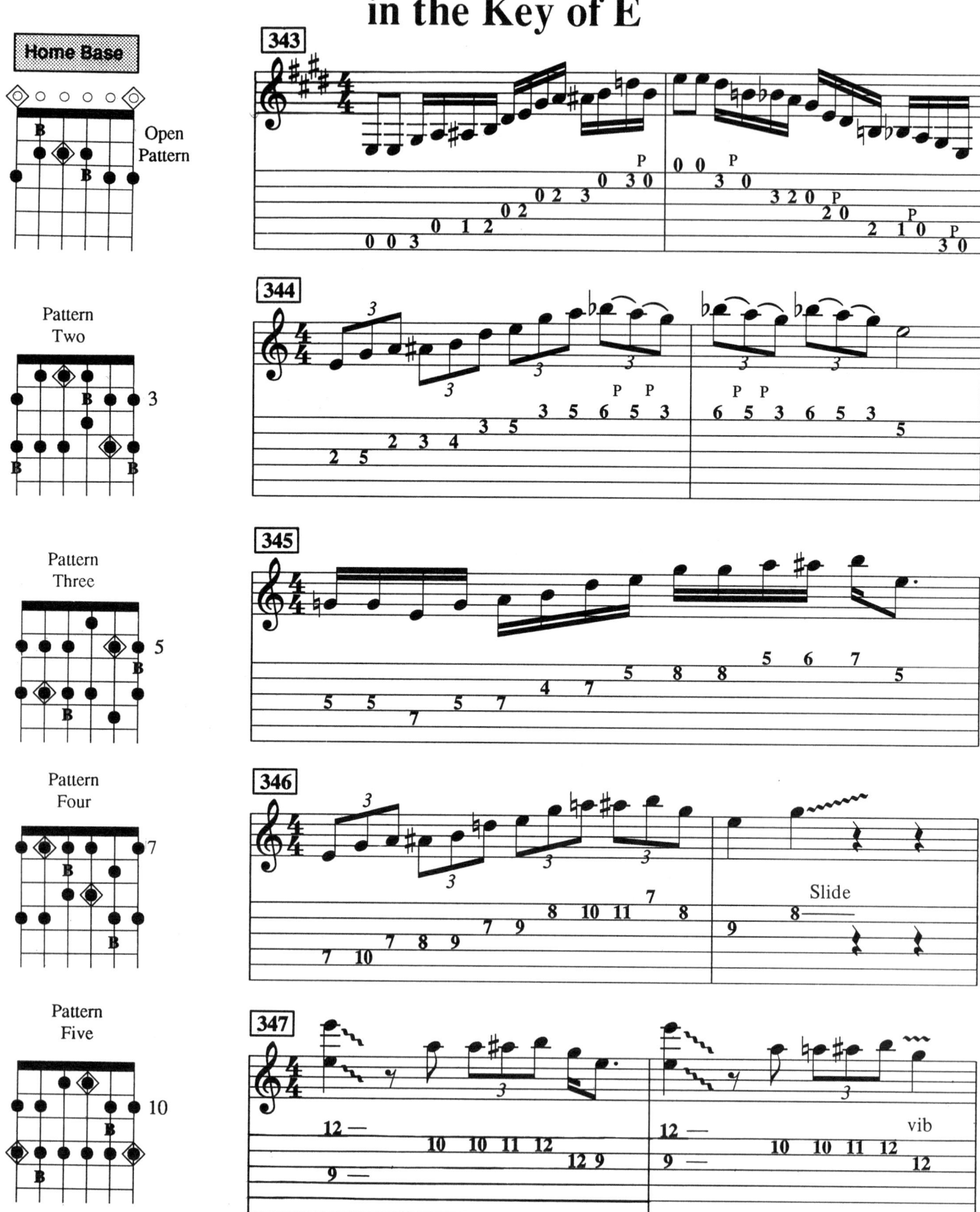

Blues Solos for Box Diagrams in F

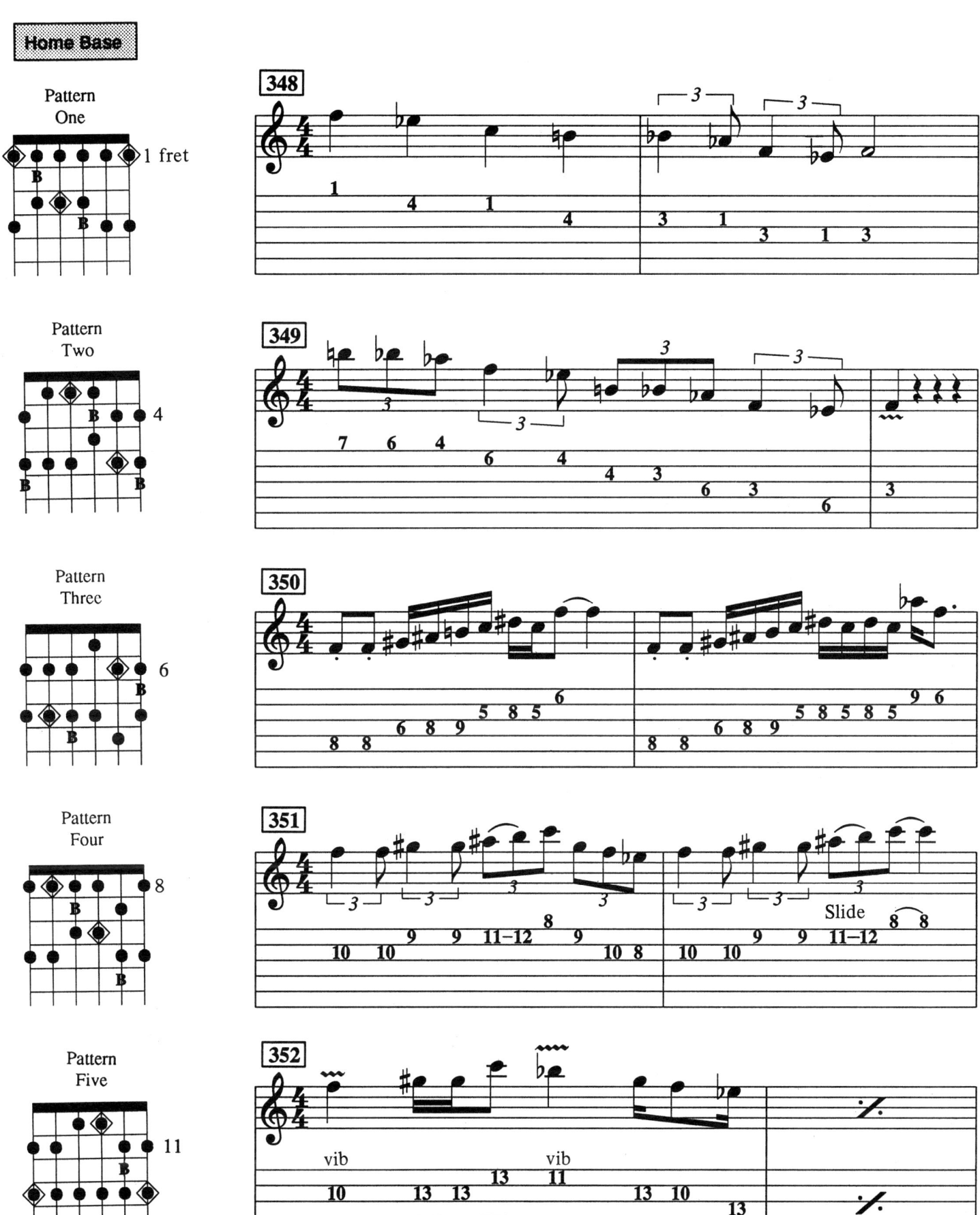

Blues Solos For Scale Box Diagrams
in the Key of F♯

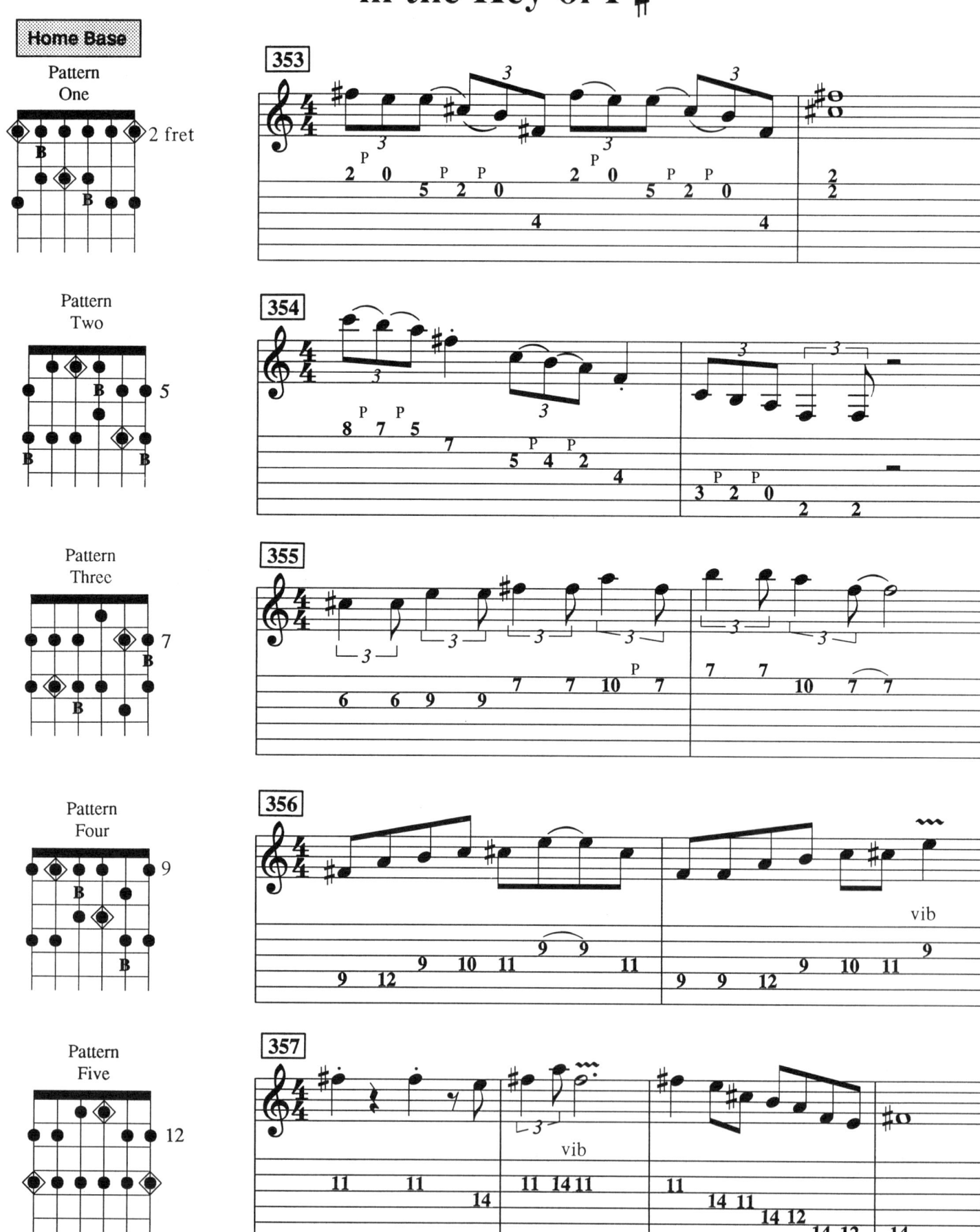

Blues Solos for Scale Box Diagrams
in the Key of G

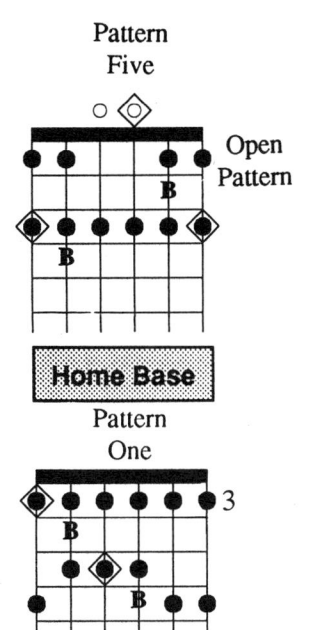

Pattern Five

Open Pattern

Home Base

Pattern One

In the Style of Z Z Top

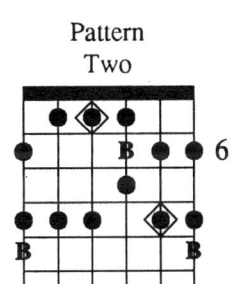

Pattern Two

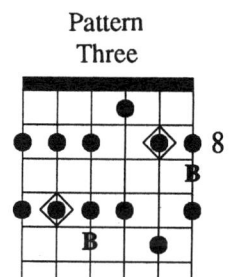

Pattern Three

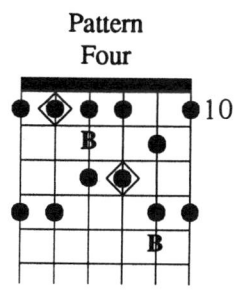

Pattern Four

Blues Solos for Scale Box Diagrams
in the Key of A♭

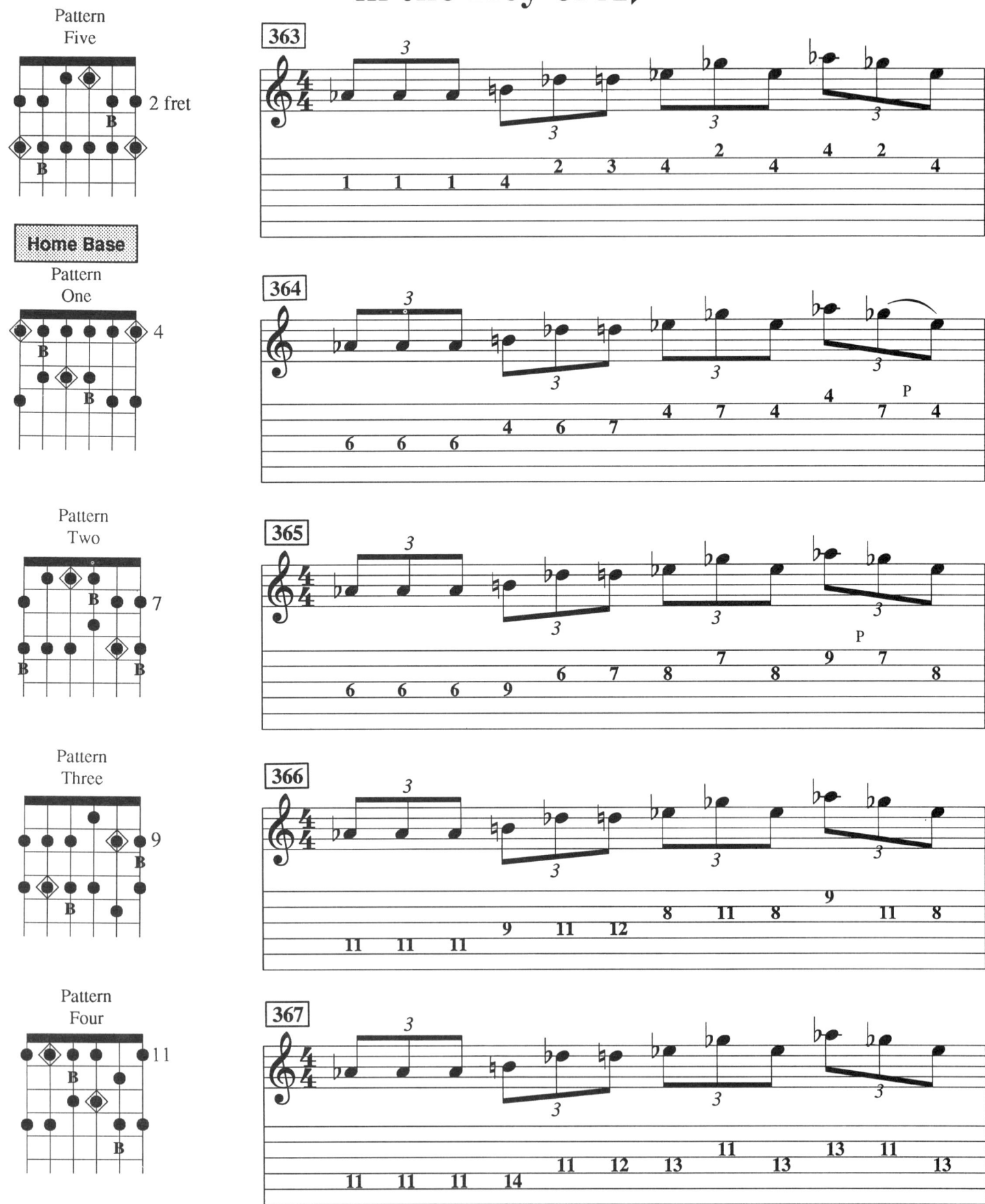

The same solo is written for each scale diagram on this page. The reason for this is to experience different finger patterns and voicings using the same solo.

Blues Solos for Scale Box Diagrams
in the Key of A

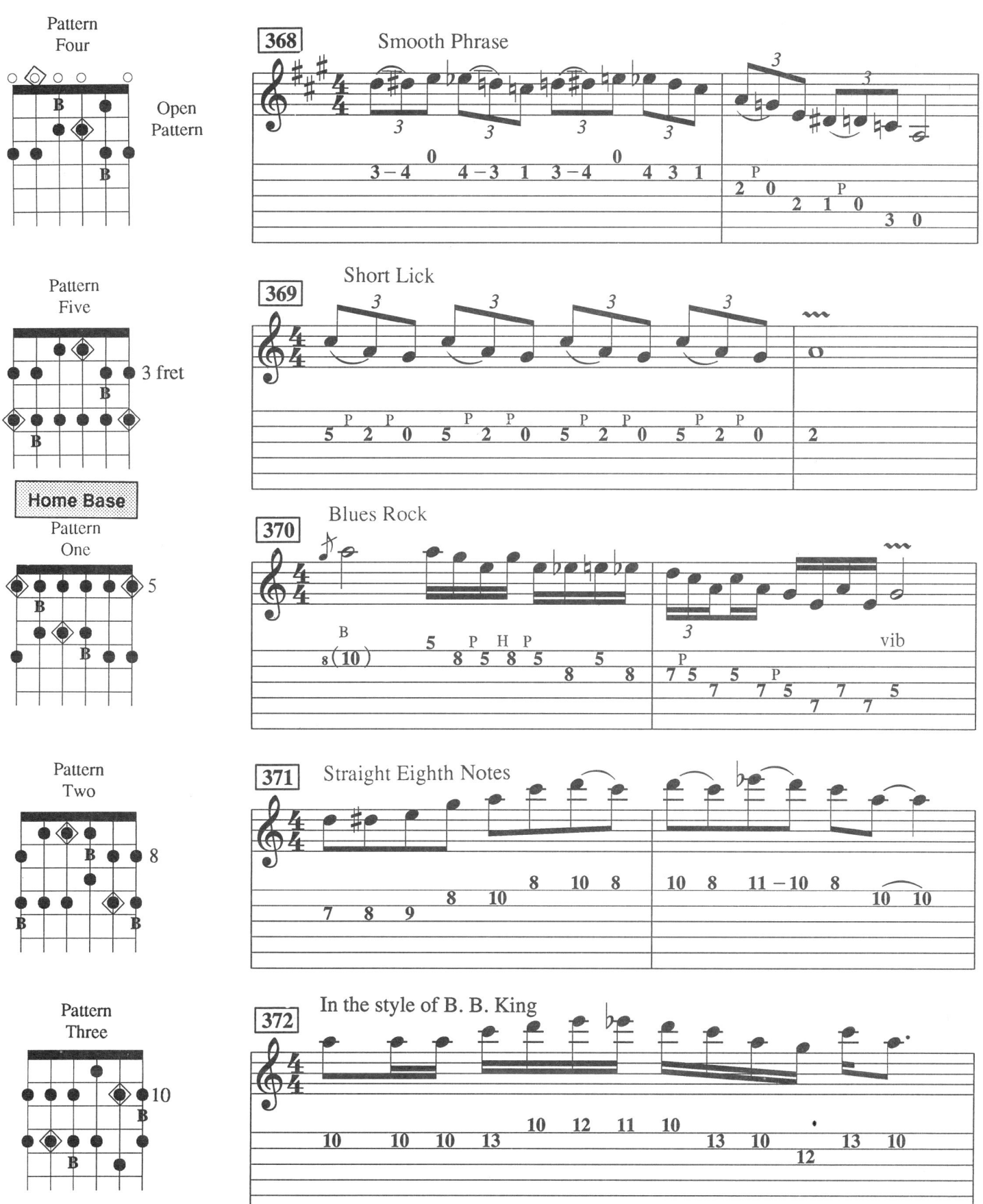

Blues Solos for Scale Box Diagrams in B♭

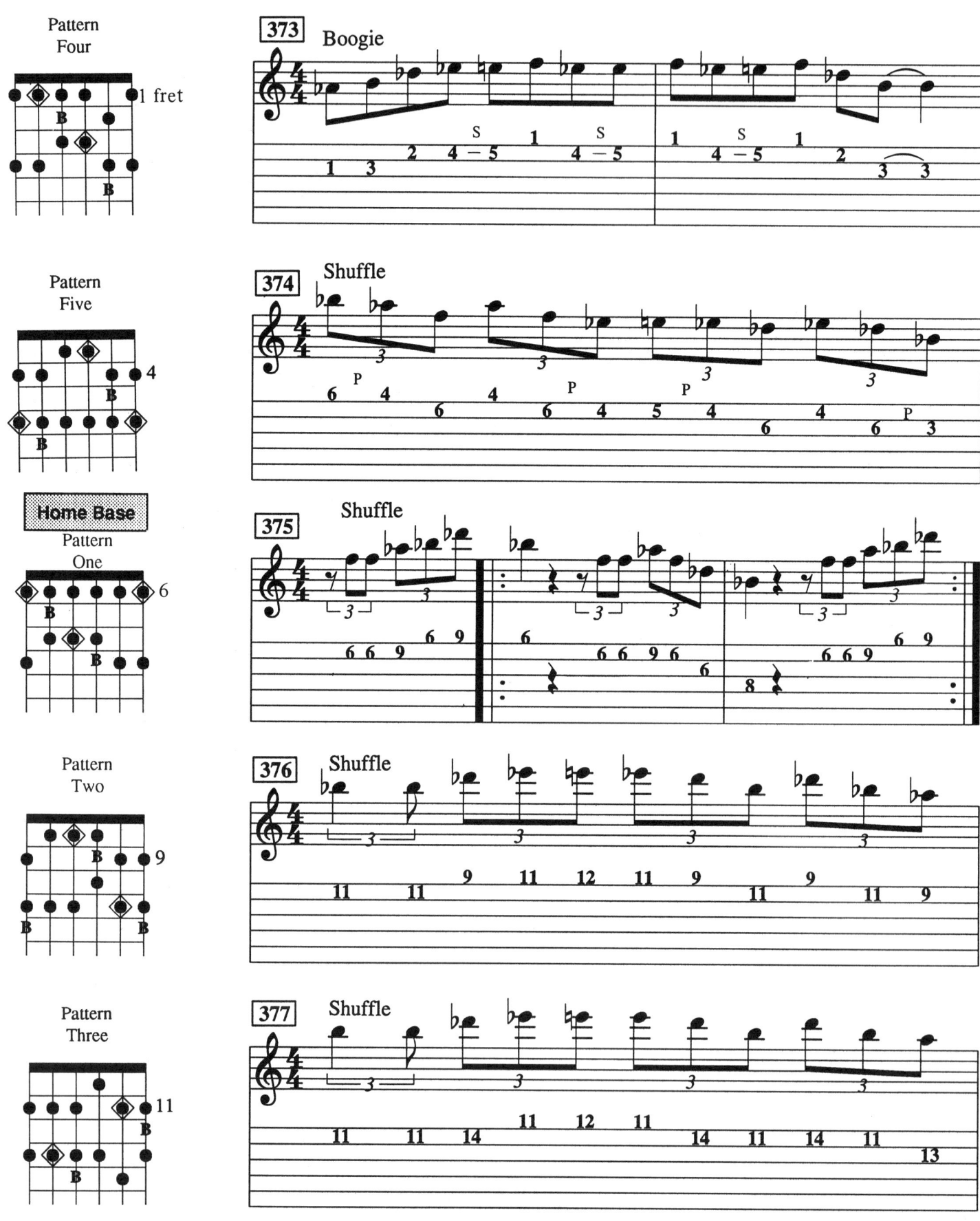

Blues Solos for Scale Box Diagrams in B

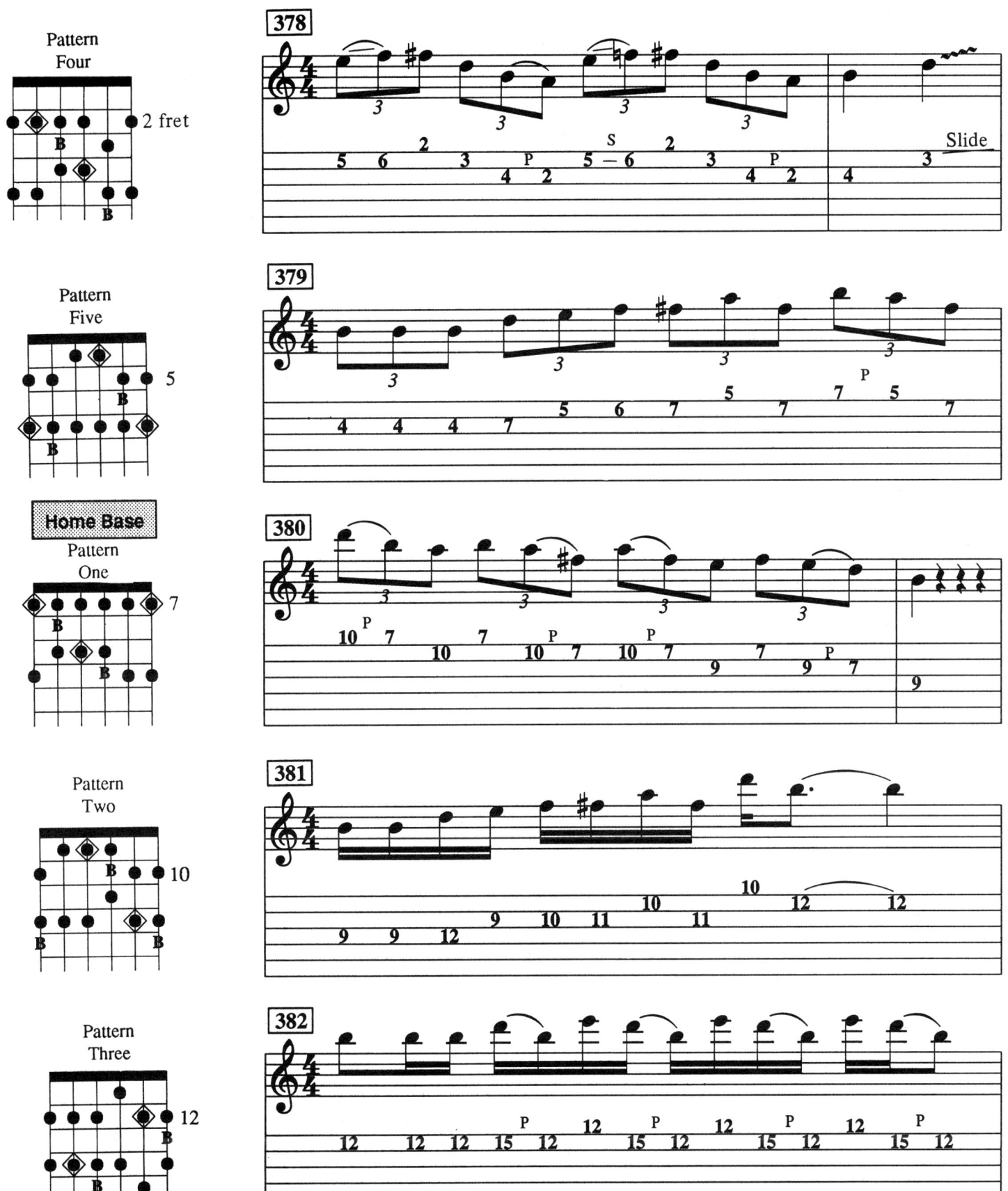

Blues Solos for Scale Box Diagrams in C

Blues Solos for Scale Box Diagrams in D♭

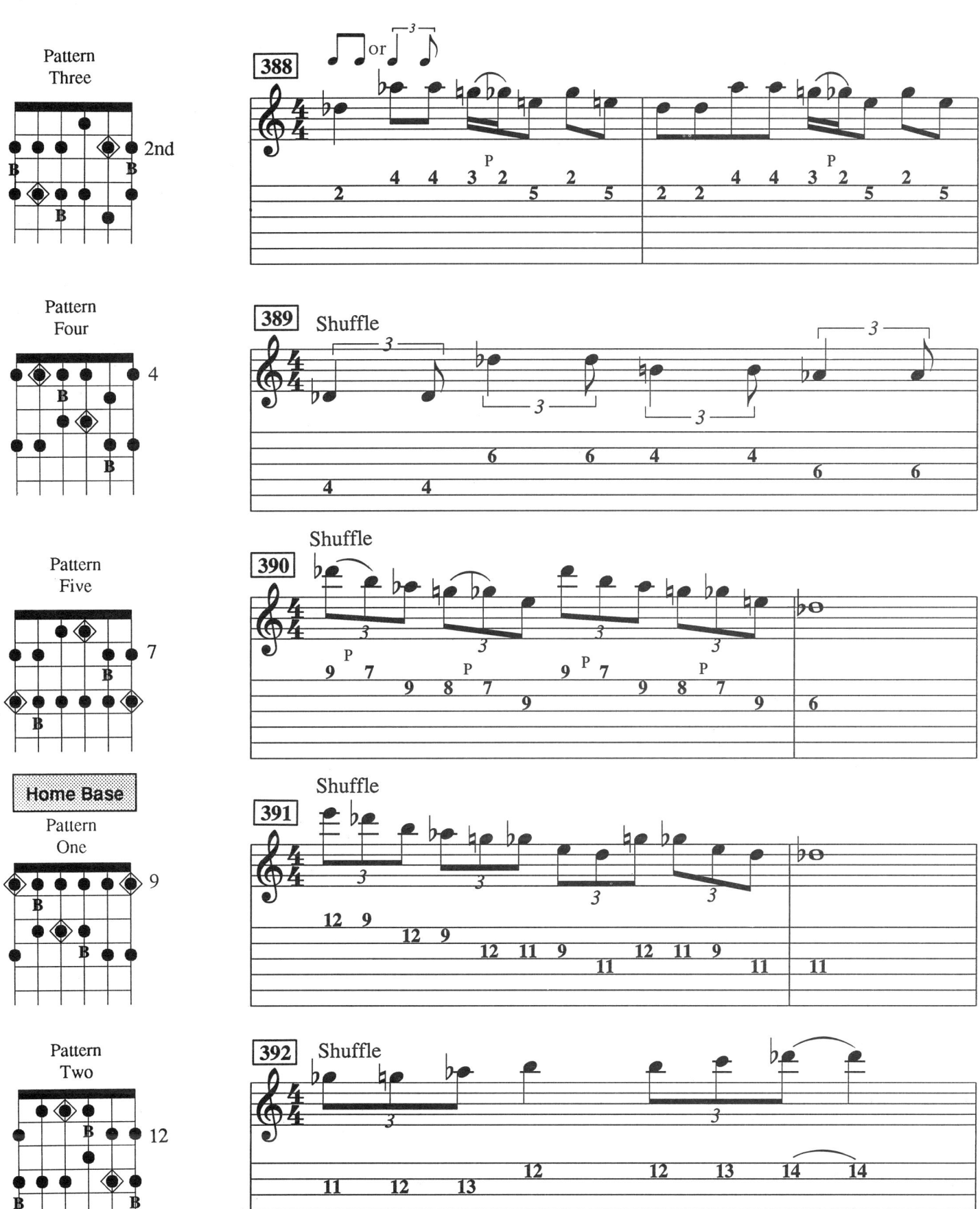

Blues Solos for Scale Box Diagrams in D

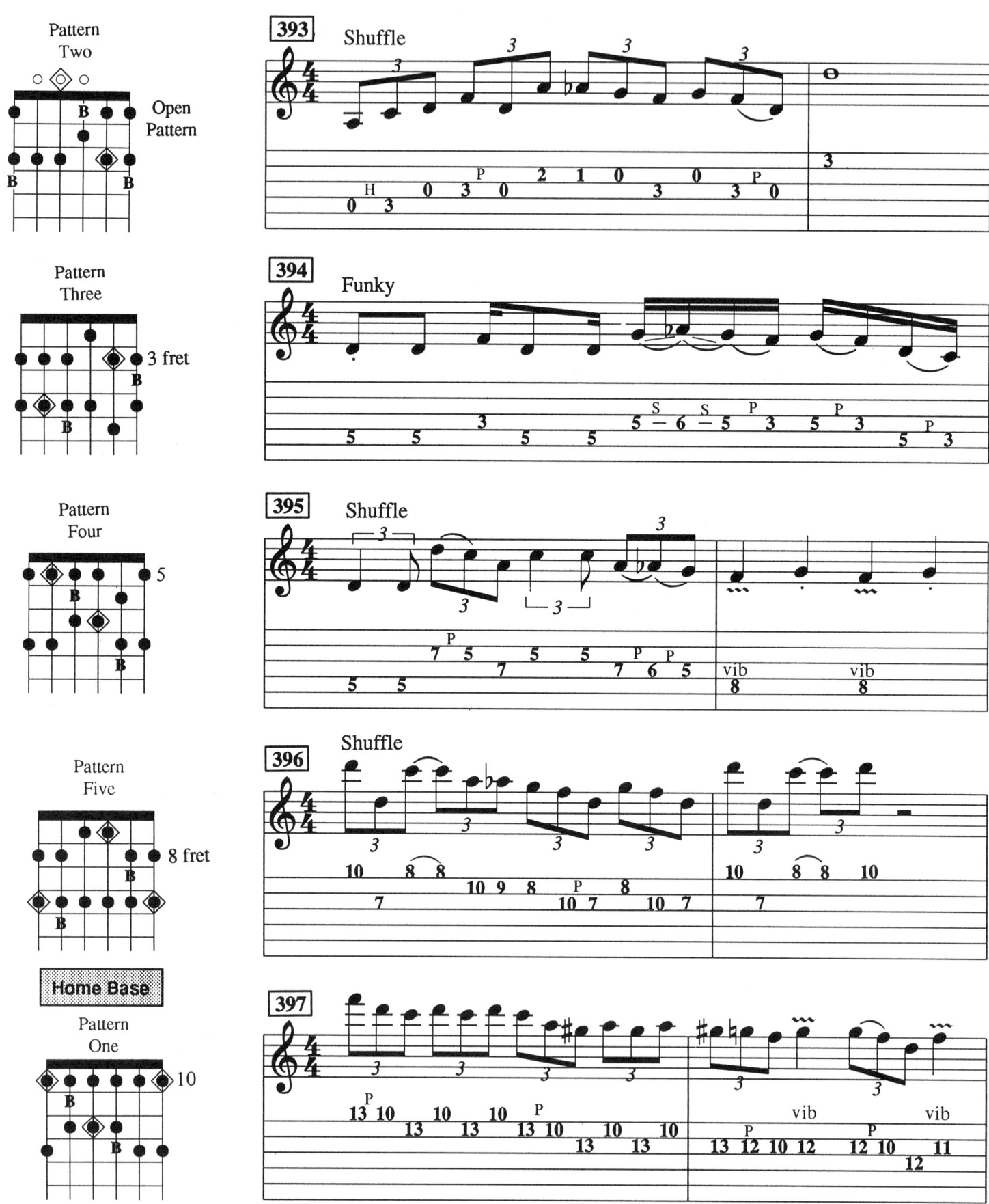

Blues Solos for Scale Box Diagrams in E♭

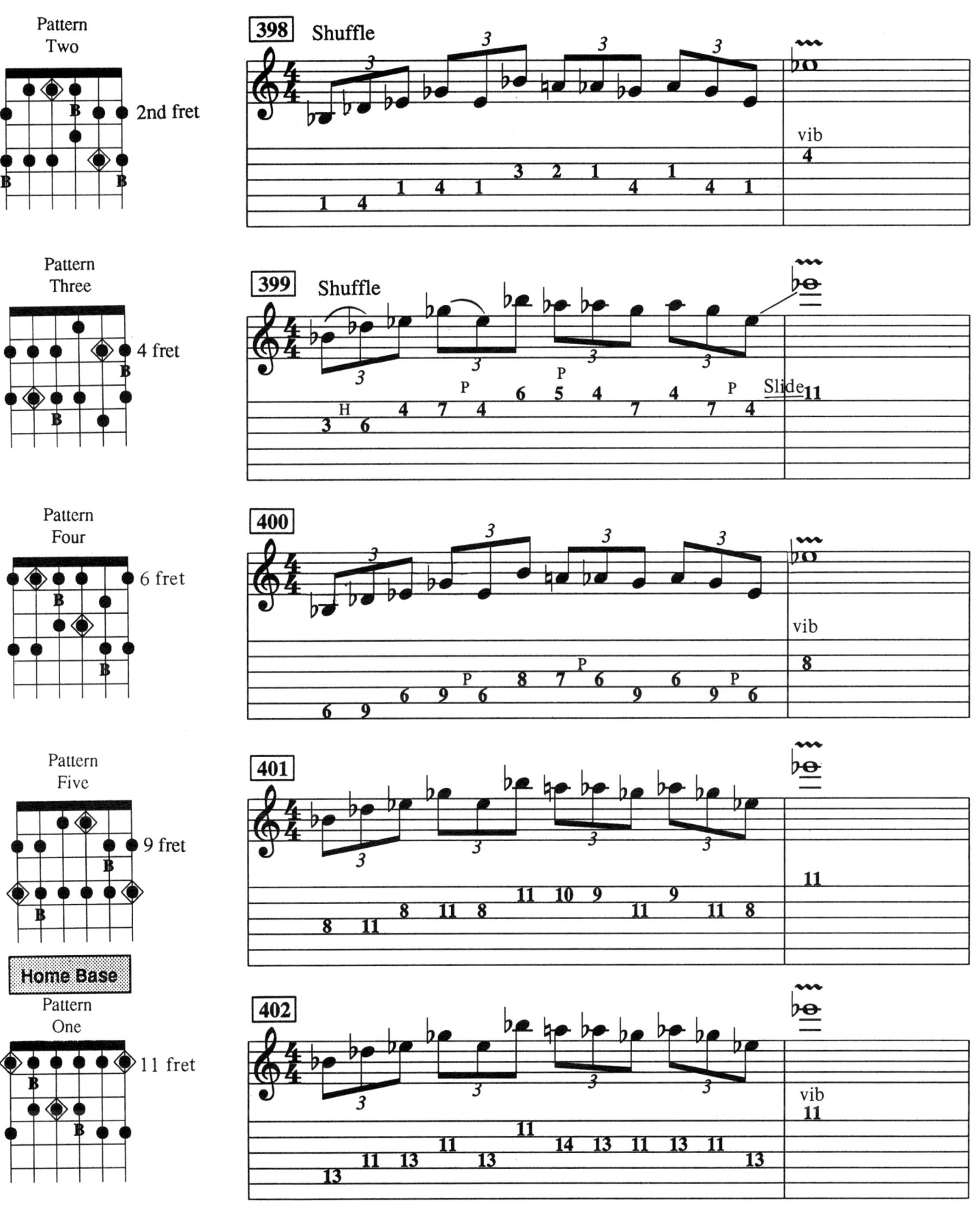

The same solo is written for each scale diagram on this page. The reason for this is to experience different finger patterns and voicings using the same idea.

Random Solos in A and E

Random Solos in A and F

Solo in the Style of Stevie Ray Vaughan

Solo in the Style of B. B. King

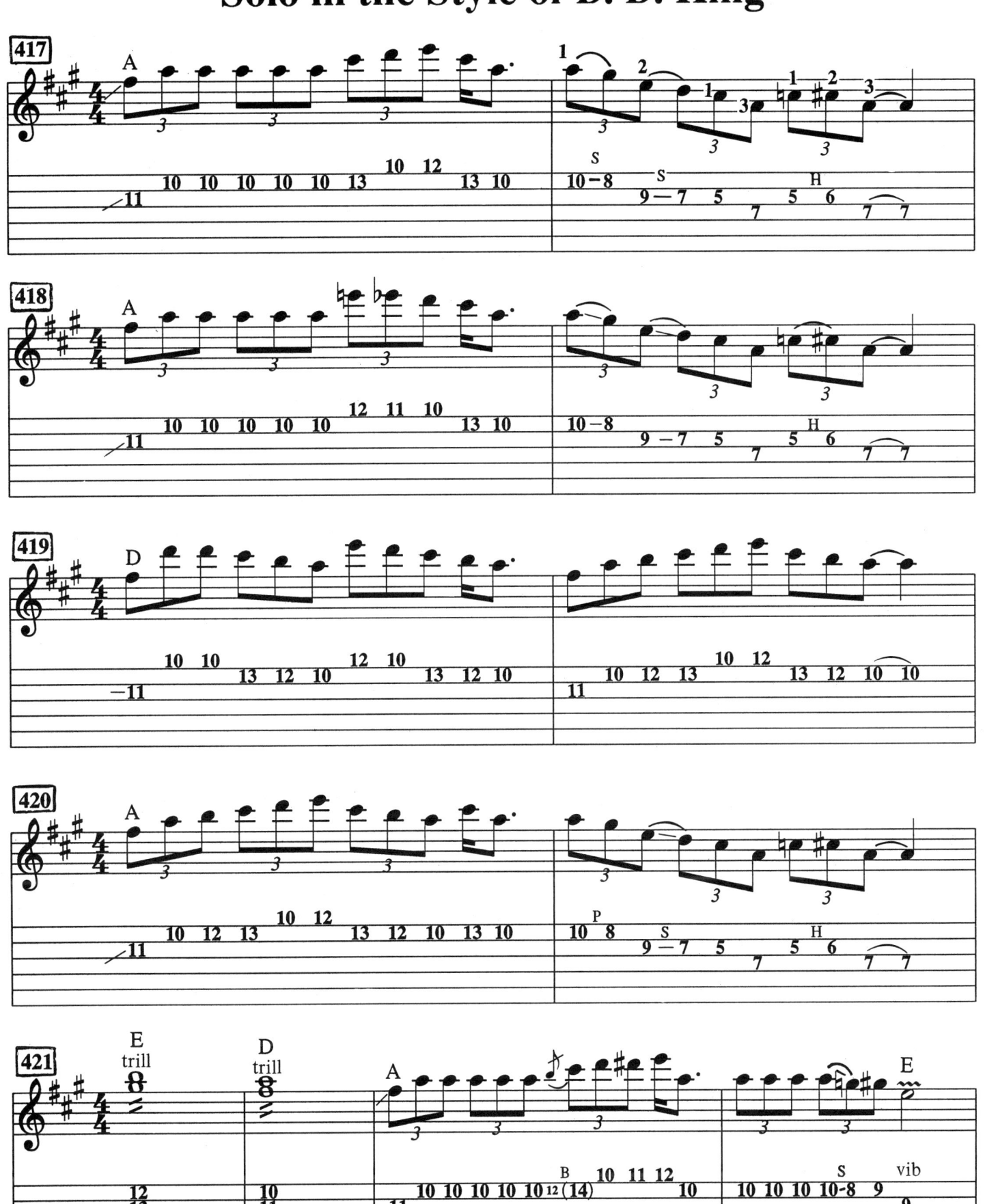

Bottleneck Slide in A

Section 14
Scale Shifting

Finding the Country Scale in the Key of G

To play country solos (scales), simply shift the home base blues pentatonic minor scale down 3 fret, or 4 frets if counting from the scale you're on.

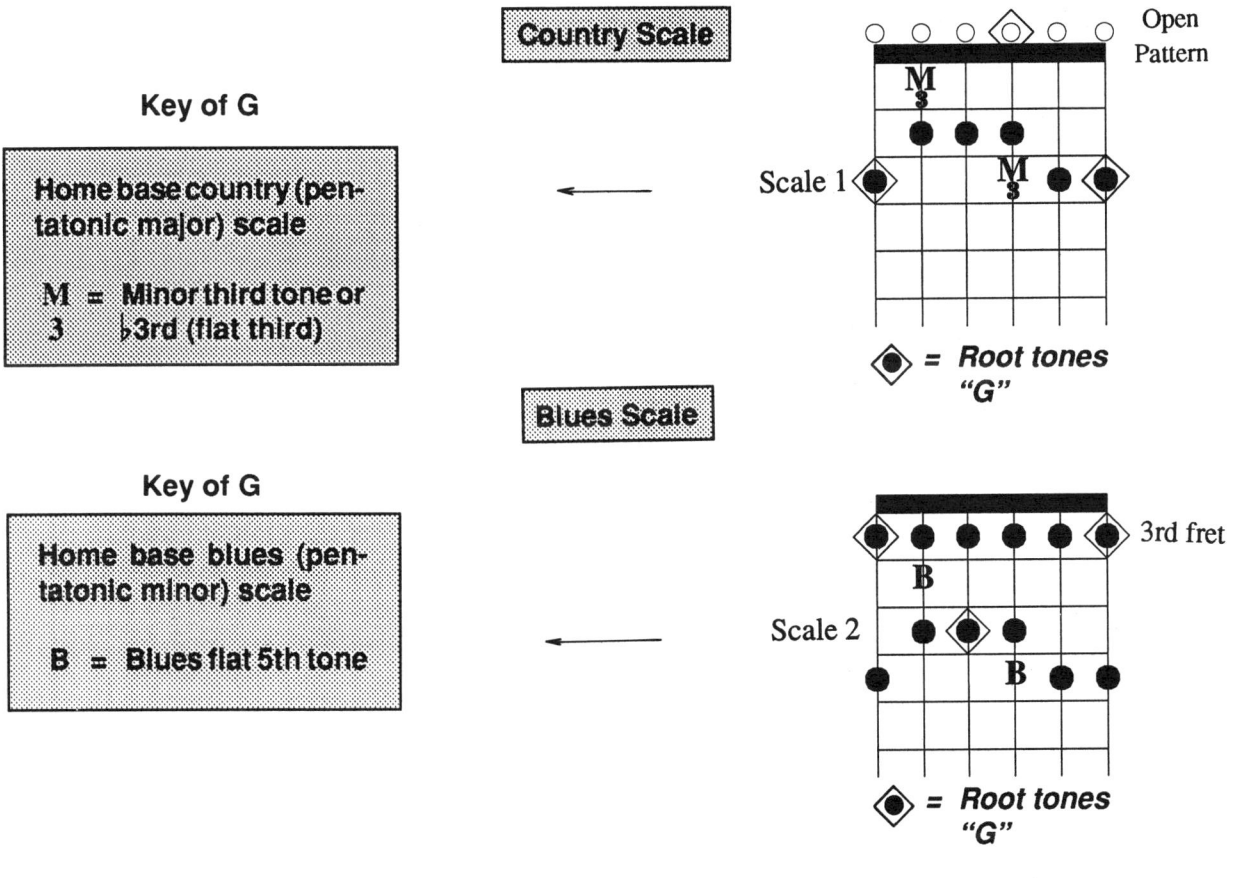

Country Scale

Key of G

Home base country (pentatonic major) scale

M = Minor third tone or
3   ♭3rd (flat third)

⬥ = **Root tones "G"**

Blues Scale

Key of G

Home base blues (pentatonic minor) scale

B = Blues flat 5th tone

⬥ = **Root tones "G"**

In this section, both scales (even though they have the same pattern when shifting) keep the root tones of the minor blues scale in order to stay in key.

When playing blues solos or rock solos, use Scale 2. When playing country solos or country-rock solos, move Scale 2 down 4 frets to Scale 1.

All blues guitarists discover this formula (one way or another) when seeking solo and sound diversity using the blues minor pentatonic scale.

Finding the Country Scale in A♭

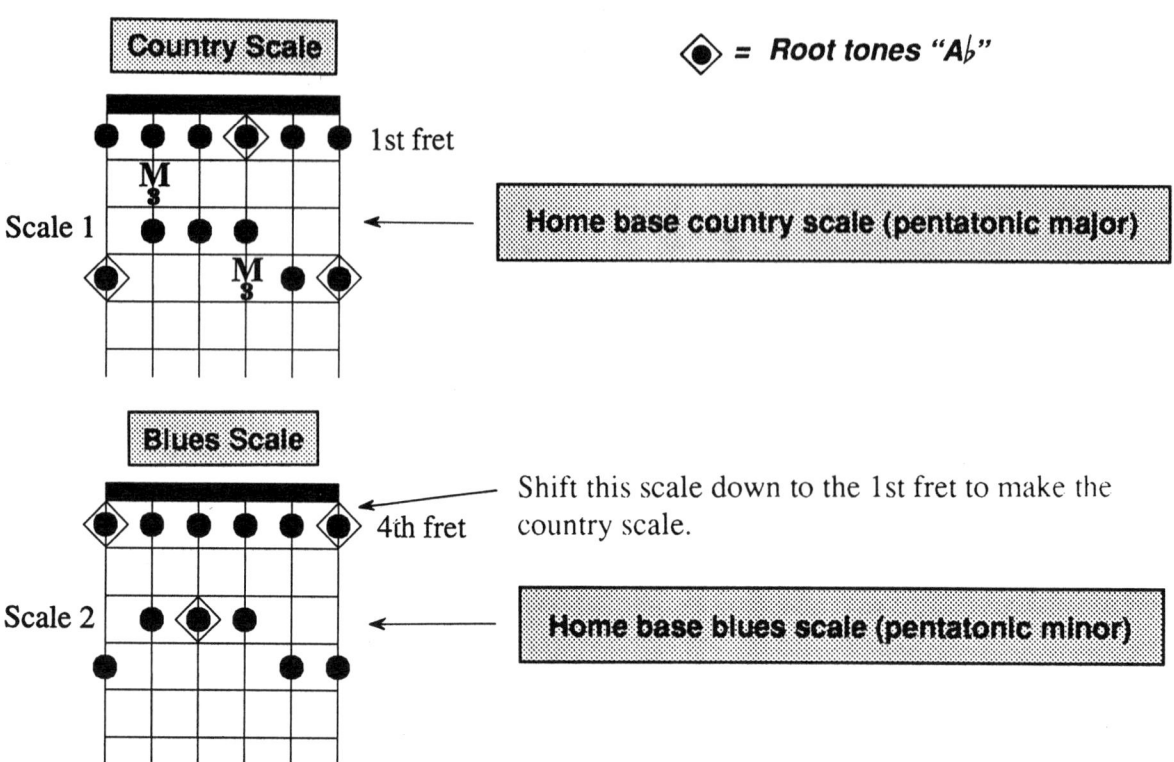

Country Scale

◈ = Root tones "A♭"

1st fret

Scale 1

← Home base country scale (pentatonic major)

Blues Scale

Shift this scale down to the 1st fret to make the country scale.

4th fret

Scale 2

← Home base blues scale (pentatonic minor)

Finding the Country Scale in the Key of A

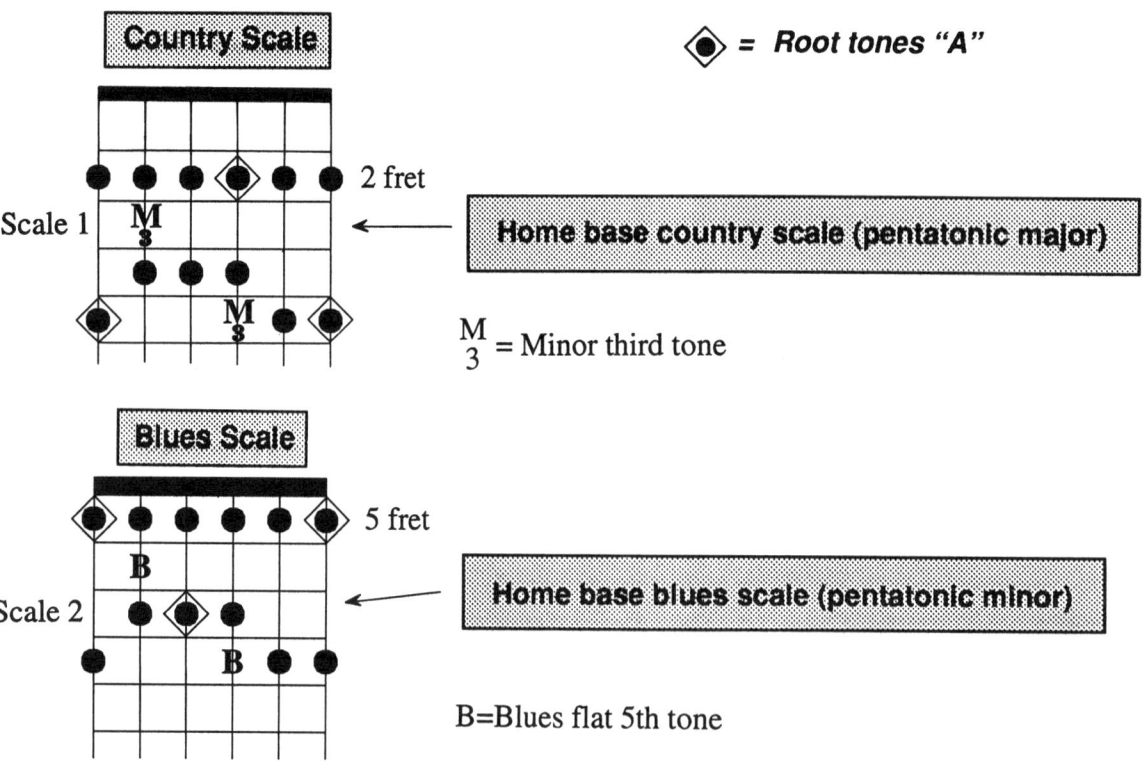

Country Scale

◈ = Root tones "A"

2 fret

Scale 1

← Home base country scale (pentatonic major)

$\frac{M}{3}$ = Minor third tone

Blues Scale

5 fret

Scale 2

← Home base blues scale (pentatonic minor)

B=Blues flat 5th tone

When the blues pentatonic minor scale shifts down 3 frets, the flat 5th becomes a minor 3rd.

Finding the Country Scale in B♭

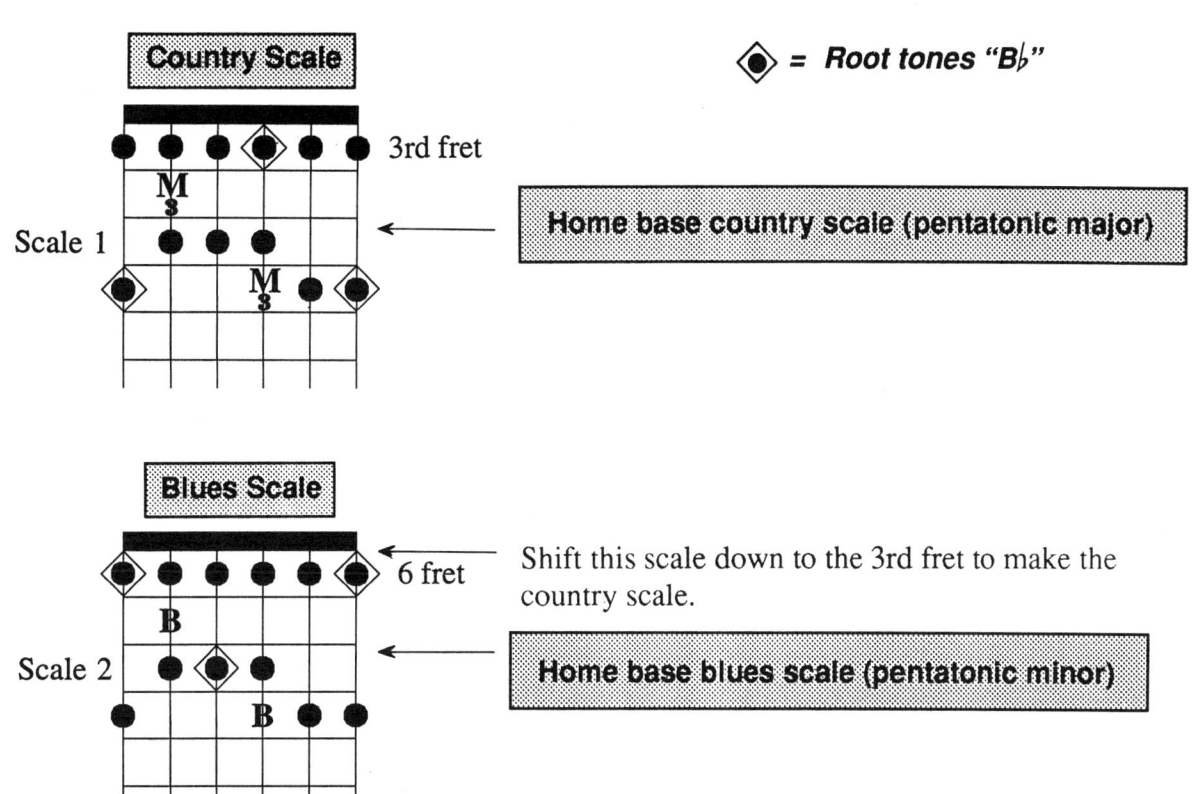

= Root tones "B♭"

Country Scale

3rd fret

Scale 1

← Home base country scale (pentatonic major)

Blues Scale

6 fret

Shift this scale down to the 3rd fret to make the country scale.

Scale 2

← Home base blues scale (pentatonic minor)

Finding the Country Scale in B

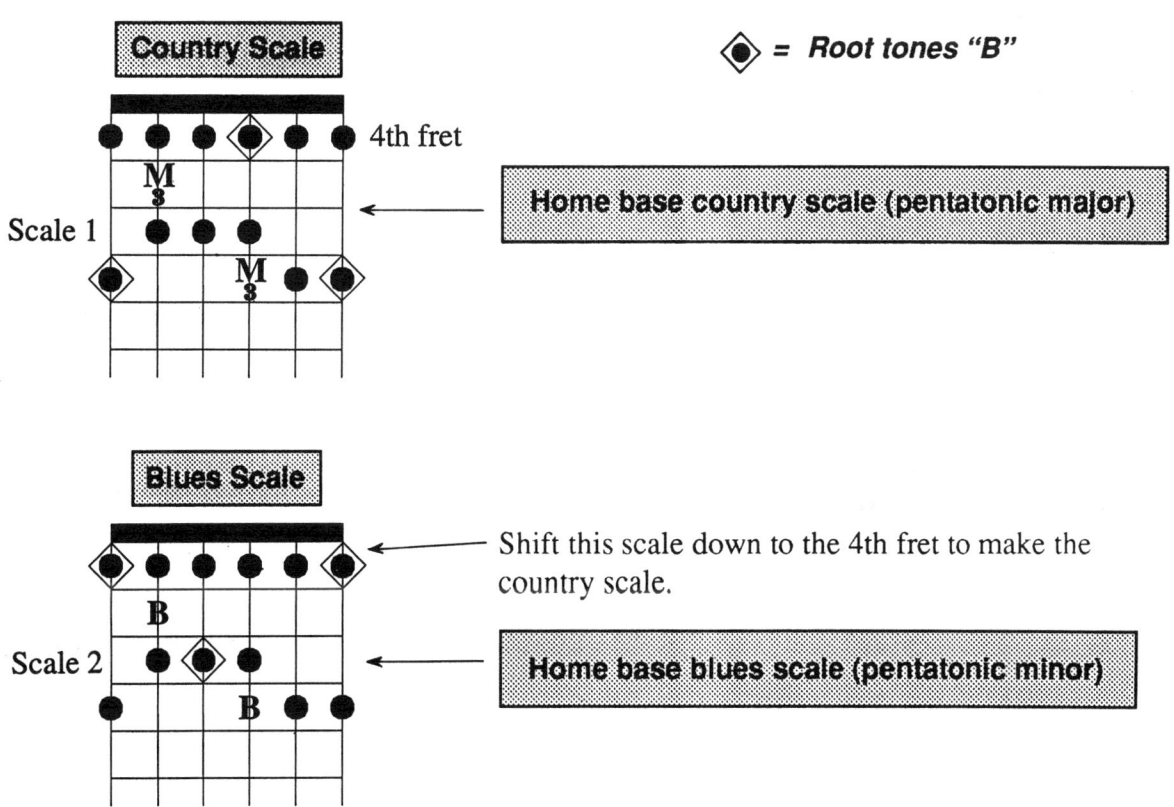

= Root tones "B"

Country Scale

4th fret

Scale 1

← Home base country scale (pentatonic major)

Blues Scale

Shift this scale down to the 4th fret to make the country scale.

Scale 2

← Home base blues scale (pentatonic minor)

Finding the Country Scale in C

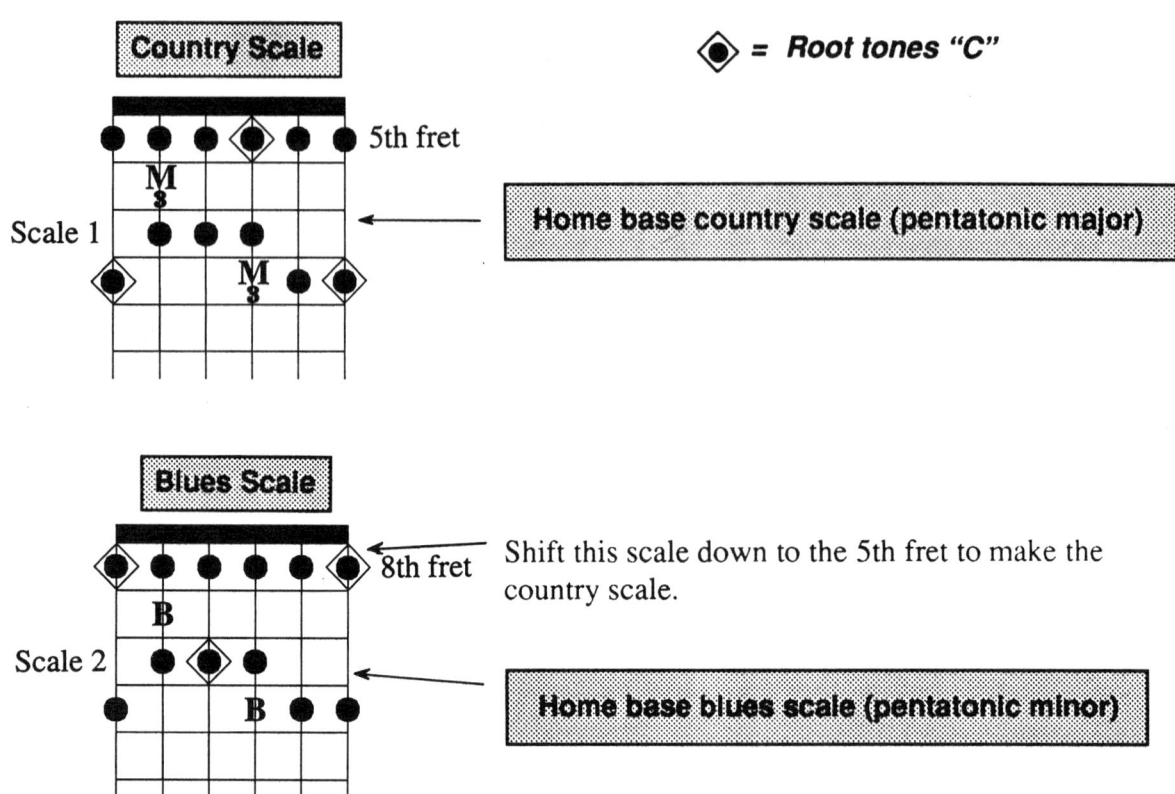

Country Scale

◈ = Root tones "C"

Scale 1

5th fret

M3

M3

Home base country scale (pentatonic major)

Blues Scale

Scale 2

8th fret

B

B

Shift this scale down to the 5th fret to make the country scale.

Home base blues scale (pentatonic minor)

More Scale Positions in the Key of C

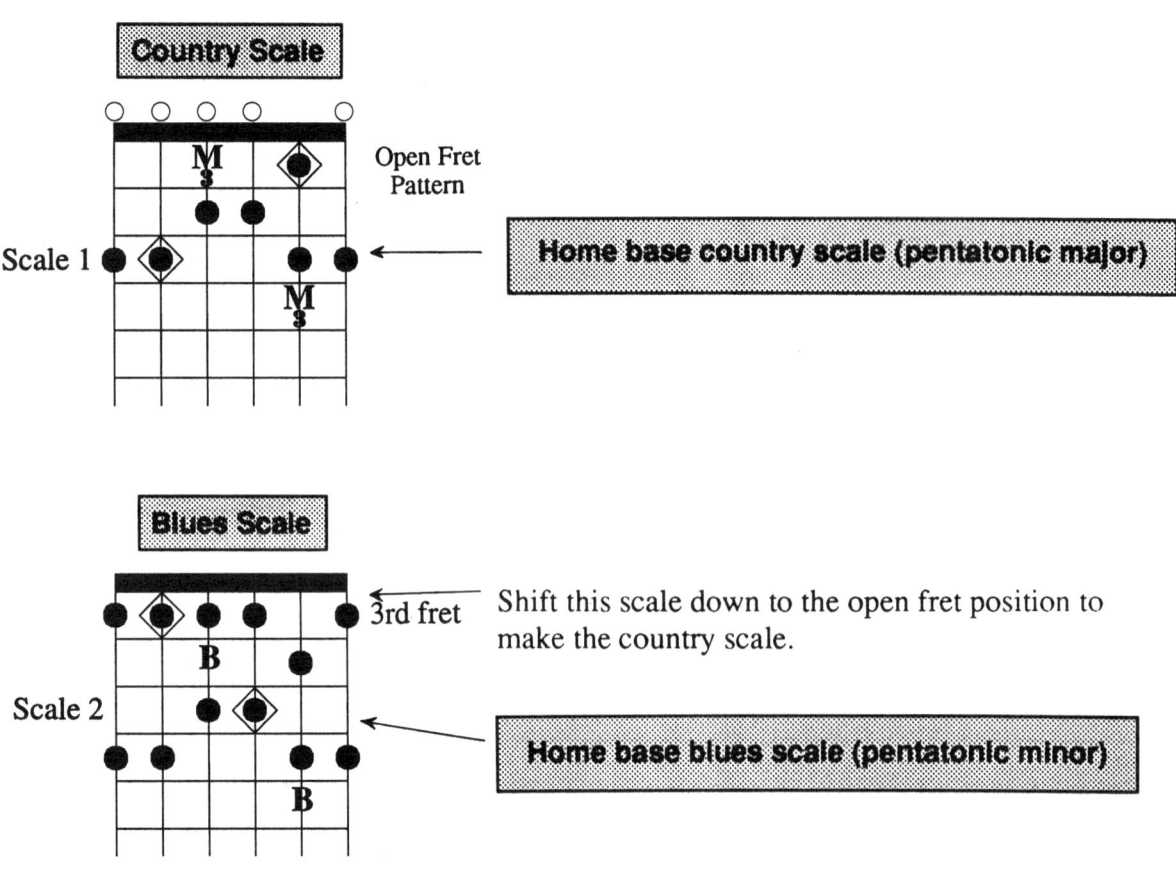

Country Scale

Scale 1

M3

Open Fret Pattern

M3

Home base country scale (pentatonic major)

Blues Scale

Scale 2

3rd fret

B

B

Shift this scale down to the open fret position to make the country scale.

Home base blues scale (pentatonic minor)

Finding the Country Scale in the Key of D♭

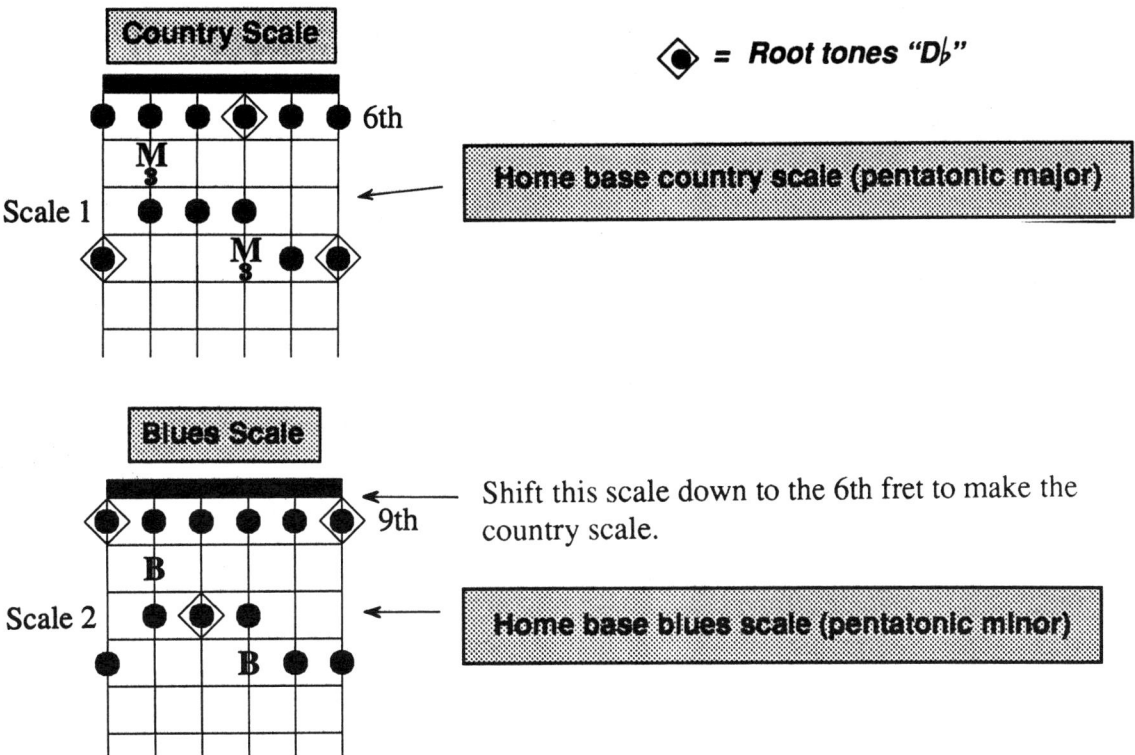

Country Scale

6th

Scale 1

◆ = Root tones "D♭"

Home base country scale (pentatonic major)

Blues Scale

9th

Scale 2

Shift this scale down to the 6th fret to make the country scale.

Home base blues scale (pentatonic minor)

More Scale Positions in the Key of D♭

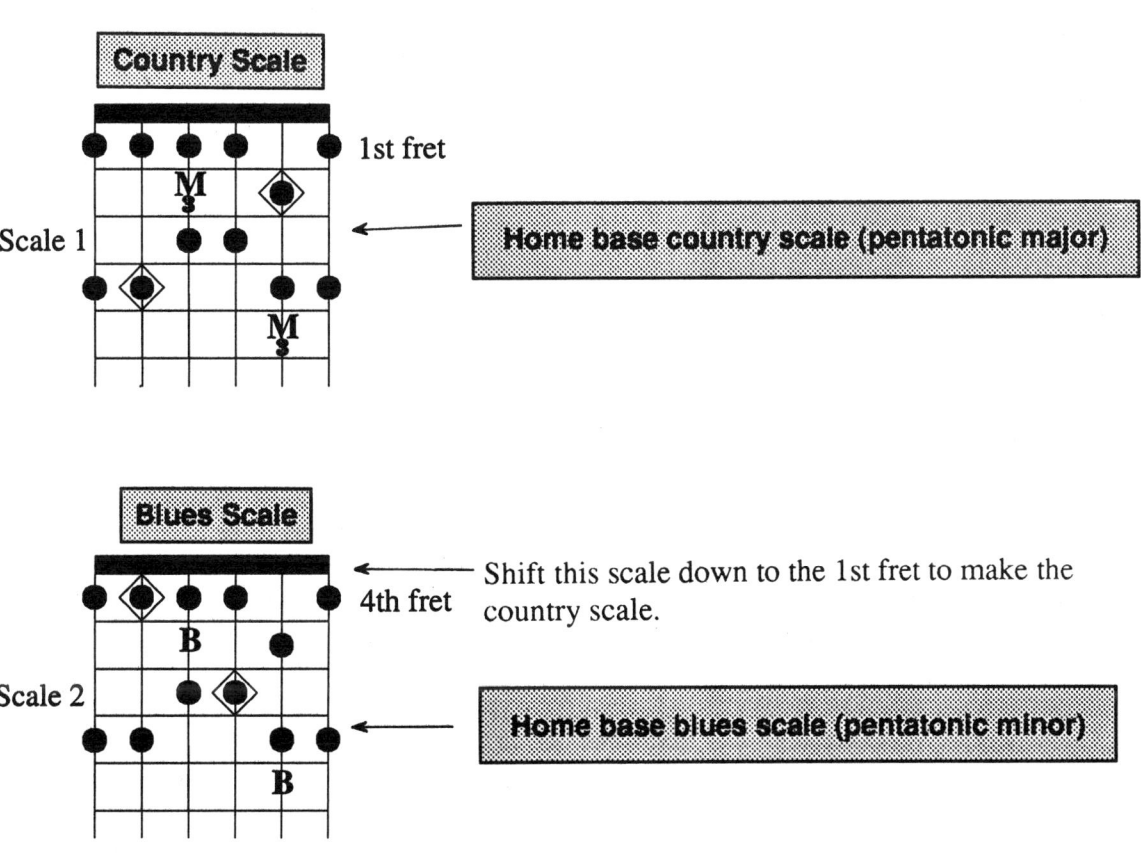

Country Scale

1st fret

Scale 1

Home base country scale (pentatonic major)

Blues Scale

4th fret

Scale 2

Shift this scale down to the 1st fret to make the country scale.

Home base blues scale (pentatonic minor)

Finding the Country Scale in the Key of D

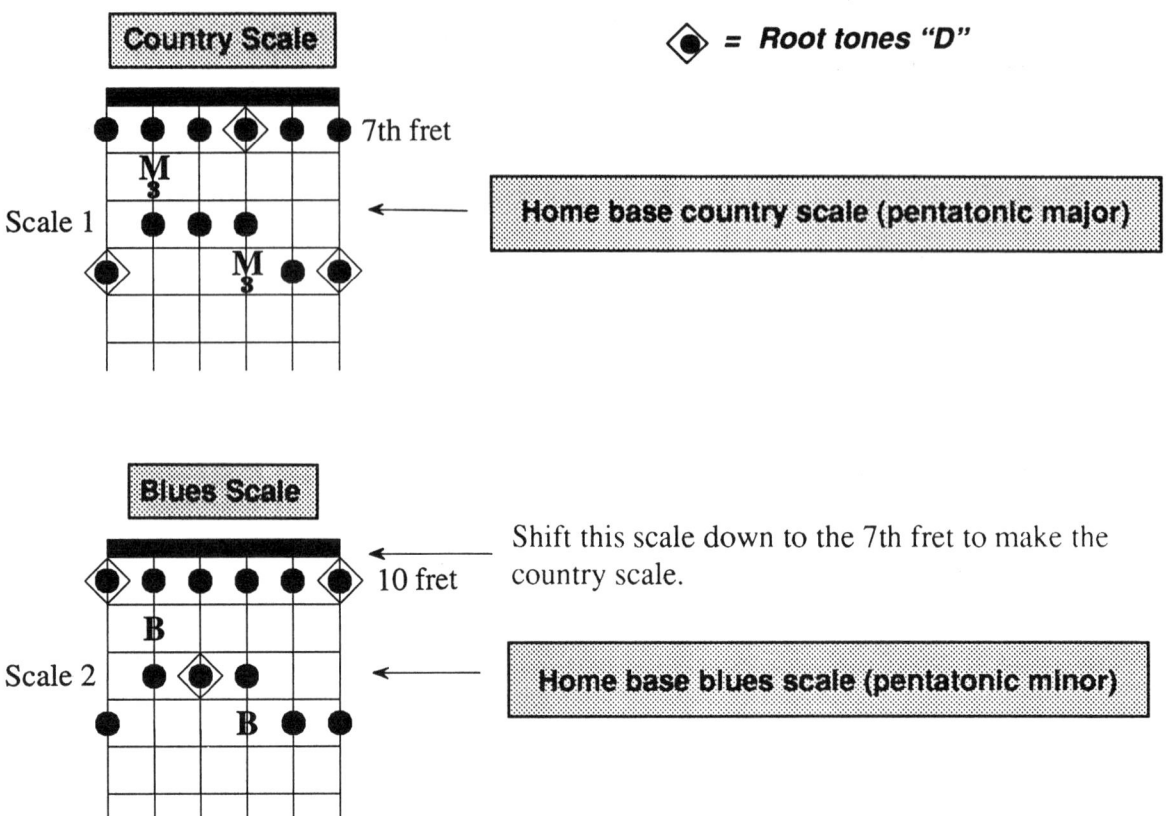

Country Scale

◈ = *Root tones "D"*

Scale 1 — 7th fret — Home base country scale (pentatonic major)

Blues Scale

Shift this scale down to the 7th fret to make the country scale.

Scale 2 — 10 fret — Home base blues scale (pentatonic minor)

More Scale Positions in the Key of D

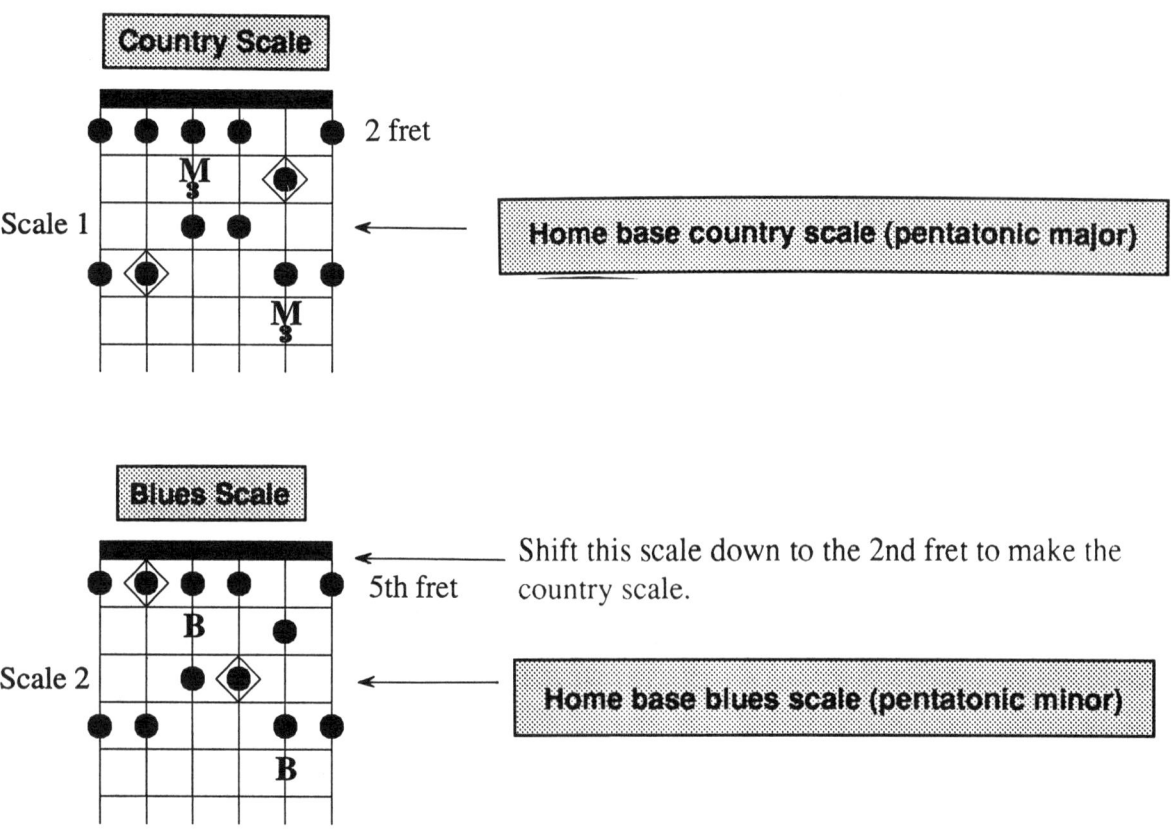

Country Scale

Scale 1 — 2 fret — Home base country scale (pentatonic major)

Blues Scale

Shift this scale down to the 2nd fret to make the country scale.

Scale 2 — 5th fret — Home base blues scale (pentatonic minor)

Finding the Country Scale in the Key of E♭

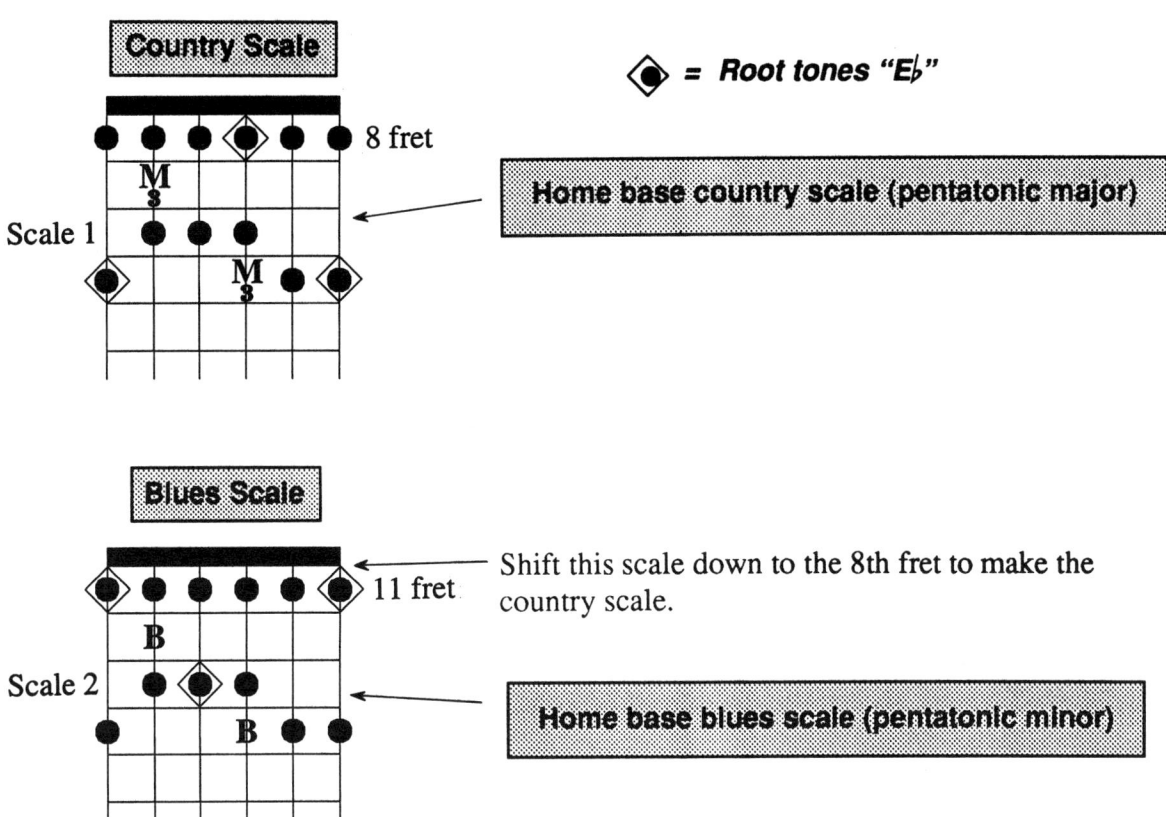

Country Scale

◈ = Root tones "E♭"

Scale 1

8 fret

Home base country scale (pentatonic major)

Blues Scale

Scale 2

11 fret

Shift this scale down to the 8th fret to make the country scale.

Home base blues scale (pentatonic minor)

More Scale Positions in the Key of E♭

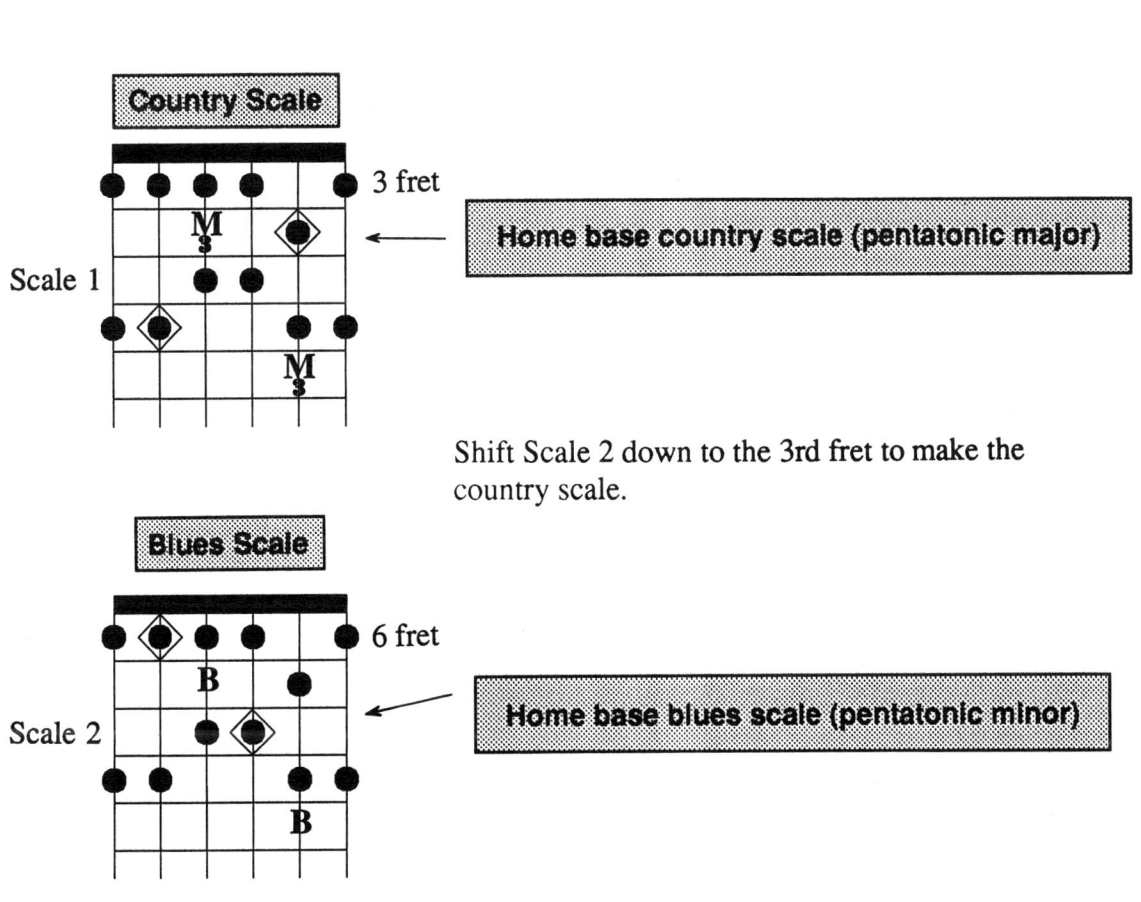

Country Scale

Scale 1

3 fret

Home base country scale (pentatonic major)

Shift Scale 2 down to the 3rd fret to make the country scale.

Blues Scale

Scale 2

6 fret

Home base blues scale (pentatonic minor)

Finding the Country Scale in the Key of E

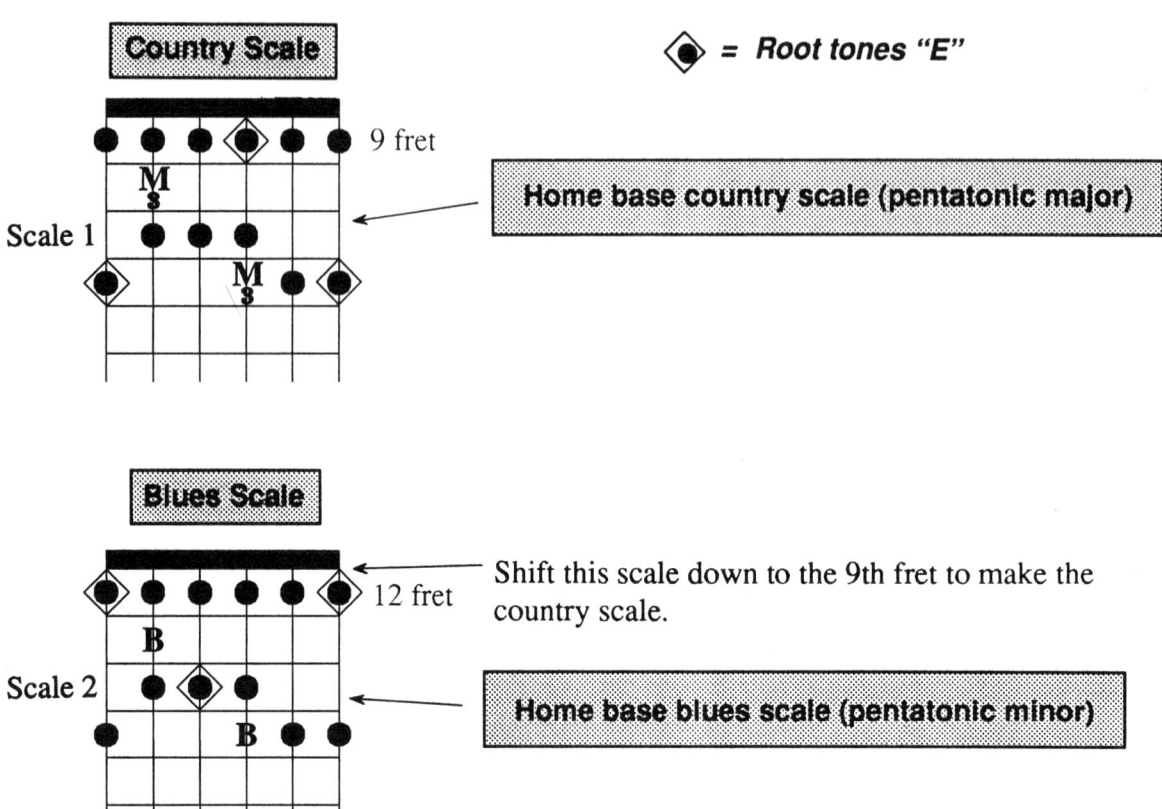

= Root tones "E"

Country Scale

Scale 1

9 fret

Home base country scale (pentatonic major)

Blues Scale

Scale 2

12 fret

Shift this scale down to the 9th fret to make the country scale.

Home base blues scale (pentatonic minor)

More Scale Positions in the Key of E

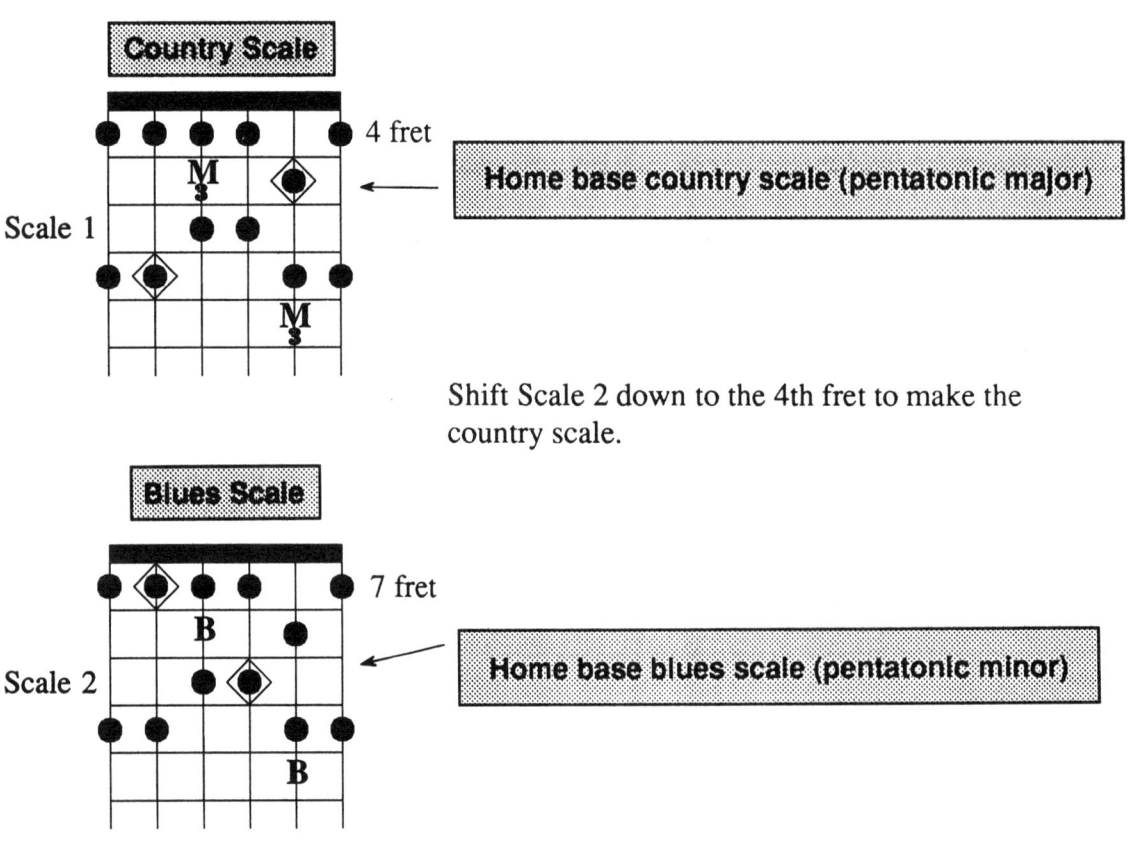

Country Scale

Scale 1

4 fret

Home base country scale (pentatonic major)

Shift Scale 2 down to the 4th fret to make the country scale.

Blues Scale

Scale 2

7 fret

Home base blues scale (pentatonic minor)

150

Finding the Country Scale in the Key of F

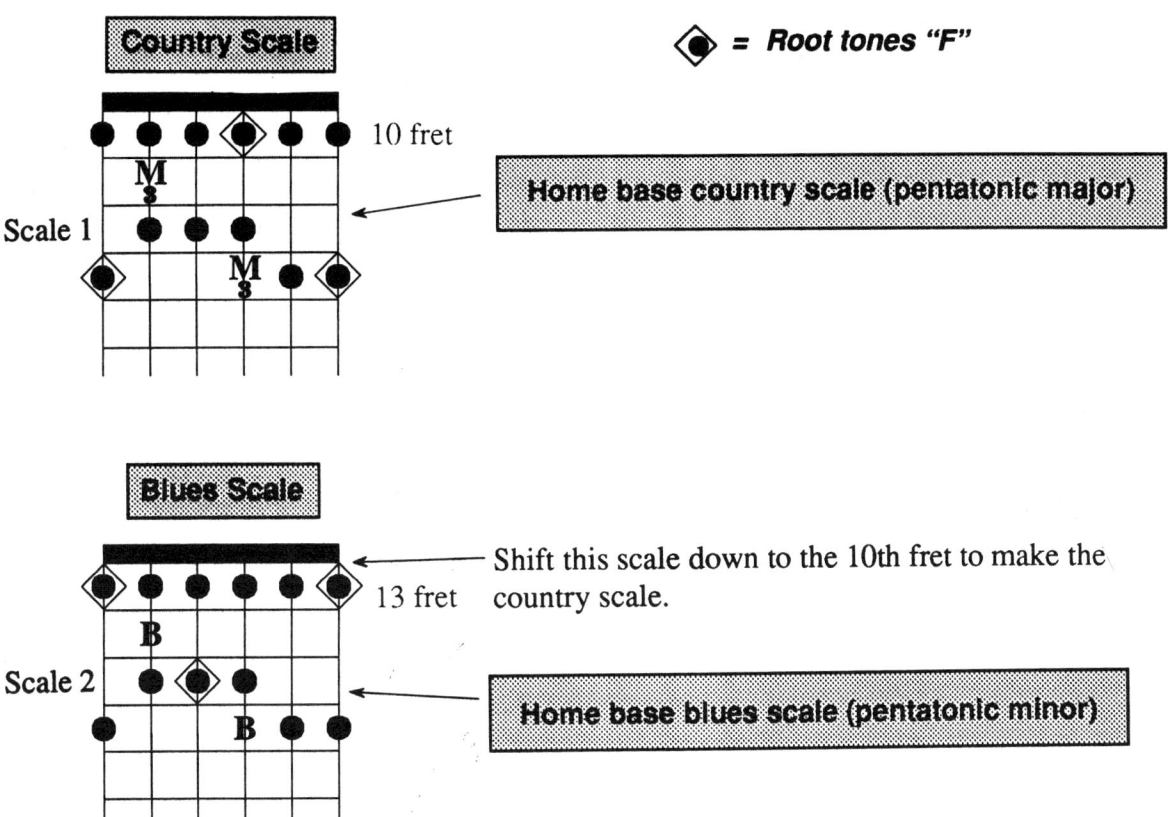

Country Scale

◈ = **Root tones "F"**

10 fret

Scale 1

Home base country scale (pentatonic major)

Blues Scale

13 fret

Shift this scale down to the 10th fret to make the country scale.

Scale 2

Home base blues scale (pentatonic minor)

More Scale Positions in the Key of F

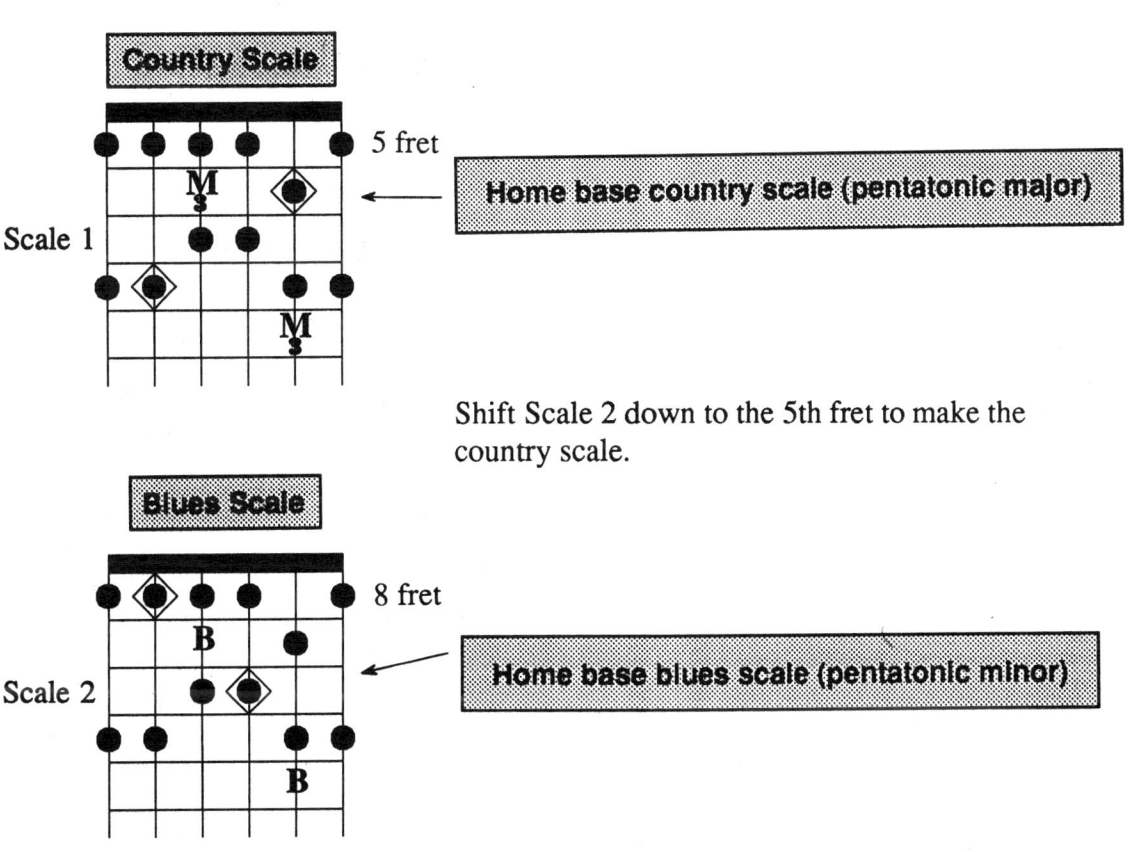

Country Scale

5 fret

Scale 1

Home base country scale (pentatonic major)

Shift Scale 2 down to the 5th fret to make the country scale.

Blues Scale

8 fret

Scale 2

Home base blues scale (pentatonic minor)

151